LONDON
MARKETS

CADOGANguides

About the Updater

Kamin Mohammadi has lived in London since the age of nine when she was transplanted from the covered bazaars of Iran to the street theatre of Portobello market where she grew up. Her subsequent progression around London has included stints living near Camden market, Shepherd's Bush market and North End Road market. She currently lives by and shops at Berwick Street market and writes articles and books about London and Iran.

Cadogan Guides
2nd Floor, 233 High Holborn,
London WC1V 7DN
info@cadoganguides.co.uk
www.cadoganguides.com

The Globe Pequot Press
246 Goose Lane, PO Box 480,
Guilford, Connecticut 06437–0480

Art Director: Sarah Gardner
Maps reproduced by permission of Geographers'
A–Z Map Co. Ltd., based upon the Ordnance Survey maps
with the permission of the Controller of Her Majesty's
Stationery Office, and drawn by
Maidenhead Cartographic Services Ltd.

Managing Editor: Natalie Pomier
Editor: Alison Copland
Editorial Assistant: Nicola Jessop
Proofreading: Dominique Shead
Printed in Italy by Legoprint
A catalogue record for this book is available from
the British Library
ISBN 10: 1-86011-3060
ISBN 13: 978-186011-3062

Contents

Introduction

01

Markets are the essence of London, mirroring its best points: cosmopolitan, unpredictable, worldly wise, exciting. Through the two millennia of its existence, this great metropolis has been sculpted by trade. From the Docklands in the east, where the booty of empire was landed, to Heathrow in the west, where much modern-day cargo comes to ground, mercantile considerations have shaped the landscape. Even in the City, where high-tech finance and glassy new office blocks now hold sway, the streets bear witness to the spontaneity of medieval trading. No town planner could have dreamt up such higgledy-piggledy thoroughfares as Milk Street, Pudding Lane and Fish Street Hill.

There is a wealth of stories to be found around the capital's markets. Ask any old Londoners from a street-trading district about their past, and chances are the lines of barrows will loom large in their memories. Take Morrie, for instance, who remembers the pre-war mayhem of the Caledonian market and, as a boy, being given a shilling to sprint and bag the best pitch for an old trader; or the two elderly women who sparkled like teenagers when reminiscing about a Saturday night on the razzle at the New Cut of the 1930s. Characters now gone, such as Bill Gallagher of Deptford and George Jeffrey of Farringdon Road, became local landmarks during their lifetimes behind the barrows.

There is no doubt now that London's local food markets are in jeopardy. Every year, dozens of traders, some of whose families had run a stall for a century or more, give up their barrows. Few young men and women are taking their places. Government and councils need to take action to reverse the decline, but so too do we, the punters, or all we'll be left with is the monotony (and expense) of supermarkets. One positive development, however, is the advent of farmers' markets, bringing nutritious, fresh food direct from farms into the city. Leaf through this book and find your nearest market. Take a trip down there one Saturday morning – you might be surprised how much fun shopping can be.

USING THIS BOOK

Don't expect markets to be exactly as described when you visit. The accounts are snapshots in the lives of constantly evolving organisms. I tried to visit each when it was in full swing – usually on a Friday or Saturday. But from week to week markets change: that is part of their appeal. There are a few general rules. January and February are the leanest months, when markets tend to finish early, and fewer stallholders turn up. Some private markets aren't even held at this time – if in doubt, phone the organizers. Throughout the year, heavy rain has a similar effect.

Opening Hours

These also vary. Ask the council when the market is open and get one answer; visit the market at different times in the week and get another. I've given the best approximate times, but it depends on both the month and the weather. If in doubt, don't go too late. There's nothing more dispiriting than arriving at a market when the stallholders have left and the rubbish is being cleared. It is like being too late for a party.

Car Parking

For every market, I have given details of nearby places to park. However, as any Londoner will know, it is often madness to look for a parking space in certain areas, and the congestion charge is now £8 per day to enter central London between 7am and 6.30pm Mon–Fri. For the boundaries of the congestion charge zone, check *www.cclondon.com*. The two most difficult and expensive districts are the City and the West End. Any market in the area run by Westminster Council (including Church Street, Bell Street, Tachbrook Street, Berwick Street, Grays Antique Market and Strutton Ground) is best reached by public transport to avoid the notoriously rapacious car clampers as well as the congestion charge.

Markets Located Within the Congestion Charge Zone

Main Wares and Specifics

'Main wares' lists the types of goods likely to be found at the market. 'Specifics' is a more subjective category, implying recommendation. I have included commodities that seem particularly well priced, unusual, high quality, or present in great variety. As food is my passion, there is an unashamed bias towards food stalls.

Food, Drink and Shopping

For each market, I list a few nearby places that serve inexpensive food and drink. There is a slant towards Indian, Chinese and pie and mash restaurants. To absorb the full flavour of these markets, a visit to a pie and mash shop is imperative. Very likely, you'll share a wooden bench with a costermonger wolfing down a plateful of mashed potato, minced-beef pie, liquor (parsley sauce) and stewed eels. I've included details of other restaurants (including more upmarket ones) worth investigating in each locality. The true companion of the street market is the small independent shop. Most street traders and small-shop owners realize they have a symbiotic relationship, both helping to attract custom to an area. Some of London's best small shops operate in the same neighbourhood, often the same street, as a market. I've tried to list the pick.

Nearby Attractions

Many London markets are near major cultural or tourist sites, which you might feel like visiting if you're in the area. Those within walking distance of the markets are listed where appropriate.

HOW MARKETS WORK

Wholesalers

Most fresh-food traders on London's markets buy their produce from the city's wholesale markets. Good fishmongers travel to **Billingsgate** five days a week, from Tuesday to Saturday (don't buy fish on a Monday); butchers go to **Smithfield**. Fruit and vegetable costermongers have a choice of **Spitalfields**, **New Covent Garden**, **Borough** and the **Western International** market, near Heathrow.

Antiques traders have a number of sources for their wares. **Bermondsey** (*see* p.150) is the most popular market, but there are also auctions around the city where goods from house clearances regularly come under the hammer. **Academy Auctioneers** (Northcote House, Northcote Avenue, W5, **t** (020) 8579 7466), **Criterion Salerooms** (53 Essex Road, N1, **t** (020) 7359 5707) and **Rosebery's** (74–76 Knights Hill, SE27, **t** (020) 8761 2522) all attract bidders from the trade. Antiquarian book traders tend to visit the **Bloomsbury Book Auctions** (3–4 Hardwick Street, WC1, **t** (020) 7833 2636), held every other Thursday.

Unfortunately, most clothes traders on London's markets seem to get their stock from a few East End wholesalers who sell a near-identical range. However, the success of Camden market has led to more traders selling handmade garments from around the world; a few even bring their own designs to market. I have described the goods sold during my visits, but there are, of course, seasonal changes: summer frocks and T-shirts make way for warm jumpers, gloves and scarves in winter.

Renting a Pitch

Most traditional street markets are still run by local councils; private operators own the rest. They charge traders rent for pitches. As this often has to pay for street cleaning, rubbish disposal and health inspection, the small patches of land aren't cheap. A Berwick Street pitch costs over £100 a week, while crafts and antiques markets in tourist areas charge upwards of £50 a day.

Rental of Stalls and Barrows

Many clothes traders buy their own collapsible stalls and erect the metal-framed constructions first thing in the morning. But there are still a few costermongers who rent the traditional wooden barrows, just as in Victorian street markets. However, wheelwright firms, who rent out these barrows and repair them when necessary, are a dying breed, and these days few new barrows are made.

Movement of Traders

At some markets, the operators expect traders to turn up every day the market is held; elsewhere, you find stallholders popping up at different markets on different days of the week. Traders at Whitecross Street during the week might appear at Chapel Market on Saturday and Brick Lane on Sunday. This is particularly common with antiques traders. If you've been to Bermondsey (*see* p.150) on a Friday, you may well see many familiar faces at Portobello Road (*see* p.54) on the Saturday.

Tips for Cheap Goods

Haggling is not common on London's street markets. If a costermonger tells you a pound of apples costs 30p and you offer 25p, some fruity language can be expected. But, for certain goods, the practice of 'making an offer' has become widespread. Traders at antiques markets are often willing to drop their prices, so the usual rules of haggling apply: don't show too much desire to buy; pretend you're streetwise; hide any signs of wealth. Clothes and household goods sellers are more likely to let you have something off the cost if you buy several items from them.

Last-minute deals are a different matter. Visit a fruit and veg market or meat stall at 'knocking out' time (last thing in the evening, especially on Saturdays) and you'll be assailed by bargains. If you have a large household, the savings can be huge. Stroll the full length of the market to find the stalls with the best prices. Hold back until the last moment if the trader has a large surplus to shift. True, these goods sometimes need to be used fairly rapidly, but the prices beat the pants off those in the supermarkets.

Some of the most memorable bargains can be found on the cheap packaged-food stalls. Often their supplies come from bankrupt stock or a failed supermarket line, and once in a while it is a luxury foodstuff. On such occasions, you might find a trader selling tins of fancy French food for the same price as a can of beans, and the beans proving more popular among the market regulars. I still remember with relish the time I came across Roquefort being sold as Danish Blue for a bargain price.

Warnings

Keep your wits about you when shopping at a London market. Pickpockets can be a problem at places that attract large numbers of tourists (Camden, Portobello, Covent Garden), and are most likely to be active when a crowd's attention is diverted by, say, a street entertainer. Although, in my experience, traders are no more likely to short-change customers than are shopkeepers or bar staff, the practice of displaying the best fruit or vegetables while serving from an over-ripe batch is not unknown.

At several of the packaged-food stalls, you may encounter food that has passed its best-before date. Few traders try to hide this fact from their regulars. The product costs half the shop price and, one could argue, markets are cutting the vast waste of society by selling such commodities. It's worth checking best-before dates and weighing the pros and cons before buying. I've always found this food perfectly acceptable. Use-by dates are more important to comply with: these apply to particularly perishable foods that become dangerous to eat if long past the date.

But most of the warnings you hear about buying goods on the street are merely the squealings of large companies feeling their profits being pinched. Markets are conspiratorial places where the customers are enticed to join in the scam: 'Let's get one over on big business and the authorities' is the gist of many street cries. Thus, if you see designer clothing or sunglasses at less than a quarter of the shop price, the chances are they're fakes. Most customers are wise enough to know this, and buy them to fool those people to whom such things as designer labels are important. True, these goods might be shoddily made and not last long, but, as built-in obsolescence is the essence of the fashion industry, the street traders provide a means of cocking a snook at the big fashion houses. Likewise, few market punters complain about the sale of bootleg CDs, DVDs or pirate computer software at knock-down prices. Go down to Brick Lane and you might find a trader yelling that everything is 'guaranteed stolen'. It isn't, but his shouts bring the crowds like flies to a hamburger, and the goods are a lot cheaper than you'd find in a chainstore.

The British are generally a painfully law-abiding lot, so it can be a pleasant surprise to find smuggled cigarettes surreptitiously sold next to bottles of dodgy whisky. But goods stolen in car and house break-ins are another matter, and London does have markets where these are 'fenced'. The ancient law of market overt gives legal entitlement to goods bought in an open market, provided the transaction takes place in daylight hours and the buyer does not know them to be stolen. But any stall full of secondhand DVD recorders, mobile phones and car radios should be viewed with suspicion.

It's easy to come a cropper, particularly when buying secondhand goods (my white-noise telephone and toaster that doesn't toast serve as warnings), but that's all part of the fun. The risk makes the bargains, when you find them, all the more enjoyable.

HISTORY
The Roman Trading Post

For most of its near 2,000-year history, London was just the square mile on the north bank of the Thames now known as the City. But from its outset as a Roman garrison and trading post, the town had a market. The historian Tacitus describes Londinium in AD 60 as a celebrated centre of commerce. Olive oil, wine, pottery, glass and marble were among the goods that came from all over the empire. Trading took place in the forum, probably close to the present Leadenhall market.

London remained in the Roman dominium until AD 410, after which Roman culture gradually disappeared from Britain. London's history during the Dark Ages is unclear but, though the town declined rapidly, it is likely that people continued to live within the walls. Bede described 7th-century London (or rather a settlement just outside the city walls) as a 'mart of many peoples'. But it was not until the late 9th century that Alfred the Great re-established London as a major town, rebuilding its defences and establishing new wharves at Billingsgate and Queenhithe.

Medieval Markets

By the 12th century, London was England's principal trading centre, with 14–18,000 inhabitants. The city had several markets, most based around Westcheap (now called Cheapside) and Eastcheap (*ceap* was the Saxon word for market). Because of its large population, London had a high demand for a wide variety of goods, including the expensive tastes of wealthy merchants or courtiers. This enabled craftsmen to specialize in ever more esoteric goods. Like no other English city, London had a large number of people who had moved off the land and were dependent on being able to buy food or raw materials, and to sell their wares.

Fairs were established at Smithfield in the 12th century (Bartholomew Fair) and Westminster in the 13th–14th centuries. They attracted numerous foreign merchants. In 1264–5 nearly a quarter of the court's purchases of cloth, furs and spices were made in London; that share increased during Edward I's reign (1272–1307).

The old chain of markets across the centre of the city was augmented by new trading areas. Each craft or trade lodged in its respective street. Mercers, saddlers, haberdashers and goldsmiths were in Cheapside; grocers in Soper Lane; drapers and secondhand clothiers in Lombard Street and Cornhill; ironmongers in Old Jewry; poulterers in the Poultry; horse-coursers and dealers in sheep and cattle at Smithfield; wine merchants in the Vintry by the river. Ready-cooked meals were prepared in the cookshops of Thames Street and Eastcheap. Foreign merchants also came to market: spice from Italy, jewellery from Egypt, furs from Russia and Norway, oil from Baghdad and wine from France. Today, the street names remain: Bread Street, Wood Street, Milk Street, Ironmonger Lane and Poultry are all off Cheapside; Garlick Hill, Fish Street Hill and Vintner's Place are closer to the river.

By 1300, London's population may have been as large as 100,000, and it was by far the biggest source of demand for agricultural produce in England. Supplies came from an increasingly wide area. Grain brought by road from the west side of the city was sold inside the walls by Grey Friars, Newgate. Grain from eastern parts was sold at Gracechurch. Londoners also bought grain and fish from the East Anglian coast and the Fenland regions of Norfolk and Cambridgeshire, using King's Lynn as the major collecting port. River trade along the Thames to London contributed to the growth of Henley and Maidenhead. The two main waterside markets were Queenhithe, below London Bridge, and Billingsgate, above it. The River Lea was another means of access to London markets.

But what was it like to walk through London's markets in the Middle Ages? One of the earliest records is a sorrowful tale of impecuniousness written in verse by John Lydgate (1370–1449). His *London Likpenny* is worth quoting at length:

...Then went I forth by London stone,
Throughout all Canwyke streete;
Drapers mutch cloth me offered anone:
Then comes me one, cryde 'Hot shepes
*   feete',*
One cryde 'Makerell, Rushes greene',
*   another gan greete,*
One bade me by a hood to cover my head:
But for want of mony I myght not be
*   sped.*
Then I hyed me into Estcheape:
One cryes 'Rybbs of befe', and many a pye;
Pewter potts they clattered on a heape,
There was harpe, pype, and mynstrelsye:
'Yea by cock! Nay by cock!' some began
*   crye,*
Some songe of Jenken and Julyan for
*   their mede;*
But for lack of mony I myght not spede.
Then into Cornhill anon I rode,
Where was much stolen gere amonge;
I saw where honge myne owne hoode,
That I had lost amonge the thronge;
To by my own hood I thought it wronge,
I knew it well as I dyd my crede;
But for lack of mony I could not spede...

Having property stolen at one end of the street and being sold it at the other has been an apocryphal tale on London's markets ever since.

Much produce was sold directly to householders in the principal markets, but middlemen gained increasing power in the city, buying from producers and selling to consumers. Cornmongers, called blades, became some of the city's wealthiest men. It was during the Middle Ages that London's craftsmen and merchants first organized themselves into guilds or livery companies, and came to exert much power over the running of the city and its markets.

Then as now, the livery companies helped run the City of London Corporation. The Corporation fiercely protected its markets, invoking charters that forbade the setting up of rival markets within six and two-third miles of the City – the maximum distance deemed possible for a trader to walk to market, sell goods and go home in a day. There are about a hundred City livery companies existing today. The Mercers and Skinners are two of the oldest companies (though few current members have much connection with the original trades), with charters granted in the 14th century.

As the markets grew, so fairs declined. In London, this happened in the 14th and 15th centuries – earlier than elsewhere – because the city's markets were able to provide on a weekly basis the luxury goods traditionally associated with annual or bi-annual fairs. St Edward's fair at Westminster, founded in 1245, had become a very restrained affair by the 15th century. Trade at St Bartholomew's cloth fair, held at Smithfield every August, became secondary to entertainment, which was so riotous that the fair was eventually suppressed by the City authorities in the 1850s.

The Wholesale Markets

The growth of London caused an increase in wholesale trade. Three of the city's great wholesale markets date from the Middle Ages: Billingsgate, Borough and Smithfield. The oldest is probably Billingsgate, which for 900 years occupied a site in the City off present-day Lower Thames Street. It began as a general market, but by the 13th century it was used mainly by wholesalers trading in coal, corn and fish. By the mid-16th century, Billingsgate was devoted exclusively to fish, and gained a reputation for the colourful language of its porters, dockers and fishwives.

Billingsgate remained on its ancient site until 1982, when archaic facilities, traffic on the newly built Lower Thames Street and the greed of prospective developers forced it out to West India Dock, near Poplar in East London. The low-crowned leather hats studded with brass nails (said to have descended directly from the helmets of bowmen at Agincourt) worn by porters to transport boxes of fish on their heads have now gone. But Billingsgate still supplies nearly all of London's fishmongers, and most of the city's eel-and-pie shops.

It's possible that Borough market has a history almost as long as Billingsgate's. The ancestor of this gourmet food market with its wholesale fruit and veg section early in the mornings is likely to have been the trading that spread onto London Bridge during the 13th century. The bridge, on which houses, shops and a chapel stood, was London's only river crossing. Its gates were closed at night, so travellers often had to stay in the Borough. Inns and traders took advantage of this gathering. A map of 1542 shows the marketplace south of St Margaret's church in the High Street. The market's charter was granted by Edward VI in the mid-16th century, and confirmed by Charles II in 1671.

A growth in market gardening in Kent in the 17th and 18th centuries benefited Borough, as it was the natural point of entry to London for the Kent farmers. By the 1750s, traffic had grown to such a volume that the market was moved to Rochester Yard, west of Borough High Street. It has remained there, still within a couple of hundred yards of London Bridge, ever since. Traditionally seen as the poor man's fruit and veg market, it still supplies many costermongers with their produce. The 'fine food' retail market is now well established at Borough and has become a big attraction for Londoners and visitors alike (see p.152).

From at least the 12th century there has been a market at Smithfield, near Farringdon, just outside the city walls. In 1173, William FitzStephen, clerk to Thomas à Becket, wrote that 'every Friday there is a celebrated rendezvous of fine horses to be sold' on the site. Sheep, pigs and cattle were also traded there. The City of London was granted the tolls from the market by charter in 1400, and the Corporation still owns it. The procession of cattle herded through Islington to market came to an end in 1852 with the Smithfield Market Removal Act. The site became a wholesale meat market, still held five days a week.

An early-morning trip to Smithfield, Europe's largest meat market, is essential for anyone interested in London's markets. The large and elaborate building (designed in 1868 by Horace Jones, who also built Leadenhall Market) is full of activity through the night, as carcasses are unloaded. Trading begins at 5am, and pubs in the area open at 7am. Smithfield is the last of the great medieval markets to remain on its original site, right by the City. Along with the equally ancient St Bartholomew's Hospital, it continues to bring life and vigour to this predominantly grey-suited district.

Rogue Traders

Much of the material concerning markets of the Middle Ages describes the action taken against 'forestallers', who bought up all the stock at a market to sell it at a profit – capitalism was not regarded as a virtue in those days. Tradesmen who gave short measure, or sold food unfit to eat, were ridden round the town in a dung cart or on horseback, tied face to tail, with the offending commodity strung around their necks. Other transgressors had to ride from Newgate to the pillory in Cornhill, where they were left for a day, wearing paper mitres carrying the story of their misdeeds. In one case from 1319, a 'William Sperlyng of West Hamme' was caught by the City wardens selling beef that was 'putrid and poisonous' from 'bodies that have died of disease'. He was placed in the pillory and the two carcasses were burnt beneath him. A couple of centuries later, the punishment for a woman who had caught fish that were too small was still more humiliating: she was condemned to ride about Cheapside with a garland of said fish around her head.

Some of the butchers' tricks were ingenious: washing old, festering meat with new blood, or selling elderly joints by candlelight. The City authorities appointed officials to patrol the markets and check for profiteering and malpractice. The carcass of a pig deemed unwholesome had its ears slit. Hygiene was a major problem in medieval London. Lack of it contributed to the city's worst catastrophe: the Black Death of the mid-14th century, which killed over half of London's population.

The 17th- and 18th-century Markets

The London markets in Shakespeare's time were described in detail by John Stow in his *Survey of London* published in 1598. He relates how trades had gradually moved from their original streets of the city:

But the brewers for the more part remain near to the friendly water of Thames; the butchers in Eastcheape, St Nicholas shambles, and the Stockes market...cooks, or pastelars, [remain] for the more part in Thames Street...poulters of late removed out of the Poultrie, betwixt the Stockes and the great Conduit in Cheape, into Grasse Street and St Nicholas shambles; pater noster makers of old time, or bead-makers, and text-writers, are gone out of Pater noster Row, and are called stationers of Paule's churchyard...horse-coursers and sellers of oxen, sheep, swine, and such like, remain in their old market of Smithfield...

Stow also reports that freshwater fish were kept alive outside the city walls in the 'towne ditch', but most fish in London's markets was dried, salted or pickled.

By the turn of the 17th century, London markets displayed a quantity and variety of food that impressed visitors from abroad. The markets went on growing as the city grew. London attracted ever more specialized goods from the provinces, and outstripped Antwerp as the great European market for exotic luxuries.

Market gardening only began to flourish in England in the 17th century, using techniques developed by the Dutch. Before then, a high proportion of fruit and vegetables was imported. Samuel Hartlib, writing in 1652, stated:

In Queen Elizabeth's time we had not onely our Gardiners ware from Holland, but also Cherries from Flaunders; Apples from France; Saffron, Licorish from Spain; Hopps from the Low Countreys...wheras now...the Licorish, Saffron, Cherries, Apples, Peares, Hopps, Cabages of England are the best in the world.

Vegetables began to form a larger part of the English diet, which had previously been dominated by bread, fish, beer and a great deal of meat. Market gardens sprang up to the north and northeast of London, and the produce was sold, as it had been for centuries, in the market near St Paul's Cathedral.

The Great Fire of 1666 destroyed nearly 400 acres within London's city walls, and subsequent rebuilding led to a major reorganization of the markets. Stalls were seen as a fire risk, so an Act of Parliament in 1674 banned street markets within the City. Cheapside, Lime Street and Gracechurch Street markets were closed. Newgate, Billingsgate, the Stocks, Honey Lane and Leadenhall were rebuilt as covered markets. Spitalfields, the wholesale fruit and veg market, was granted its charter in 1682, and was held on its site to the east of the City until 1991 (*see* p.117). In the ensuing decades, markets developed outside the City at Whitecross Street, Leather Lane, Hoxton Street, Petticoat Lane and near Brick Lane.

The City authorities often invoked their charters to prevent markets setting up in competition with their own. As a result, several of London's early suburbs had shops before a market. Until well into the 18th century, however, markets were the normal place for Londoners to buy food.

The property boom that followed the Great Fire soon covered much of the space between the City and Westminster with housing. Most of this land was owned by the nobility. As well as becoming housing developers, they were keen to earn revenues by running markets. One of the first such charters was granted to the Earl of Bedford in 1670 to run Covent Garden (see p.28). This was followed in 1680 by St James's market (near what is now Piccadilly Circus), built by Henry Jermyn, and Hungerford market (on the south side of the Strand), owned by Sir Edward Hungerford. Newport market (near Leicester Square), Carnaby market (near Carnaby Street), Brooke's market (near Leather Lane, see p.40) and Clare Market (the name still exists, near Aldwych) were all inaugurated in the late 17th century. The Haymarket (on the road of that name near Trafalgar Square) also dates from this period. All have now gone.

The trend continued into the 18th century. Grosvenor market (off South Molton Street), Mortimer market (off Tottenham Court Road) and Oxford market (north of Oxford Circus; the name Market Place remains) all helped to feed London's burgeoning population. By the beginning of the 18th century, London was already the biggest city in western Europe, with about 600,000 inhabitants – 10 per cent of the entire nation. In 1724 Daniel Defoe wrote of the 'general dependence of the whole country upon the city of London for the consumption of its produce'.

But, as the 18th century continued, the city's population stopped rising so dramatically, because of the huge death rate in the slums. Overcrowding, open sewers, dirty drinking water and a widespread addiction to gin killed thousands who had recently migrated to London from the country. Two contemporary writers give a picture of the markets of the period. First, Ned Ward's description of Fleet market:

We mov'd on til we came to Fleet Bridge, where nuts, ginger-bread, oranges, and oysters lay pil'd up in moveable shops that run upon wheels, attended by ill-looking fellowes, some with but one eye and others without noses. Over against these stood a parcel of Trugmoldies [old former prostitutes], Straw-Hats or Flat-Caps, selling socks and furmity [wheat boiled in milk], night-caps, and plum-pudding.

A still more unsavoury tale is related by Tobias Smollett in his novel *Humphry Clinker*, published in 1771:

It was but yesterday that I saw a dirty barrow-bunter in the street, cleaning her dusty fruit with her own spittle; and who knows but some fine lady of St James's parish might admit into her delicate mouth those very cherries which had been rolled and moistened between the filthy, and perhaps ulcerated, chops of a St Giles's huckster?

The fact that market gardeners filled their carts with 'night soil' from the city to fertilize their crops did little to reassure nervous gentlefolk of the period.

Large supplies of fruit came from the Kent orchards, which expanded rapidly in the 18th century. More foreign fruits also reached London, with oranges and lemons from southern Europe becoming widely available for the first time. But Londoners were still great meat-eaters. It has been estimated that during the first half of the 18th century nearly 80,000 head of cattle came to the city's market each year. St James's market, Clare Market, Newgate and Leadenhall were all important meat markets. By the end of the century, city dwellers could also buy a variety of cheeses from traders, including Double Gloucester, Cheddar, Cheshire and Stilton.

The Victorian Era

London and its markets were utterly transformed by the Industrial Revolution. The railways enabled people and produce to travel speedily into the city. Wholesale markets were started by rail companies near King's Cross, Stratford, Paddington and St Pancras stations to sell fresh food from around the country. (The last of them, Stratford, closed in the early 1990s.) The population of what became known as Greater London soared from just over a million in 1801 to over 6.5 million by the end of the century. As scores of suburbs sprang up near to rail and, later, tube stations, traders moved in to cater for the new residents.

Henry Mayhew, in his magnificent work *London Labour and the London Poor*, described the markets of the 1850s in painstaking detail. Several of his discoveries are worth noting. He lists 37 markets, 10 in south London, 27 north of the river. At these he counted 3,911 traders. The largest markets were at Tottenham Court Road, which had 333 traders, New Cut (now Lower Marsh, *see* p.165), with 300 traders, and the Brill (near Chalton Street, *see* p.174), also with 300 traders.

Many stallholders sold what would now be called fast food. In the Victorian street market this included hot eels, fried fish, baked potatoes, ham sandwiches (an innovation from the 1840s), meat pies and, as in John Lydgate's time over 400

years before, hot sheep's trotters. Oysters (then cheap) and whelks were also commonplace. Traders often described themselves in terms of the article they sold. A coster once enquired of Mayhew: 'Is the man you're asking about a pickled whelk, sir?'

Watercress was one of the cheapest and most plentiful foods. In winter, most fruit stalls carried an old saucepan with a fire inside, to roast chestnuts and apples. Hot elder-wine stalls and ginger-beer stands could be seen across the city; coffee stalls, heated by charcoal, were also common; and fresh milk from the cow could still be had in St James's Park. But by the 1850s the number of traders selling 'eatables and drinkables' was already declining, partly as a result of the growth in the number of shopkeepers selling penny pies. London's eel-and-pie shops, which sprouted up towards the end of the century, soon finished off the hot-eel sellers of the street.

Sellers of sheet music would sing their songs at the markets; boys would fire percussion caps at targets to win nuts; buskers joined in the mêlée – shopping and entertainment couldn't be separated. Mayhew describes one class of commodities being sold as 'pretended smuggled goods', a trick which is still echoed in the 'guaranteed stolen goods' occasionally advertised at Brick Lane. The largest Victorian markets were held on a Saturday night and Sunday morning, after the working men had received their week's pay. Trading on a Sunday was allowed to continue until church services began at 11am. Then 'the policemen in their clean gloves come round and drive the street-sellers before them.'

Costermongers were originally sellers of apples (the word 'coster' comes from a type of apple), but now the term applies to all market traders who sell fruit and vegetables. From Victorian times costermongers have been seen as the aristocrats of street trading. In some East End boroughs, the costers elected leaders to protect their rights from competitors. These leaders became known as pearly kings and queens, after the tradition, started in the 1880s, of successful costermongers wearing pearl buttons sewn onto their dresses and suits. The Pearly Kings and Queens Association was founded in 1911 as a charity to help old and destitute costers. On the first Sunday of October at 2pm, London's remaining pearly kings and queens gather for a harvest festival thanksgiving service, now held at St Martin-in-the-Fields church, off Trafalgar Square.

The 20th Century

Towards the end of the 19th century, several of London's markets were forced out of the main streets by traffic and tramlines. During the 20th century, traders have continued to be shoved from pillar to post. Markets have changed streets or even districts, making it difficult to trace their lineage. Bermondsey market, for example, moved to its present site after the Second World War; before that it had been held near the Caledonian Road, in north London, since the mid-19th century; before that it had been an appendage to Smithfield market since the Middle Ages.

By 1900 it is estimated that London had about 60,000 street traders. After the First and Second World Wars many demobbed servicemen tried their hands at market trading but, as with the more recently unemployed who have tried to switch to the job, few succeeded. There's a knack to selling on the streets, and the life is hard.

Many markets weren't officially recognized until 1927, when the London County Council (General Powers) Act gave the councils the authority to license street traders and pass hygiene legislation. During the Second World War, several of London's market streets were badly damaged by bombing, and redevelopment has forced many more traders off their pitches since. Hydra-like, most markets have continued to survive, even on unpromising concrete sites. Some have thrived; the postwar influence of various immigrant communities has breathed new vigour into a number of traditional markets, especially Brixton (*see* p.124), Shepherd's Bush (*see* p.64), Ridley Road (*see* p.114) and Whitechapel (*see* p.121).

But several have closed, or are dying. These days, Lambeth Walk market has pretty much died out, with only a couple of traders turning up; in Mayhew's day there were 104 stallholders. At Hammersmith market, the fishmonger's John Tydeman ceased trading after 101 years in 1998; there are now no stalls left. Other Victorian markets that have given up the ghost are Burdett Road, E3, which has basically disappeared, and Chatsworth Road, E5, which is revived once a year at a market festival.

SAVE OUR MARKETS

The traditional street markets are now under attack as never before. A combination of modern shopping habits, depopulation, gentrification and council indifference has hit street trading hard. Like small shops, whose numbers have fallen from more than 100,000 in the

1960s to only about 30,000 at the turn of the 21st century, markets are in crisis.

Superstores

Compared to many of England's towns, where 800-year-old markets are in danger of closing following the arrival of an out-of-town superstore, London has much to be grateful for. Relatively few superstores have been built in inner London – there simply isn't room. Yet large shopping centres are taking trade away from the markets. Stallholders in Soho's Berwick Street, plumb in the West End, believe that Brent Cross and Lakeside shopping centres, miles away on the outskirts of London, are damaging their businesses. A new threat is the rapid growth of smaller supermarkets in central London, notably the Tesco Metro, Sainsbury's Local and M&S Simply Food chains.

Food traders have fared worst. The supermarkets' share of the fruit and vegetable market has leapt alarmingly. Wholesale as well as retail markets are being badly hit, because most of the fresh produce sold by supermarkets is transported direct from growers to central depots, bypassing New Covent Garden and Spitalfields.

Farmers are also suffering. Supermarkets require producers who can supply all their outlets through the year. Small suppliers who concentrate on regional foodstuffs and seasonally available produce aren't wanted. Neither are many varieties of crop. Supermarkets insist that their fruit and vegetables are uniform in appearance and have a long shelf-life. Some of the tastiest varieties of English apple are ignored because they don't take well to being kept in carbon dioxide for six months. In addition, the pressure supermarkets exert on producers to provide ever-cheaper meat has caused

farmers to cut corners. BSE, increased salmonella and foot-and-mouth disease have been just some of the consequences.

True, supermarkets offer convenience and variety. But this has been more than outweighed by a homogenizing process caused by the concentration of ownership. Increasingly, four firms are coming to dictate what we eat and how much we pay for it. The social and environmental costs of supermarkets' policies are high. These include the use of prodigious amounts of packaging (according to the Consumers' Association, we pay about 10 per cent higher prices because of it, and supermarkets don't bear the cost of disposing of it), and excessive 'food miles' (the distance raw ingredients must travel before reaching the consumer). Air and noise pollution, increased congestion, more accidents and vast quantities of government money spent on road-building are consequences of supermarkets' transport policies. Supermarkets might benefit some consumers, notably car-owners, but it is at the expense of other, more vulnerable members of society: the old, the car-less, the poor.

In contrast, London's traditional street markets are concentrated in some of the most deprived parts of the city. Costermongers have always made a living by bringing food to the poorest sections of society. They usually buy their stock from the nearest wholesale market, and the most packaging you'll get is a plastic bag for your spuds. The seasons also make their presence felt more on the markets, though less so in London than in rural districts. Spring greens are followed by summer fruits; autumn marrows make way for the Kentish cobnuts and boiled beetroot sold near Christmas.

The domination of retailing by ever fewer companies does not only affect the markets. The high streets of Britain's towns and London's boroughs are starting to look identical. Butchers' shops and bakeries are closing; fishmongers and greengrocers are nearing extinction. Worthwhile and satisfying jobs are disappearing, as shopkeepers and stallholders are replaced by battalions of weary checkout assistants. Personal service is being lost. Above all, we're in danger of losing variety and a way of life.

Battles with Government

With a few noteworthy exceptions, London councils rarely seem to value the markets in their care. Starved of funds, they are prone to look kindly on supermarkets, who are prepared to build amenities in exchange for planning permission. Revenue raising often takes precedence over conservation. Many traders in central London believe that Westminster Council would rather have parking meters on its streets than markets, as the meters raise more cash. But more often councils simply neglect their markets, taking them for granted, failing to respond when pitches are left empty, doing nothing until it is too late.

National government seems little better, whichever political party is in control. The Conservatives' huge road-building programme in the 1980s helped subsidize out-of-town superstores; and through the 1990s street markets were treated as if they were little more than an anachronism. Market traders can't match the muscle of the supermarket companies (nor are they able to match their donations to both major political parties), and so can expect no subsidies themselves when times are hard. The European parliament, too, seems to work in the interests of multinational companies, passing directives that are easy for large corporations to comply with, but crippling for small shops and market traders.

The Flight from the City

After over 40 years of decline, the population of central London is slowly beginning to climb again, which is good news for the city's street markets. Less pleasing is the fact that businesses are continuing to relocate away from the centre, partly because of transport problems. This has caused many of central London's lunchtime markets to decline. The American phenomenon of the 'doughnut effect' is a warning of what can happen to the city centres if businesses and shops move out. Conurbations acquire deserted holes in their centres, where those on low incomes live with few amenities, and where crime is rampant.

Gentrification and Touristification

It is fast becoming a general rule that seekers after 'genuine' street culture, those wishing to see communities about their daily business (not play-actors performing for tourists) should shun the great sights, avoid all that is deemed quaint or beautiful. Rather they should search for the ugly and the unfashionable. Above all they should travel to districts not mentioned in guide books. London is a big enough city to encompass both the worst of the synthetic self-parodies and the most lively of unspoilt street culture. Traditional street markets tend to be at the centre of the latter. Visit some of the markets listed here and you'll learn a great deal more about London's culture than you will from queuing with the hordes at the Tower.

But there is a danger that markets themselves could be repackaged for tourists and lose their *raison d'être* as providers of essentials for local people. The success of Camden market (now the fourth most popular tourist attraction in London) has caused a number of crafts markets to be set up, most notably at Greenwich, Merton Abbey Mills and St James's Piccadilly. These new markets, though mostly geared to tourists, have not displaced any existing traditional street trading. More worrying are the developments at Earlham Street and Rupert Street, where traditional markets have all but been taken over by stalls for tourists.

The gentrification of an area has a more ambivalent effect on street markets. Where the tastes of the new arrivals are represented on the stalls, as at Columbia Road and Northcote Road, the market continues to be a success. When the market fails to respond to the changing population, it is in danger of dying once its old constituency disappears.

Market Predictions

The future for London's markets is not entirely gloomy. Go to Brixton, Portobello, Wembley, Ridley Road, Camden or Brick Lane, and you will find entertainment and a sense of occasion that supermarkets couldn't hope to compete with. Within limits (perhaps exceeded at Camden, Petticoat Lane and Portobello), the crowds are an attraction in themselves; in a supermarket crowds are a mere nuisance. And in a market there is no sense of behind-the-scenes manipulation by middle managers, advertisers and corporate strategists. On the streets you are confronted by stallholders who usually own their business. They can be wily, but at least the transaction is on a human level, a kind of joust.

To survive, street markets, particularly those specializing in food, need to adapt. Over the past thirty years, the huge increase in the number of women working outside the home has led to a rapid growth in the consumption of convenience food, and to fewer people being able to shop during office hours. Supermarkets have responded by offering a wide range of ready meals, and by staying open later. Market traders rarely have the resources to provide chilled or frozen ready meals, but, with the notable exceptions of Borough, Portobello, Camden and Merton Abbey Mills, they have also been slow to offer any takeaway food more imaginative than a hot dog or a burger. And it is rare that you'll find stallholders trading after 6pm.

London, meanwhile, has become a city of food lovers. Restaurants have proliferated and the quality of cooking has soared. It is at this specialized level that markets can compete. The remarkable success of farmers' markets in Britain is indicative of this trend and is cause for great hope among market devotees, showing there is strong demand for high-quality food from small producers. When this guide was first published in 1996, farmers' markets were a US phenomenon yet to be established in Britain. However, by 2006 there were well over 550 farmers' markets held regularly across the country, including many in London (*see* p.179). These markets, where a wide variety of food is sold directly to the public by the producers, join the organic markets set up at Spitalfields, Portobello, Greenwich and Camden in the 1990s. Such initiatives forge links between producers and consumers (cutting out supermarket middle men), benefiting both. With luck, their success will encourage a move back towards seasonal and locally grown food, reviving once again the glorious expectation of fresh asparagus in May and strawberries in July. Such a shift in demand will cut the unnecessary transportation of goods halfway across the globe.

But specialized food markets cater mainly for more affluent consumers. Most of London's traditional markets cater for low-income groups. Many are sited in areas of high unemployment, where locals aren't prepared to pay a premium for organic produce. If London's local markets are to survive, they have to appeal to their local population. As is the case in France (and some rural areas of Britain, notably north Devon), small producers must be encouraged to take stalls on London's traditional markets. The Women's Institute markets of rural Britain also show the way. Farmers' markets should be allowed to combine with the established street markets, rejuvenating the latter while gaining prime retail sites for themselves. At present we are in danger of creating a type of social apartheid between those who shop at farmers' markets and those who frequent traditional street markets.

Councils often seem to think that all it takes to inject new life into a market is to pedestrianize it and install some street furniture. But often it is a case of too little too late. More fundamental measures need to be implemented urgently:

- Councils should inform local people about their markets, and the low prices to be found there. The multi-million-pound advertising budgets of the supermarket chains obviously cannot be matched, but younger consumers especially need to know that there is an alternative. At present, Waltham Forest Council seems almost alone in widely promoting its traditional street market, Walthamstow.

- Councils should keep an eye on the markets they own. If food stalls are deserting them, traders should be enticed back with rent-free pitches to ensure the market remains balanced and attractive.

- Markets should be allowed and encouraged to stay open until late in the evening, as they did from Victorian times to the outbreak of the Second World War, enabling people to shop locally after finishing work. The benefits to the local community would be manifold. Not only would the market provide a meeting place and entertainment for those too young or without enough money to drink in a pub, thereby keeping them out of mischief, but it would also ensure that more people were out on the streets at a later hour, thus making the area safer, especially for women. Any outlay by the council would easily be counterbalanced by a decrease in local crime.

- Local people from various ethnic groups should be encouraged to take pitches. The success of Brixton, Shepherd's Bush and Ridley Road points the way. There are still local markets in multi-ethnic areas of London that are dominated by a dwindling number of (occasionally xenophobic) old coster families. As a result, local people of Afro-Caribbean and Asian origin – many of whom come from cultures well used to street trading – shop elsewhere.

- Cheap local parking should be provided wherever possible, to allow markets to compete with out-of-town superstores. The success of markets such as Wembley shows the attraction of plentiful nearby parking.

Market-led Recoveries

Councils too often see their markets as a liability, instead of a valuable resource capable of bringing prosperity to an area. In the 21st century, shopping is increasingly a leisure activity. Markets have always been an entertainment in themselves, so councils should capitalize on this. Camden Lock is the best-known example of a market reviving the fortunes of a declining area, but it is not the only one. Many chainstores left Peckham in the recession of the early 1990s, but the low prices on its markets are helping to bring back the crowds; and Deptford's market, where new traders were supported through a training programme, attracts people from miles around.

The danger is, of course, that successful markets in a previously run-down district can entice chainstores back into the area to compete for the crowds. However, when the market is flourishing, and the supermarkets are suitably near, both can thrive, as Ridley Road, Chapel Market and Walthamstow High Street all show.

With the tremendous popularity of farmers' markets, some councils are beginning to realize that markets can be a powerful tool in regenerating an area. Exmouth Market (*see* p.33) is one example of a new 'Continental' market run by private contractors on what was a traditional council-run market street (the original market lasted from Victorian times until the end of the 1990s). The new market caters to the affluent residents that have recently moved into the area and seems to be thriving. It's sad, however, that the last of the original traders thought the local council (Islington) gave them inadequate support in fighting to save the old market. Similar developments have taken place at Broadway Market in east London (*see* p.174), which now has a farmers' market on the site of a failed traditional market. It's possible that a similar fate awaits Tachbrook Street (*see* p.47). True, it is good to see the new markets thriving, but there is a suspicion that some councils are keen to see the death of the old-style markets and to use the designated market streets for something more profitable.

If this book is anything, it is a celebration of variety. The variety still to be found in London's markets is one of the joys of the city; each market district is distinctive – something that a street of chainstores will never be. Markets humanize their surroundings and, like street-corner pubs, act as a focus for the local community, providing a meeting place and free entertainment, as well as supplying daily essentials at a low price. If allowed to trade into the evening, they could also help create a safer environment.

To avoid losing all this in the 21st century, government, councils and stallholders need to take action, but so do consumers. Boycotts of specific goods or companies for ethical reasons have gained in popularity during recent years. Perhaps now it is also time to switch our patronage from the retail multiples to local markets and shops. We have nothing to lose but our chains. We have a world to gain.

Central London

BERWICK STREET AND RUPERT STREET

Berwick Street, between Broadwick Street and Peter Street; Rupert Street, between Brewer Street and Archer Street, W1.

Transport: ⊖ *Piccadilly Circus, Tottenham Court Road, Oxford Circus; buses 3, 6, 7, 8, 10, 12, 13, 14, 15, 19, 23, 24, 25, 29, 38, 55, 73, 88, 94, 98, 139, 159, 176, 390, 453.*

Open: *Mon–Sat 9am–6pm.*

Best time to go: *Busiest at Thursday and Friday lunchtimes; best-value fruit and veg after 4.30pm on Saturday.*

Parking: *Very difficult; within the congestion charge zone; Soho's one-way streets can flummox the most experienced cabbie. There's a limited number of parking meters on some Soho side streets (try Soho Square); otherwise, there's a multi-storey car park (expensive) on Brewer Street.*

Main wares: *Berwick Street – fruit and veg, fish, flowers, cheap electrical goods, socks, gloves, underwear; Rupert Street – new and secondhand clothes, CDs and videos, watches, jewellery, greetings cards.*

Specifics: *Cheap and varied fruit and veg, herbs and spices, bread.*

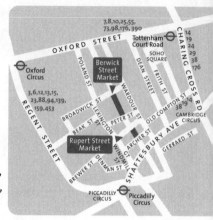

'They'll never get rid of the Berwick,' an old woman who had lived in Soho all her life told me a dozen or so years ago, over a drink in the Blue Posts. Few would have disagreed then – Soho without Berwick Street's boisterous costermongers was unthinkable. Yet, in the past decade or so, central London's best market has been facing the biggest threat in its history.

Street trading in Berwick Street probably started in the 19th century, when shopkeepers began displaying their goods on the roadside. But it wasn't the first market in the area. From the mid-17th century until the 1720s, a hay market had been held around the corner in Broadwick Street. French Huguenots, Greeks, Italians and Jews all helped populate this cosmopolitan but modest district. By the 1890s, several of these expatriates, or their descendants, had opened eating houses serving their native cuisines. As the market traders attempted to supply the ingredients, Berwick Street earned its reputation for selling a bewildering variety of fruit and vegetables. Tomatoes were said to have made their first appearance on a London street market here in 1880; grapefruit followed in 1890.

The spirit of Victorian Berwick Street survived into the 1930s. Teignmouth Shore called it 'one of the queerest sights in London', and describes 'barrows laden with fruits, vegetables, fish, meats, garments of all sorts, ironmongery; lit at night by flaring naphtha-lamps; an amusing and almost picturesque sight'.

In the late 19th century, Soho also became a centre for entertainment, as several theatres and music halls opened nearby. The area's reputation as a red-light district also dates from this period. The potent mix of food and sex has been a feature of Soho ever since. In the 1980s, local pressure groups managed to curtail the number of Soho premises used by the sex industry. In the late 1990s, though, the soft-porn traders multiplied; where Camisa's (a great little Italian deli) once was, a sex video shop now resides. The market continues outside unabashed.

With 80-odd stalls packed both sides of the narrow thoroughfare, Berwick Street used to be a scene of exuberant mayhem. Many a time I've been jostled along here, squeezed against a barrow as the rubbish cart edged its way through. In 1995, however, Westminster Council banned stalls from the eastern side of the street, halving the number of pitches to 41. Wanting congestion to be cleared, and eager to accept the larger pitches offered, the traders reluctantly went along with the plans. No one was forced out, but no new licences were granted until there were only enough traders to fill one side of the street. This didn't take long. The older generation of costers called it a day, while, according to a council official, many of the younger traders only keep their pitch for a couple of years, seeing it as a stepping stone to getting a shop. No doubt the market is now more ordered and seemly, but it has been gravely wounded.

'In ten years' time, all you'll see is parking meters along here,' said one coster at the time. Meters, clamp-removal fees and parking fines net Westminster Council a sizeable income. Revenue raising appears to be the councillors' top concern, so the market is seen as little more than a drain on resources. Customers arriving by car must pay hefty parking charges, and new stallholders aren't even provided with storage facilities for their barrows.

It's easy to understand why the traders feel despondent. True, the street is now pedestrianized, but there are few sign-posts pointing the way to the market, and the number of stalls continues to dwindle. So how can Berwick Street be saved? For a start, the council should allow the market to stay open later in the evening, as it did before the war. An entirely new crowd of people flocks into Soho at night, attracted by its restaurants, theatres and cinemas. The market would add to the nightlife, and local people would also be able to shop there after work. Were Berwick Street allowed to tap these markets, it might flourish again.

It is certainly worth saving. Although the bustle has diminished, dozens of stalwart traders still offer the cheapest fruit and veg in the West End. 'Fill yer boots with bananas, 50p a pound,' yells Paul outside the Endurance pub, while his mate Charlie, a Berwick Street star with a voice like a foghorn, sings the praises of 'sparragrass'. Charlie, known as Norman (after Norman Wisdom), is small and wiry. He never stands still, leaping around the stall, deftly tipping a scoop of 'avos' into a bag while foraging in his market trader's money-bag, a denim pouch with a zip-up pocket for notes. A passing group of schoolgirls goads him on as he explodes into action, hollering his heart out.

Some of the lowest prices can be found at the Peter Street end of the market, while the stalls further north tend to concentrate on quality and variety. Watch out for over-ripe produce (those mushrooms at £1 for 3lb look a little too brown), prowl the street checking price against price, and you'll usually get a bargain. Try finding five avocados for £1 in a supermarket; or two pineapples for £1.50. Many of the traders lay out bowls at the front of their stalls containing grapes, bananas, peaches or peppers, which they sell for £1 a bowl.

Food, Drink and Shopping

Cafés and Fast Food

Dim sum (Cantonese snacks and dumplings) is served from noon until 5pm at **Golden Dragon** (28–9 Gerrard Street). **Bar du Marché** (19 Berwick Street) is a modish café-bar with French windows opening onto the market. There are several cheap Japanese noodle bars on Brewer Street, **Ryo** at No.84 being one of the best. **Beatroot**, at 92 Berwick Street, is a good-value veggie café.

Restaurants

Soho has the highest concentration of restaurants in London. The most fashionable place for tea or dim sum is the gorgeous **Yauatcha**, at the north end of the market on the corner with Broadwick Street (Nos.15–17). It has 150 varieties of tea as well as lovely little pastries. For a treat, visit **Quo Vadis**, Marco Pierre White's restaurant at 26–29 Dean Street. **French House Dining Rooms** at 49 Dean Street is a slightly less expensive option for fine French cuisine. For seafood and spit-roasts, you will need to go round the corner to **Randall & Aubin** (16 Brewer Street), which is a converted Victorian butcher's.

Livebait Café Fish (36–40 Rupert Street) is a lively café/restaurant with good fish and seafood dishes. Wardour Street has several good restaurants: **Satsuma** (No.56) is a trendy Japanese diner; **Soho Spice** (Nos.124–6) serves Indian food and **Spiga** (Nos.84–6) is an excellent place for Italian food.

Pubs

Traders usually drink in either the **Blue Posts** or the **Endurance**. More convivial and more crowded, however, is the **White Horse**, a Victorian pub at the corner of Rupert Street and Archer Street.

Shops

Lina Stores (18 Brewer Street) is one of London's best Italian delis, great for fresh pasta, sausages and balsamic vinegars. Brewer Street also contains **Anything Left-handed** (No.57), a quirky shop providing lefties with scissors, peelers and such like, and the **Vintage Magazine Shop**, which sells memorabilia.

Chinese, African, American and European chefs from local restaurants come to root around for ingredients: kaki fruit, sharon fruit, custard apples, sweet potatoes, dried chillies, Nashi pears from Japan, fresh figs, Italian plum tomatoes, oakleaf lettuces and golden passion fruit are just some of the varieties offered.

Stalls come and go, but they are usually dominated by fruit and veg sellers, and there's a large stall offering all sorts of dried fruit and nuts. Prices seem to get lower as you go south towards Peter Street, but mostly they are uniformly reasonable. At the north end of the market is a solitary fish trader, whose catch might include prawns, tuna, rainbow trout and scallops, and a little further up, outside the Blue Posts pub, there is a popular crêpe stall operating most days.

It is the traders selling goods other than food who have been most severely affected by the reduction in the number of pitches, but you can still find a flower seller, a trader in cheap electrical goods (batteries, clocks and extension plugs), a socks and underwear pitch, a stall selling an array of wheely cases and bags, and a chap selling secondhand CDs. Jewish refugees fleeing the pogroms of Eastern Europe settled in Soho towards the end of the 19th century. Several engaged in the rag trade. Mr Borovik keeps the tradition going from his shop (at No.16), though he has relinquished the two pitches he ran.

From Berwick Street, head south through narrow, seedy Walker's Court to **Rupert Street**. A few years ago, Rupert Street was pedestrianized and cobbled. This, coupled with its position near the tourist hot-spot of Shaftesbury Avenue, has encouraged a rash of stalls sporting Union Jacks and selling football scarves. London and pop T-shirts sell for £5.99 each or two for £10. Most of the dozen or so traders sell fashion-wear: their stock includes leopardskin leggings, cheap silver jewellery, socks and jumpers, leather belts with grotesque buckles (favoured by adolescent advocates of heavy metal), feather boas, chunky woollen sweaters, hats and gloves. An army-surplus pitch is stocked with fatigues, rucksacks and camouflage T-shirts. There's also a second-hand stall with vintage Levi's, and jackets in leather, suede and velvet (from £20).

The CD stall is worth inspection. A huge number of CDs are laid out in boxes. A knot of dedicated enthusiasts flick through scores of records by little-known artistes. From here they will move on to **Cheapo Cheapo Records** (53 Rupert Street), thence to Berwick Street, London's prime quarter for independent record shops.

There's something tawdry about Rupert Street in comparison to Berwick Street. Traders rarely shout their wares; in the alleys by the market, you're more likely to hear the infamous Soho hiss, 'Show sir?', uttered by shivering young women in doorways. I can't leave the market on this low note, so I return to Berwick Street and head for the Endurance pub. It's already dark, but

several traders take their time packing up to catch the after-work crowds, including Charlie and his mate. Still they shout 'Mangoes to make you tango, kiwis to make you, er, wee wee.'

I sit drinking a pint and am astounded at Charlie's energy. Even when there are no customers, he races about, bellowing 'Aye aye, eh oh' – I can hear him now, above the jukebox – and throwing empty boxes across the street. Over 12 hours before, at dawn, he had unloaded a lorry with the same vigour. He draws on a cigarette with gusto and polishes an apple. Berwick Street will survive as long as his like are here. Without the market Soho, and London, will be a greyer place.

CHARING CROSS COLLECTORS' FAIR

In the Pricewaterhouse Coopers car park, under Charing Cross Arches (entrance on Northumberland Avenue, next to the Playhouse Theatre, or opposite Embankment tube), WC2, **t** *(01483) 281771.*
Transport: ⊖ *Embankment, Charing Cross; buses 3, 6, 9, 11, 12, 13, 15, 19, 23, 24, 29, 53, 77, 77A, 88, 91, 139, 159, 176, 453.*
Open: *Sat 8.30am–5pm.*
Best time to go: *Early.*
Parking: *Difficult; within the congestion charge zone (but this is not applicable on Saturdays). There's an (expensive) underground car park on Bedfordbury (see map, p.26).*
Main wares: *Old coins, stamps, cigarette cards, postcards, phonecards.*

Until the Arches Shopping Centre was built, this captivating market was held underneath the very arches that were

cast of *I Claudius*, particularly Caligula – can fetch prices of up to £2,000, while others bearing the image of less well-known yet, historically, equally important figures – Augustus, the self-styled founder of the Empire (£100–120), Constantine, the first Christian Emperor (£30), and Marcus Aurelius, Gibbon's philosopher-king (£20–30) – are considerably cheaper.

If imperial currency doesn't take your fancy, why not pick up an honest-to-goodness socialist Russian rouble from 1924 for £24, or an example of Royal largesse in the form of a collection of Maundy money from 1895 (£68) – still in the original box as handled by Queen Victoria. But, to get more cash for your cash, head for the pile of old British pennies. These now seem unfeasibly large and heavy, yet only cost 10p each and include many well-worn Victorian coins. A Georgian example, however, will set you back about £10. Otherwise, try the

made famous by the Flanagan and Allen song. The spanking-new postmodern redevelopment of Charing Cross station put paid to the stallholders' harmless fun. After a temporary exile to London Bridge station, they descended out of sight. You'll now find them down a concrete staircase in an underground car park.

In a strange way, the bunker-like surroundings suit the cabal-like atmosphere. A pleasant hum of hushed conversation pervades the place, as traders enthuse about their stock. About 40 trestle tables are set up, with nearly half of them holding displays of old coins – financial relics from the last 2,000 years of commerce. The spare change of the Roman Empire is particularly well represented. There are enough coins here to have paid an entire legion: copper and silver *denarii* bearing the imprint of almost every emperor. Prices vary according to the face on the metal, although perhaps not always as you would expect. Coins featuring the most famous emperors – Julius Caesar and the

Food, Drink and Shopping

There are a few sandwich bars along Villiers Street, running between Embankment and Charing Cross stations, but the best bet for a budget meal is the **Café in the Crypt**, below St Martin-in-the-Fields church off Trafalgar Square (*see* p.27). There's also a pleasant café in Embankment Gardens.

Stanley Gibbons (399 Strand) and **The Stamp Centre** (79 Strand) should also be visited by earnest philatelists on a Saturday outing to the market, but numismatists will have to wait for a weekday to visit **A. H. Baldwin & Sons** (11 Adelphi Terrace) and peruse its collection of coins, tokens, medals and decorations.

Nearby Attractions

Trafalgar Square, the National Gallery, the National Portrait Gallery and St Martin-in-the-Fields are all nearby. *See* The Courtyard, St Martin's, p.27, for further details.

'rummage trays' of assorted ancient coins at 50p, £1, £2, etc. If you go early, before they have been thoroughly pillaged, you can pick up some bargains.

Foreign coins and banknotes are also up for sale or for swapping. Some traders keep their specimens in plastic sachets; the zealots file them meticulously. Watch out for the small emergency banknotes produced by many German cities around the end of the First World War. Often brightly coloured and beautifully designed, they are ludicrously cheap. There are also a few antiquities – Romano-British brooches – plus medieval pilgrims' badges and so on. This is the sort of place where you can start collecting for your own museum: begin with a copper axe from 1500 BC (£145), a Celtic toggle (£25) or a Tudor belt buckle (£25). Some of these stallholders must spend every waking hour dredging the Thames or combing fields with metal detectors.

A decent distance away from the other traders is a single stall full of phonecards. The prices charged for these slices of modern technology are surprisingly high: £80 for four unused Irish cards emblazoned with an advertisement for Beamish stout – the equivalent of four coins from the reign of an unfashionable Roman emperor. Quite a number of devotees gather round, their excitement feverish. Another trader who ploughs a lonely furrow deals in regimental cap badges, while nearby is a chap with

hundreds of cigarette cards. My favourite set is of 1930s radio performers, including legendary stars like Stainless Stephen and Arthur Askey.

Just as the temptation to snigger at these careful collectors becomes urgent, you're likely to get drawn in. A couple of stalls specialize in old postcards arranged by British county and city. Both the photos and notes written on the back, often in beautiful handwriting, provide fascinating historical records. I now have my £3 purchase in front of me. The photo shows an old hall – long since demolished – of a Norfolk village. The note, probably written from the hall, tells the correspondent that harvest began that day, 23 August 1907.

My bucolic daydream is interrupted by an inadvertent elbow from the elderly gent scrutinizing the next stall. The remaining traders deal in stamps, and he is poring over first-day covers, deftly using magnifying glasses and tweezers. As with the coins, stamps come from all over the world, and prices start low – 50p for an assortment of 100, £1 for world covers. Indeed, none of the quoted prices is written in stone. When I expressed an interest in a particular item, the stallholder immediately told me the post-haggle price (about 20 per cent cheaper) because he 'didn't see the point of all that rigmarole'.

Nonetheless, high finance is not unknown. Dealers come here from all over the world to meet gents in wax jackets with Jiffy bags full of bronze-age spear-heads. At such times, large wads of bank notes change hands. For the most part, however, the market's habitués are genuine enthusiasts and gentle eccentrics. Browsing among them is a treat.

THE COURTYARD, ST MARTIN'S

Courtyard of St Martin-in-the-Fields church, off Trafalgar Square, WC2,
t *(020) 7766 1100.*

Transport: ⊖/⇌ *Charing Cross; buses 3, 6, 9, 11, 12, 13, 15, 23, 24, 29, 53, 77A, 88, 91, 139, 159, 176, 453.*

Open: *Mon–Sun 10am–6pm.*

Best time to go: *Saturday, early afternoon.*

Parking: *Very difficult; within the congestion charge zone; there are a few parking meters on Chandos Place, or try the (expensive) underground car park on Bedfordbury.*

Main wares: *Crafts, novelty goods, clothes, London souvenirs.*

Specifics: *Antique woodworking tools, secondhand books.*

Try not to approach the Courtyard market from the Trafalgar Square entrance, for this is where it flaunts its tawdry side. While most of the 30 or so stallholders deal in goods loosely described as 'ethnic', the first pitches are full of tosh for trippers – the busby-

Food and Drink

The **Café in the Crypt** of St Martin-in-the-Fields (entrance on Duncannon Street) is the best-value venue for meals and snacks in the area. It has a coffee bar and buffet counter.

A more pricey, classy Modern European option is to be found across the road at **The Portrait Restaurant**, on top of the National Portrait Gallery, with breath-taking views of Whitehall.

The **Lemon Tree** on Bedfordbury is a cosy backstreet pub adorned with opera posters (it is next to the rear entrance of the Coliseum, home to the English National Opera).

wearing doll, the policeman's helmet, the London tea towel and the London T-shirt.

Things aren't so desperate near the Adelaide Street entrance, behind the church. Here you're soon immersed in a multicultural mélange of goods, often sold by equally exotic traders. There are usually plenty of African, Asian and Latin American crafts to be found: colourful children's clothes from Peru, woollen hats from Afghanistan, carved wooden face masks from Africa and embroidered silk dresses from Thailand. Attached to one stall is a collection of rainsticks. They are made from cactus plants found in the Atacama desert of northern Chile; the spines are pushed into the hollow stem, which is filled with small stones. When the stick is up-ended, the pebbles tinkle over the spines, making a sound like falling rain. No doubt this is reassuring in the Atacama desert. One stall sells antique woodworking tools, including spirit levels, and there are two secondhand book stalls.

More general crafts on view might include inexpensive Celtic jewellery,

Nearby Attractions

National Gallery, *Trafalgar Square, information line* **t** *(020) 7747 2885, www.nationalgallery.org.uk;* ⊖ *Charing Cross, Leicester Square, Embankment;* **bus** *see Trafalgar Square.* **Open** *Thurs–Tues 10am–6pm, Wed 10am–9pm.* Fantastic collection of western European painting from the 13th–19th centuries. Artists represented include Leonardo da Vinci, Raphael, Titian, Rubens, Rembrandt, Caravaggio, Turner, Constable, Monet, Van Gogh, Cézanne, Picasso and many more.

National Portrait Gallery, *St Martin's Place,* **t** *(020) 7306 0055, recorded information* **t** *(020) 7312 2463, www.npg. org.uk;* ⊖ *Charing Cross, Leicester Square, Embankment;* **bus** *see Trafalgar Square.* **Open** *Mon–Wed, Sat and Sun 10am–6pm, Thurs and Fri 10am–9pm; extra charge for some exhibitions.* Collection of portraits ranging from the Tudor period to the present day. There are some real gems here as well as some pretty awful stuff.

St Martin-in-the-Fields, *Trafalgar Square,* **t** *(020) 7930 0089, www.stmartin-in-the-fields.org;* ⊖ *Charing Cross, Leicester Square, Embankment;* **bus** *see Trafalgar Square.* **Open** *Mon–Sat 10am–8pm, Sun 12–6pm. Lunchtime recitals Mon, Tues and Fri at 1.05pm.* Completed in 1726, this church is the oldest building in Trafalgar Square.

Trafalgar Square, ⊖ *Charing Cross, Leicester Square, Embankment;* **bus** *a mind-boggling number of buses stop nearby.* The home of Nelson's column is now pedestrianized to the National Gallery.

'hand-crafted' wooden chess sets, silk ties, and hats with dreadlocks attached. But several of the traders display the sort of goods that are commonplace at London's Camdenesque markets: Russian dolls, hippyish clothes, pot pipes (and king-size Rizla papers), aromatherapy goods, colourful bedspreads, woollen coats, suede and leather jackets, and watches with rotating smiley faces. Prices tend to be high.

The Courtyard market was inaugurated in the late 1980s, following in the footsteps of, but not quite managing to emulate, the Piccadilly market (*see* p.45) which is also held in a churchyard. It's a pity that there's little originality among the stalls, as the setting is sublime. A church has stood on the site for nearly 900 years, although the present neo-classical edifice was built by James Gibbs in 1722–6. Nell Gwynne (1687) is buried within. Young musicians give free lunchtime recitals in the church on Mondays, Tuesdays and Fridays (from 1.05pm to 2pm), which can well be combined with a visit to the market.

How much better it would be if more of the stalls trading on the vast, venerable paving slabs around the church contained old books. The market would then echo the ethos of old Paternoster Row, by St Paul's Cathedral, which for centuries was a centre of book publishing.

COVENT GARDEN

Covent Garden, WC2.
Transport: ⊖ *Covent Garden; buses 6, 9, 11, 13, 14, 15, 19, 23, 24, 29, 38, 77A, 91, 139, 176.*
Parking: *Very difficult; within the congestion charge zone; there are a very few parking meters along Chandos Place, otherwise try the expensive underground car park on Bedfordbury, or the equally expensive multi-storey on Upper St Martin's Lane.*

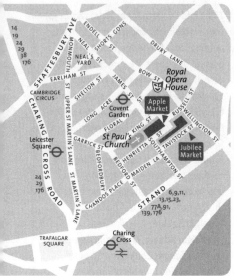

Did London sell its soul when the great wholesale markets were banished from its centre? Were the moves a practical necessity, or did the prospect of lucrative redevelopment hold sway? The argument has continued since 1974, when the fruit, vegetable and flower wholesalers who had traded at Covent Garden for 300 years were relocated to Nine Elms in south London (see p.137).

The produce market began at Covent Garden (named after a medieval monastery's allotment) in the mid-1650s. About 15 years earlier, Inigo Jones had completed London's first square, a magnificent creation with Italianate arcades around its edges. (Only the much-altered St Paul's church remains of Jones's work.) Fashionable and wealthy folk were keen to bag a residence in the district. To cater for them, traders set up stalls in the gardens of Bedford House to the south of the square. The market received official status in 1670, when the owner of the land, the Earl of Bedford, was granted a licence. (The dukes of Bedford owned the market until 1918.)

Markets and posh districts rarely survive side by side for long. As the number of traders grew, the fashionable residents left to settle in the newly built squares around St James's. By the mid-18th century, Covent Garden was known for prostitutes, duels, gambling dens and gangs of aristocratic yobbos known as Mohocks. Coffee houses also flourished; Boswell, Pope, Fielding and Garrick frequented them. Although a row of permanent shops was built inside the square, much of the trading was still carried on in the open air, from temporary stalls and wooden huts.

In 1737, the closure of the Stocks market in the City increased Covent Garden's trade. About 10 years later, £4,000 was spent on new market buildings. Herbs, lavender and live hedgehogs, as well as fruit and veg, could be bought here – the hedgehogs were kept as pets to eat beetles. As London grew, so did the market, and after the Fleet market (near Fleet Street) closed in the 1820s the trade increased still further.

By now, Covent Garden was the largest fruit and veg market in the country. Overcrowding was still a problem, so in the 1820s Charles Fowler was commissioned to design a new market building. The elegant results, though altered and enlarged, remain today. Tuscan colonnades and yellow stonework are topped by an expansive glass and iron roof which allows light through to the cobbled and paved thoroughfares below.

It is a beautiful place, but less than 30 years after its opening in 1831 it had reached capacity. And the market continued to grow. Other buildings were constructed during the late 19th century, and they were joined by the Jubilee Hall in 1904. But, as the 20th century progressed, the increasing number of fruit and vegetable lorries had to contend with taxis, buses and commuter cars every morning. The decision to move out to the suburbs was taken in 1966, and the wholesale market came to an end here in November 1974.

The market buildings reopened in 1980, their interiors converted into small shops and boutiques selling expensive clothes, 'lifestyle accessories' and gifts. The renovated Piazza almost immediately became a major tourist attraction. What had been lost was the morning bustle of people engaged in useful work, helping to feed the stomachs of London from the heart of London, and reminding office-bound Londoners of the food-distribution process. But there have also been benefits. Covent Garden has been in the vanguard of the movement to Europeanize London and reintroduce street life to the capital. The loosening of licensing laws has helped, and now, for most of the year, people dine and drink alfresco in London's oldest square, while street entertainers and buskers attract crowds onto the cobbles outside St Paul's Church.

And there are still markets in Covent Garden – of sorts. True, they are touristy, expensive and often naff, but at least they keep the streets vital. If you're looking for bargains, or wish to view Londoners about their daily business, steer clear. If you want to see London at its most cosmopolitan, however, come and brave the crowds.

Apple Market

The Market, Covent Garden, WC2,
*t (020) 7836 9136. **Open** Mon–Sat*
*10am–7pm, Sun 11am–6pm. **Wares** Crafts,*
clothes, novelty goods. On Mondays there
is an antiques and collectibles market.

Food and Drink

There are dozens of places to eat and drink within a couple of hundred yards; most are crowded and overpriced. **Punch & Judy**, in the Market, is a popular pub with a terrace for great views of the action in the Piazza. Another pub is the **Cross Keys**, a cosy, cluttered old place at 31 Endell Street. If you simply want to hang out and drink coffee, head for Neal's Yard, off Neal Street.

The best fish and chips are to be found at **Rock & Sole Plaice**, a 5-minute walk away at 47 Endell Street. **Mode** at No.57 is a friendly café serving salads, sandwiches and pasta. *See also* Earlham Street, p.31.

The Apple Market occupies the refurbished central building of Charles Fowler's old market. Along each side of the central space are shops selling things like crafts, designer clothes and posh toys. These sorts of goods also dominate the stalls, where you'll find hand-painted enamel jewellery, leather purses and handbags, knitwear, glassware and a variety of novelty goods. Some designers travel halfway across England to sell here – striking metal coat-stands and mirrors framed by tarnished steel come courtesy of a craftsworker from Nottingham. You might also come across original watercolours for sale, depicting clichéd English rural scenes or London landmarks – many of the artists here are happy to take commissions if you want something a bit more individual. Clocks with faces of oxidized (green) copper, or delicately carved wooden flowers, are destined to be bought and given as presents, while there is no shortage of original, sparkling jewellery, lovingly hand-crafted, that may tempt you to treat either yourself or a loved one.

Jubilee Market

Jubilee Hall, south side of Piazza, off Southampton Street, WC2, t (020) 7836 2139. Open Mon 5am–4pm, Tues–Sun 10am–5pm (sometimes ends earlier). Wares Antiques, secondhand goods, bric-a-brac (Mon); clothes, souvenirs, records (Tues–Fri); crafts, clothes (Sat, Sun).

Built in 1904 as a market for foreign flowers, Jubilee Hall was extensively rebuilt in the mid-1980s using money raised by traders. It is now open on two sides; to the rear are cafés and sandwich bars (including a good pizzeria), while a few permanent shops stocked with wooden furniture and various ornaments line the eastern side.

Market buffs should come here on a Monday. Few other London markets are at their best on this day of the week, and the antiques stalls that set up on Mondays are far more enticing than the general and craft goods you'll find here during the rest of the week. You'll have to get here pretty early, though, to bag the best bargains.

Not all the pitches are always taken on Monday, but the market's scope is wide, with stock ranging from cheap secondhand baubles and bric-a-brac to antiquities. There's plenty of old jewellery, much of it silver and with semi-precious stones. You'll also find a few stalls with a crazy mix of stuff: a pot dog, a lurid pink belt from the 1960s and a deconstructed Victorian china doll, for instance. Better still are the stalls run by collectors. One long-standing trader concentrates on old coins. An Edward III silver ha'penny costs £25, Roman bronze coins are £5, and there's a tray-load of coppers for 10p each. Another voluble chap has been coming here for years with his stock of old woodworkers' tools, pleasingly weathered

Nearby Attractions

London Transport Museum, *The Piazza, t (020) 7379 6344, www.ltmuseum.co.uk; ⊖ Covent Garden; buses 14, 19, 24, 29, 38, 176 to Charing Cross Road; 6, 9, 11, 13, 15, 23, 77A, 91, 139, 176 to the Strand. Open Sat–Thurs 10am–6pm, Fri 11am–6pm, last entry at 5pm; adm adults £5.95, children free.* Entertaining museum celebrating all London transport. *Closed until spring 2007.*

Royal Opera House, *Bow Street, t (020) 7304 4000, www.royaloperahouse.org; ⊖ Covent Garden; buses 14, 19, 24, 29, 38, 176 to Charing Cross Road; 6, 9, 11, 13, 15, 23, 77A, 91, 139, 176 to the Strand. Front-of-house areas open 10am–3pm. Box office open Mon–Sat 10am–8pm. Guided backstage tours Mon–Sat 10.30am, 12.30pm and 2.30pm; £9.* London's opera house is now in its third incarnation, with 10 restaurants and bars, the most impressive of which is in the 1859 Vilar Floral Hall.

Theatre Museum, *Russell Street, t (020) 7943 4700, www.theatremuseum.org; ⊖ Covent Garden; buses 14, 19, 24, 29, 38, 176 to Charing Cross Road; 6, 9, 11, 13, 15, 23, 77A, 91, 139, 176 to the Strand. Open Tues–Sun 10am–6pm. Guided tours at 11am, 2pm and 4pm.* Exhibits illustrating the history of the English stage, plus 'Theatre Rights', a whole host of interactive displays of theatrical paraphernalia. The museum also hosts a variety of workshops for aspiring thespians and free make-up displays each day (you need to telephone in advance for times).

with age. A punter is inspecting the batch of old spirit levels. They are giving a wonky reading. 'Are you on the level here?' he asks. 'No, none of the dealers are,' is the quick-witted reply. At one stall a couple of dealers are haggling over the price of a silver pen. Nearby, a stallholder has a fascinating collection of newspapers and magazines from the 1930s and 1940s. The second-hand postcard stall is also a weekly fixture, its stock divided into sections such as 'David Bowie', 'shopping adverts' and 'railway'. Collectors of 1960s watches, penknives, toy cars, military medals and old kitchenware could also find a Monday trip to Covent Garden rewarding.

Traders come from all over southern England. It's easy to imagine these respectable middle-aged folk running a quiet antiques shop in Winchester or Rye. Monday is their day out, and they make time for a chin-wag. By 2.30pm many of them have called it a day.

From Tuesday to Friday a general market is held in the Hall. There's little remarkable among the new clothes, handbags, souvenirs, watches and cheap jewellery. Some stalls sell tacky souvenirs from far afield: glittery pyramids from Egypt, stone sculptures from Africa. The trader with a collection of fake perfumes is busy, while nearby someone is selling a range of fountain pens. Soap is carved off blocks, like Cheddar cheese, at another, while another still spills with the delight of most toddlers: all manner of shiny stickers. Loud pop music emanates from the Pleasuredome, which sells cut-price CDs. And velvet dresses can be snapped up for under a tenner at one pitch. The army surplus stall, with its sweat-soaked khaki, might be worth a sniff – if you like that sort of thing.

The weekend crafts market is moderately better. Look for the handmade walnut jewellery boxes; some of the designer jewellery with which to fill them merits inspection, too. But you need to be wary: a highly skilled craftsworker might occupy one stall, a dreadful charlatan the next. And prices everywhere are high.

EARLHAM STREET

Earlham Street, between Shaftesbury Avenue and Seven Dials, WC2.

Transport: ⊖ *Covent Garden, Leicester Square; buses 14, 19, 24, 29, 38, 176.*

Open: *Mon–Sat 10am–4pm.*

Best time to go: *Friday lunchtime.*

Parking: *Very difficult; within the congestion charge zone; there's an (expensive) multi-storey car park on Upper St Martin's Lane.*

Main wares: *Flowers, new clothes.*

Seven Dials, that star-cluster of seven streets to the east of Cambridge Circus, was built by the property developer and Master of the Mint, Thomas Neale, between 1693 and 1710. It was intended to house fashionable Londoners near to Covent Garden and Soho, but by the late 18th century had become a notorious hide-out for thieves. The street market on Great Earl Street, later to become Earlham Street, probably dates from this period.

The district's reputation didn't improve in the 19th century. Charles Dickens described the poverty he found at Seven Dials in *Sketches by Boz*. The building of Shaftesbury Avenue and Charing Cross

Food, Drink and Shopping

Belgo Centraal (50 Earlham Street) is an immensely popular basement eating hall specializing in mussels, chips and Belgian beers. The **Two Brewers** on Monmouth Street is a cosy place for a drink. The best venue for coffee – whether drinking in or buying to take home – is the **Monmouth Coffee Company** (27 Monmouth Street). **Mon Plaisir** (No.21) serves tasty French provincial dishes. Good and low-priced vegetarian food can be had at **Food For Thought**, a café on nearby Neal Street (No.31). Neal Street and its environs have some of the best shops in Covent Garden.

Foodies should make a pilgrimage to **Neal's Yard Dairy** (17 Shorts Gardens), with its unparalleled collection of British and Irish cheeses; and **Carluccio's** (28a Neal Street), one of the classiest (and most expensive) Italian foodshops around. In Neal's Yard itself stop off for a delicious alfresco lunch at **Neal's Yard Salad Bar** with its stunning vegetarian fare, unusual wheat-free breads and huge range of fresh juices and smoothies.

Koh Samui (65 Monmouth Street) is a hip womenswear shop that stocks delectable clothes from individualistic labels; and **Screenface** (No.48) is the make-up artists' favourite shop.

Road in 1886 helped clear this squalid and impenetrable slumland, though in doing so it increased homelessness.

These days the area has been smartened up, and forms a backwater of the West End. The Seven Dials column, at the focus of the junction, supports six sundials; the pillar itself is the seventh. Removed in 1773 after (false) rumours circulated that a large stash of money was buried underneath, the column was replaced in the 1980s as part of the renovation of the area. Since then, many stylish new boutiques have opened in the old terraces, and the district is in danger of being absorbed into the Covent Garden tourist circus. But a few relics of another age – including a couple of old neighbourhood shops and a street market – still survive.

About a dozen traders set up stall on the west side of this short backstreet, away from the incessant traffic of Shaftesbury Avenue. Sadly the shellfish stand and the fruit and veg seller have gone, replaced by a mix of stalls that would seem more at home in Camden or the Apple Market of Covent Garden (*see* p.29). One trader sells bumbags and rucksacks, while another deals in sportswear and utility-style clothing. Cheap, bright, designer jewellery attracts a few passers-by; pieces range from fluorescent yellow rings emblazoned with a letter of the alphabet to heavy pendants and crucifixes. At a nearby stall a chap flogs wooden toys: Russian dolls depicting leaders from Lenin to Yeltsin, together with pecking wooden chickens and drumming bears.

One of the most popular stalls is packed with CDs. There's a good choice of rock, pop and dance (with Beatles albums selling for £10). Next, a clothes stall specializes in clubwear, with shiny metallic silver trousers a highlight. There are two jewellery stalls, one of which sells leather studded bracelets and other punk rock accessories. Nearby, old arts and crafts books are laid out on a table. Nearest to the monument is a large flower stall that's been here for years. It stocks a wide variety of blooms, including orange ranunculus, tulips, roses and vibrant gerbera, plus foliage for home decoration.

This small collection of stalls might not be worth travelling far to visit, but if you're in Covent Garden you should take the 5-minute stroll to Earlham Street if only to view one of its shops. **F. W. Collins** (at No.14) started trading in 1835. It's an old-fashioned hardware shop, bursting with disparate bits and pieces – from nuts and bolts to a large tin bath. Collins sometimes takes a stall at the market, its good-quality wooden brooms, gleaming dustbins and coal scuttles highlighting the tawdriness of some of the other stalls' wares.

During successive property booms over the last quarter-century, rents and business rates in this area have soared. Several shops selling essentials for local people (there's still a primary school and housing to the east of Seven Dials) have closed down, making room for yet more ephemeral, exorbitantly priced boutiques.

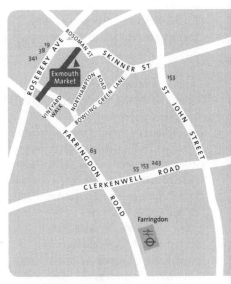

EXMOUTH MARKET

Exmouth Market, near the junction of Farringdon Road and Rosebery Avenue, EC1.

Public transport: ⊖ *Farringdon; buses 19, 38, 55, 63, 153, 243, 341.*

Opening hours: *Thurs–Sat 10am–5pm.*

Best time to go: *Lunchtime on Friday or Saturday.*

Parking: *Within the congestion charge zone. There are a few parking meters along Easton Street, northwest of the market. Otherwise, try the underground car park on Skinner Street, or the multi-storey car park on Bowling Green Lane – both are expensive.*

Main wares: *French foodstuffs, shellfish, bags, jeans.*

Specifics: *French cheeses and sausages.*

Were the grunting traffic of the Farringdon Road and Rosebery Avenue intersection to catch its breath and for a moment be silent, you might almost hear the slap of colliding cultures at Exmouth Market. Here, over the past decade or so, a market has died and a market has been born; stores servicing the needs of nearby flat-dwellers have gone (though several remain), while cutting-edge shops, bars and restaurants have opened to cater for Clerkenwell's new population of trend-savvy 'creative' office workers.

This short street was named after Admiral Edward Pellow, made first Viscount Exmouth in 1816. The market most likely dates from the middle of the 19th century. Like Earlham Street in Covent Garden, street trading here fell on hard times when slum clearance reduced the local population. For many years, Exmouth Market got the overspill from the Farringdon Road book market, which died with the passing of its last trader, George Jeffrey, in 1994. When the first edition of this guide was published (1996), there were still about a dozen traders in secondhand clothes and old books populating the newly pedestrianized street. By 1999, however, only a couple of stallholders remained. These included Paul Grant, a picture framer, who blamed Islington Council for spending money attracting trendy businesses into the street, but paying scant attention to the market. Now, the only stalls from the old market to be found are the three near the junction with Farringdon Road, providing hot food: a Thai food stall, one selling crêpes, and Jollof Pot, dishing up Ghanaian food.

On Exmouth Market, gentrification started when **Al's Bar Café** opened on the street in the mid-1990s. Yes, it was a café, but it served focaccia as well as egg and bacon – and fashionable bottled beers. Al's has since been joined by such classy restaurants as **Moro** along the street (Nos.34–6), where Spanish/North African cuisine might include poached hake in paprika sauce for £15, and **Cotton's**, a smart Caribbean restaurant where a two-course lunch can be had for £10. Nearby, there's a branch of the Spanish delicatessen **Brindisa**, with its stock of top-notch Iberian delicacies. Pizza chains Strada and Pizza Express also have outlets along the street.

Yet there are still businesses that once co-existed with the old market. Pie and mash has been sold at No.46 since 1930; a splendid plateful at **Clark's** comes to just £2.75 with liquor (green parsley-based gravy). And at No.29 **Farringdon Tool Supplies** still has garden forks hanging from its fascia, and shiny mop buckets displayed out in the street – as it has for decades past.

Into this demi-gentrified brew, Islington Council tossed, in autumn 2001, another ingredient. Making use of the thoroughfare's 'designated street market' status, it

Food, Drink and Shopping

As well as those establishments mentioned in the text, there's **Ayla's** at No.45a, an old-style caff where cod, chips and peas cost £4.20. Nearby, at 159 Farringdon Road, is **The Eagle** pub, the prototype for London's 'gastropubs' and still extremely popular for its pricey but high-quality food. **The Exmouth Arms**, on the corner of Exmouth Market and Spafield Street, is a decent pub, attracting blue-collar workers quaffing pints of lager.

Typical of the new wave of shops is **Space EC1** at No.25 with its mix of kitsch and stylish home accessories, while **Tom Faulkner** at No.66 sells handmade metal furniture. **Tohum Organic** at No.54 is an organic grocer and deli with a café serving salads, sandwiches and fresh juices.

licensed stallholders from France to set up a 'continental market'. Up to a dozen traders – most of them from Lille – now set up stall on three days a week.

'That's made from donkey?' I ask, getting a sideways glance from a neighbouring customer as I point at the sausage marked '*L'ane*'. '*Mais oui,*' replies the unconcerned trader, picking up the specimen, cutting a sliver and proffering it. He has about 20 varieties of sausage, including examples made from wild boar and venison. The donkey sausage has an overpowering peppery coating and I prefer the unalloyed meatiness of the pork-with-herbs version.

Next is a trader in freshly ground coffee, who also displays big vessels marked '*thé*' and tins of beeswax. Across the street, a couple of young lads have scrawled a notice over their barrow: 'old-fashioned waffles filled with *cassonade* and made with love and pride'. '*Ca va?*' calls one as I pass.

The cheese stall here has a splendid choice of a score or more French beauties, mostly from the north. Camembert, Pont L'Evêque and Reblochon *fermier* are joined by a *Tomme au marc de raisins* proudly displaying its discolouration: the badge of age and sweat. A makeshift yet magnificent lunch could be made by combining the fruits of this stall with those of the next, where a dozen or more types of bread are sold by the piece (walnut and raisin loaf) or by weight (wholemeal rye sourdough).

A Thai noodle van seems incongruous in this setting, though other stalls selling colourful shopping bags made from natural fibres, machine-washable cushions and faded denims encrusted with sequins all have a vaguely Gallic flavour. The remaining stall emphasizes the theme, displaying myriad types of French sweets: bonbons in Tupperware, boxes of chocolate truffles, coils of luridly coloured candies, and bars of nougat.

That there is yet to be a British market in Paris shows the relative strength of street trading in the two countries, but Exmouth Market has gained a new vigour following the advent of the French traders. With luck, the market will thrive and attract more local traders. The signs are good. Bruce Neave of Islington Council has commented: 'We even have people coming over from the City by taxi in their lunch hours to shop.'

Just east of the market on the middle stretch of the street is the Church of the Holy Redeemer, an impressive late-Victorian structure built in Italianate style. There is another reminder of Clerkenwell's Italian community at 56 Exmouth Market; from 1818 to 1828 this was home to the famous clown Joseph Grimaldi.

GRAYS ANTIQUES

58 Davies Street and 1–7 Davies Mews, W1, **t** *(020) 7629 7034.*
Transport: ⊖ *Bond Street; buses 7, 8, 10, 25, 55, 73, 98, 176, 390.*
Open: *Mon–Fri 10am–6pm.*
Best time to go: *Thursday and Friday afternoons.*
Parking: *There's an (expensive) underground car park at the London Marriott Hotel, entrance on Duke Street.*
Main wares: *Antique silverware, jewellery, glassware, toys, ancient artefacts, commemorative china.*
Specifics: *Dinky toys, thimbles, Middle Eastern antiquities, watches.*

J. Bolding & Sons, Victorian brass founders, metal merchants and manufacturers of sanitary appliances, might flush their heads down their own toilets in surprise if they knew the use to which their factory off Oxford Street had been put. The ground floor and basement of this large 19th-century building are now given over to the antiques trade and, together with nearby premises on Davies Mews, house up to 200 dealers. It is a peach of a place for browsing.

Grays is run by the firm Antiques Hypermarket, which also owns Alfie's Antiques Market (*see* Church Street, p.79). Situated on the edges of expensive Mayfair, it is perhaps not surprising that some of the jewellery stalls seem off-puttingly glamorous. A top-hatted doorman now greets customers to the building. On the whole, however, Grays is not an intimidatingly pricey or pompous place. True, you won't find bargains, but many of the traders have high-quality stock, and several display pristine, esoteric exhibits that are likely to get collectors flustered with pleasure. Most of the traders accept credit cards and there is a bureau de change downstairs.

The stalls are permanent structures, and many have glass counters. In the basement of 58 Davies Street, down a carpeted staircase, is a large floor full of traders. A china bell commemorating the auspicious marriage of Princess Anne and Mark Phillips costs £38 at the stall specializing in royal wedding memorabilia (particularly Andrew and Sarah mugs). As with many of the goods at Grays, the 'best price' is likely to be appreciably lower – just ask.

A huge variety of jewellery is kept down here, some of which was first sold 70 or 80 years ago at Mayfair shops. More interesting are the collections garnered by enthusiasts. Your eye might be caught by the Chinese ceramics at **Wheatley Antiques**, or the selection of Cartier and Rolex watches on display at three of the stalls downstairs. Other stalls include a bookshop with first editions of Dickens in its window, an engraver, painted tiles, all manner of cufflinks and an antique lace shop selling lace tablecloths, dresses and napkins. There is a decent café in the basement, and a WC.

> ## Food, Drink and Shopping
>
> **Rasa** (6 Dering Street), a plush but outstanding restaurant, specializes in vegetarian South Indian Keralan food; starting at noon it stays open through the afternoon. **The Hog in the Pound** pub, at Davies Street's junction with South Molton Street, may be touristy, but it does have outdoor seating. **Borders** (second floor, 203 Oxford Street) is a civilized licensed café within a bookshop; fashionable European snacks are served all day.
>
> Window-shopping at the designer fashion shops around South Molton Street or the millionaires' jewellery shops of Old and New Bond Street is a pastime pleasing to many.

On the ground floor it is not difficult to find more displays of jewellery and silverware: lockets, cruets, cufflinks, pipes, rings and magnifying glasses; petrol-fuelled cigarette lighters, bejewelled hatpins and antique pocket watches. **Pearl Gallery**, opposite the entrance, has an impressive collection of pearl jewellery. **A+T Jewellery** handmakes jewellery to your specification. **Arca's** collection of little wooden boxes with inlay work in silver and gold is also worth a look.

The Mews section of Grays, scarcely 50 yards down the street, has still more stalls both on the ground floor and in the basement. Downstairs, there's also the chance to see the Tyburn, an old London stream that now runs entirely underground. Marshalled in a straight line through the room, it is home to a shoal of well-fed goldfish.

Toys and ancient artefacts are the highlights down here, along with the Victory Café, which has had a trendy makeover (listen to the Wurlitzer jukebox and peruse the mural of 20th-century figures as you munch on penne, button mushrooms and cream). **Colin Baddiel** sells a selection of model cars, boats and London buses – the discontinued iconic Routemaster bus. **Wheels of Steel** also attracts many devotees to its collection of old model train sets dating back to the 1920s. Nearby, **Sarah Sellers** has a display of Victorian china dolls that seems almost scary. At one end, behind the stream, is the popular **Vintage Modes**, selling vintage clothing from the Victorian era onwards, including pieces from all over the world, such as old Afghani tribal costumes. A stall next door sells vintage jewellery.

Fragments of antiquities from Roman Britain are displayed at one stall, including a lozenge-shaped enamelled knob. **Padogan**, meanwhile, concentrates on ancient and Islamic art, and **Peter Sloane** has a cache of ancient Eastern art including sculptures of Hindu gods. There are cabinets in the basement displaying a range of collectibles such as Staffordshire figurines, Clousseau teddy bears and Victorian dolls.

The ground floor of the mews is also chock-a-block with traders in esoteric objects. Highlights include: **CF Seidler**, where you can buy military items such as medals, swords, guns and caps from the early 16th century to the Third Reich; **Jane Stewart's** collection of pewterware (from buttons to mugs); paintings from the 19th and early 20th centuries (most with a price tag of £1,000–5,000); a Roman forearm and hand with bronze bracelet costing £10,000; Chinese ceramics; oriental art; and two stalls selling ancient artefacts from Afghanistan (from one of which you can also get a detailed account of the political situation in that country). In addition, **Michael's Boxes** sells ceramic boxes, and there is a bookstall, **Biblion**.

The market is not held at weekends, which enables several of its traders to transport their wares to Portobello Road (see p.54) every Saturday. Many also attend Bermondsey market (see p.150) on Friday mornings, so, if you're thinking of visiting on that day, it's best to come in the afternoon.

A fair number of people, mostly European and American tourists, visit Grays, but it rarely gets unpleasantly crowded – odd when you consider that it is only a stone's throw from the turmoil of Oxford Street. Why London's most boring shopping street is also its busiest is one of the city's most mystifying conundrums. But, if you find yourself struggling amid the chainstores and slow-moving, slow-thinking crowds, don't despair: there is an escape along Davies Street, where the traders are all charming.

LEADENHALL

Whittington Avenue, off Gracechurch Street and Leadenhall Street, EC3.

Transport: ⊖ *Monument;* ⊖*/DLR Bank; buses 15, 17, 21, 25, 35, 40, 43, 47, 48, 76, 149, 133, 141, 344, 521.*

Open: *Shops vary, but most are open Mon–Fri 7am–4pm. There's a food market on Fridays 10am–4pm.*

Best time to go: *Midday, before it gets too busy.*

Parking: *Very difficult; within the congestion charge zone; try the (expensive) Vintry underground car park on Bell Wharf Lane (just east of Southwark Bridge).*

Main wares: *Fish, flowers, suits, newspapers, tobacco.*

Specifics: *Fish, shellfish, deli goods.*

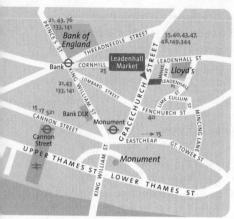

Leadenhall is the oldest of London's surviving retail markets by centuries. The trouble is, it's scarcely a market any longer. The current structure is a grand Victorian arcade, built in 1881 by Sir Horace Jones, who also designed the wholesale market buildings at Smithfield and old Billingsgate. The businesses inside are divided into permanent premises – shops, in other words. But Leadenhall deserves to be included for three reasons: its rich history, its fresh-food shops and its Friday food market, which is a tiny version of Borough.

Before noon, the market can be a quiet place, but the peace is deceptive; listen carefully and you can hear the muffled roar of an immense city. London began here: when Sir Horace laid the foundations of his arcade, the remains of a Roman basilica and other administrative buildings were unearthed. In the Middle Ages, Leadenhall lay on the edge of the great markets of the City of London. Just examine the street names to the south and west of here: Cornhill, Poultry, Cheapside (*ceap* was Saxon for market), Bread Street, Fish Street Hill, Milk Street.

The name Leadenhall comes from the lead roof of a mansion on the site that belonged to the Neville family in the 14th century. According to John Stow's 1598

Survey of London: 'in 1408 Robert Rikeden of Essex and Margaret his wife confirmed to Richard Whittington [the Lord Mayor of pantomime fame] and other citizens of London, the manor of Leaden Hall. In 1411, Richard Whittington confirmed the same manor to the mayor and commonalty of London, whereby it came to the possession of the city.'

The market itself dates from the late 14th century, when one Hugh Neville was allowed to hold a market for his tenants. After the city came to run it, the trading area was reserved for outsiders – country people, provincials and even foreigners – to come and peddle their produce. From the first it was noted for poultry. Gradually other foodstuffs came to be sold here, and in 1444 the draper and one-time mayor Simon Eyre built a granary on the site. He also constructed a chapel on the east side of the building. Stow relates that every market day before noon priests 'did celebrate Divine service there to such market-people as repaired to prayer...' This practice ended in 1484, when the market buildings were destroyed by fire.

By Elizabethan times, Leadenhall had been rebuilt. It was still the market for

Food and Drink

Several snack/sandwich bars trade in the market: **Chop'd** (Nos.1–3) is popular for its salads and soups; **Hamilton's** cocktail bar and restaurant (No.28) is one of the poshest; the tiny **Regis Snack Bar** (No.34), on Leadenhall Place, is one of the oldest. Also within the market buildings is the **Leadenhall Wine Bar** (No.27), where Spanish tapas are served from noon.

Should you not find anything you want to eat at Leadenhall, **Noto Ramen House** (Bow Bells House, 7 Bread Street), a Japanese noodle bar, is a short walk away.

traders from outside London, but the poultry dealers were now joined in the street outside by traders in meat and dairy produce. They spilt out onto Gracechurch Street, almost joining up with the general market held there. Inside the market enclosure, hardware, leather and cloth were sold.

The market was destroyed once again in the Great Fire of 1666. It was soon rebuilt, and the new structure enclosed an open space divided into three. The beef market took up one section, poultry and fish another, while the third contained general shops. This system more or less continued until Sir Horace was commissioned to design the new building.

Structurally, the market has changed little since the 1880s. Four avenues, entered through tall, stone arches, meet in a central crossing. Ornate ironwork graces the interior, and glass roofing allows light onto the cobbled street below. At ground level, the building is divided into shops; no trading takes place on the street apart from the shoeshines outside the Lamb Tavern (see p.40) and the Friday market.

The best of the four avenues is approached from Gracechurch Street. By the entrance is **Nicholson and Griffin**, an old-fashioned barber's which now caters for women as well. In its basement premises, you can view part of the Roman basilica on which Leadenhall is built. Inside the market, the first shop is occupied by **Butcher & Edmonds** (1–3 Grand Avenue), a traditional butcher's with hares hanging up and a superb choice of game birds in season. Sawdust is strewn on the floor, and butchers in starched white tunics get down to business behind the counter: plucking pheasants, dressing turkeys, drawing mallards. The turkeys are proud barrel-chested birds; the chickens corn-fed.

Nearby Attractions

Bank of England Museum, *entrance on Bartholomew Lane, t (020) 7601 5545, www.bankofengland.co.uk;* ⊖ *Bank;* **buses 21, 43, 76, 133, 141. Open** *Mon–Fri 10–5.* A history of the Bank of England, with some interactive exhibits, such as the foreign-exchange game for risk-free dealing.

Lloyd's of London, *Lime Street, www.lloydsoflondon.co.uk;* ⊖ *Monument;* **bus 40. Closed** *to the public.* Spectacular 'inside-out' architecture by Richard Rogers, designer of Paris's Pompidou Centre.

The Gherkin aka Swiss Re, *30 St Mary Axe, www.30stmaryaxe.com;* ⊖ *Liverpool St/Bank.* **Closed** *to the public.* The Gherkin is not only architecturally innovative, but also London's first environmentally sustainable skyscraper. It was designed by Sir Norman Foster, who also brought light to the Reichstag in Berlin and the British Museum's Great Court.

Monument, *Monument St, t (020) 7626 2717;* ⊖ *Monument; bus 15. Viewing platform, accessible by spiral staircase, open daily 9.30am–5pm; adm £2, £1 for under 16s, under 5s free.* Commemoration of the Great Fire by Christopher Wren. The view from the top, although obscured somewhat by the surrounding office blocks, is enjoyable, especially at dusk.

St Katherine Cree, *Leadenhall St;* ⊖ *Aldgate.* Built in the 1620s, this was one of the few church buildings to survive the Great Fire of London.

Nearby, **H. S. Linwood & Son**, the fishmonger's (6–7 Grand Avenue), has a vivid, mouthwatering display outside its lock-up shop (with Royal Warrant proudly on show). Enormous crabs and monstrous lobsters bask in the spotlight on crushed white ice. Cheeses from all over Europe draw the crowds at 4 Leadenhall Market, along with all cheese-related accessories, such as gourmet crackers.

Chamberlains (25 Leadenhall Market) sells sea creatures such as fresh lobster and swordfish, and has a restaurant next door. The solitary florist's, **A. Booth**, sells pot plants, wicker baskets and cut flowers from No.16. Two other old-school businesses at Leadenhall are **Kandies** (No.58), a 'tobacco blender and cigar importer' according to the sign over the tiny kiosk; and **Leadenhall News Ltd**, its miniature premises simply bursting with magazines.

By 12.30pm the market is crowded. There's a high suit-count as stockbrokers, insurance dealers from the nearby Lloyd's Building, merchant bankers and their ilk spill out of the offices and into the snack bars, or come for a whisky and cigar at the **Lamb Tavern** (selling excellent Young's real ales) or the **New Moon** (a pleasantly murky, wood-lined pub). Several drink out on the avenue, where the smell of beer mixes with that of meat. Shoeshines vie for their attention.

On Fridays, stalls appear that sell a variety of fresh food and gourmet goodies. This food market is still quite small and aimed at satisfying the lunchtime crowd or tempting the city gent to take deli delights home for supper, but it brings a touch of the old market back and the punters love it. There's **Yumchaa**, selling delicate loose-leaf tea in exotic combinations (at £6 a bag it's aimed squarely at the money crowd), a stall selling salamis, foie gras and honey from France, and another devoted to the olive oils of southern Italy. You can try cured wild beef from Dartmoor or wild-boar salami from Italy and, to finish, pick a beautifully presented fruit tart or a bag of homemade fudge in a range of unusual flavours such as Baileys or Strawberry Swirl. If you need

beautifying, check out **Grace's** stall with her handmade organic miracle cream.

Leadenhall remains an Epicurean oasis amid the humming air conditioning of the finance factories. But it may not stay this way for long. New businesses coming into the market are acutely aware of the customers they can attract within this most wealthy square mile in Britain, and few want to sell food. Chains inside the hall include **Jigsaw** (No.31), **Hobbs** and **The Body Shop** (No.26). **Gieves & Hawkes**, the Savile Row tailors, have a branch nearby (18 Lime Street). The **Leadenhall Suit Co** within the market also offers bespoke tailoring. There is a photo shop, too, as well as **The Leadenhall Gift Shop**, which sells horrendous porcelain creations.

But, while poultry is still sold at Leadenhall, and reeking water from the fishmonger's flows onto the cobbles, the vestiges of the ancient market remain.

LEATHER LANE

Leather Lane, between Greville Street and Clerkenwell Road, EC1.

Transport: ⊖ *Chancery Lane, Farringdon; buses 8, 17, 25, 45, 46, 55, 63, 242, 243, 341, 521.*

Open: *Mon–Fri 10.30am–2.30pm.*

Best time to go: *11.30am, before it gets too busy. This market caters for the lunchtime trade and many traders don't set up until after 11am, so don't go early.*

Parking: *Difficult; within the congestion charge zone; there's a multi-storey car park (expensive) on Saffron Hill.*

Main wares: *Women's clothes, pot plants, jewellery, handbags, children's clothes, menswear, books, electrical goods, fruit and veg.*

Specifics: *Women's office wear.*

London office workers are a strange species. Spot them on the tube first thing on a Monday morning and their grey faces and tired, melancholic expressions would lead you to believe that these corporate foot-soldiers were being overworked and used up in the cause of the company. Catch sight of them at Leather Lane market at lunchtime, however, and they present a very different picture as they cram into the narrow street, shuffling past the stalls while devouring a sandwich or pie. The bustle is invigorating; the market brings colour back to their faces.

Leather Lane attracts office staff (mostly from finance institutions and the nearby Inns of Court) like worker-bees to a honey pot. This ancient street has played host to a market for well over 300 years. There are several explanations for its name. Maybe it derives from *leveroun*, French for 'greyhound', perhaps the name of a local inn. On the other hand its etymological grandparent could be *le vrune*, Flemish for 'district'; in the late 13th century, the street demarcated two districts, forming the western boundary of the Bishop of Ely's garden. Most historians agree that the derivation has nothing to do with leather, even though leather sellers have long

Food, Drink and Shopping
Cafés and Fast Food

There's a plentiful supply of takeaway food shops along Leather Lane. The **Tiffin Sandwich Bar** (No.24) sells all manner of food, from Indian to Italian via Mexican, kebabs, meat pies and sandwiches. Salt-beef sandwiches on rye are £2.90. **Traditional Plaice** (No.83) is a traditional fish-and-chip restaurant by the corner of Portpool Lane and Leather Lane.

Bars

The **King of Diamonds Market Bar** on Leather Lane's southern stretch is a congenial spot for a drink, though a more old-fashioned venue for a glass of wine and a meal is the **Bleeding Heart** wine bar, a short walk away on Bleeding Heart Yard, off Greville Street. For a modern, clubby bar, try **Clerkenwell House**, 23–27 Hatton Wall, over two floors.

Shops

The northern end of Leather Lane enters Clerkenwell, long a home to London's Italian population. At 138–40 Clerkenwell Road is England's oldest Italian deli, **L. Terroni & Son's**, which has a great choice of foodstuffs and alcoholic drinks.

been a feature of the market, and you can still buy leather goods here today.

Like Whitecross Street (*see* p.48), Leather Lane was never a major thoroughfare, so stalls haven't been forced off the street by traffic or trams. In 1692 it was joined by a meat market opened by Lord Brooke. This survived until the late 19th century, when it succumbed to competition from the new deadstock market at Smithfield. Today only the name remains; Brooke's Market is a small square off Dorrington Street to the west of Leather Lane (access from Baldwin's Gardens).

Mary Benedetta, in her *Street Markets of London*, describes the Leather Lane of 1936. Surprisingly little seems to have changed, though less food is now sold on the stalls. Office clerks already made up many of the punters. In those days the majority of them were men, so the clothes stalls were full of braces, belts and men's suspenders, rather than today's skirts, tights and women's suits. The electrical goods traders then sold wireless sets; now they sell little portable CD players. A few toby men, whose job it was to set up traders' stalls, remained, and at that time traffic still used the street as a short cut between High Holborn and Clerkenwell Road.

In 1936, the razor-blade seller called out: 'They won't cut steel, they won't cut corns, they might cut off a bullock's tail, if someone holds the horns.' Today the poetry has changed and the rhyming gone askew, but you might find a gravel-voiced trader doing a form of cockney rap: 'Here's the best material, the best made, the boxer *shorts*. Marks insult you, have a look, sort them out today, *c'mon!*'

A great deal of building was carried out along the southern stretch of Leather Lane in the 1970s and 80s. To reach the market from High Holborn, walk down a wide pedestrianized passage between new office blocks, where Gamage's (a famous Victorian department store housed in a warren of old buildings) stood until 1972. The official stalls start at the junction with Greville Street, where the street widens for about 30 yards, allowing room for a few rows of semi-permanent stalls with corrugated roofs. There's a well-stocked household goods pitch with useful bits and pieces such as household cleaners, razors and Superglue. Children's clothes are sold nearby, while another trader has a large supply of wool suits for women, tights and underwear. Doing

Nearby Attractions

Smithfield Market, ⊖ *Farringdon; buses 17, 45, 46.* London's meat market has been in this spot since the 14th century, though there's not a lot of gore to see these days.

St Paul's Cathedral, *t (020) 7236 6883, www.stpauls.co.uk;* ⊖ *St Pauls.* **Open** *Mon–Sat 8.30am–4pm;* **adm** *adults £9, children £3.50. Guided tours at 11am, 11.30am, 1.30pm, 2pm; adults £3, children £1.* One of London's most prominent landmarks, Wren's cathedral is perhaps most famous for surviving the Blitz and for the Whispering Gallery in its great dome.

brisk trade is a dealer in cheap sweets, biscuit and chocolates, and next door is a stall draped in bath towels, with, in pride of place, a towel emblazoned with the legend 'fancy a shag?'.

Leather Lane has the best choice of women's clothes to be found at any of London's lunchtime markets, with several unusual lines among the mass-produced stuff. Styles range from the vaguely prim to the almost saucy via the nearly trendy. Women's suits are sold at a number of stalls, and there's also a good selection of woollen jumpers, pashminas, smart cashmere coats, jeans, jackets and lingerie. There are some quite funky clothes too, such as jeans with designs in gold glitter and sequinned skirts (three for a fiver). The range of men's clothes is smaller but there are always plenty of ties, socks and underwear, plus the odd checked shirt and lots of sweatshirts and track pants for pre-office workouts.

As you continue northwards, the street narrows and the crowd thickens. Much of Leather Lane is lined with Victorian terraces, interspersed with more recent buildings, including some 1970s blocks. Back at street level, women's shoes and jewellery are much in evidence on the stalls. Among the more everyday items you might find something out of the ordinary, such as fancy hats, fluffy boas and slinky party dresses. Perfumes, hair accessories and handbags are also snapped up, and there's a stall of bestseller paperbacks for office juniors to read surreptitiously under the desk. A bargain bookseller's called **Original Soho Bookshop** has permanent premises on the street, with a licensed sex shop selling erotica and leather goods downstairs.

Over the years, the amount of food available on the market has declined, but there are fruit and veg stalls which sell exotic fruit such as figs and mangoes. Near the Clerkenwell Road end, a traditional fruit and veg pitch still caters for locals from the neighbouring Peabody Estate, while a more recent addition to the market, the organic food stall, sells pesticide-free maple syrup, rice, herbal teas and organic popcorn. At the other end of the market there's a stall selling fresh fruit juices, carrot juice and beetroot, as well as seeds and nuts.

Greetings cards, cheap CDs and children's clothes are also sold along Leather Lane, and a couple of stalls have pot plants, cut flowers and flower bulbs. There's plenty of opportunity for office workers to buy each other gifts here: a wind chime, a candlestick holder or a set of spoons.

ST JAMES'S AND PICCADILLY

St James's Churchyard, Piccadilly, W1, t (020) 7734 4511; and between Hyde Park Corner and Queen's Walk, W1.

Transport: ⊖ *Piccadilly Circus, Green Park; buses 8, 9, 14, 19, 22, 38.*

Open: *St James's Tues (antiques) 10am–6pm, Wed–Sat (arts and crafts) 11am–7pm; Piccadilly Sun 9.30am–4pm.*

Parking: *Difficult; within the congestion charge zone; try the (expensive) under-ground car park at Arlington House, on Arlington Street.*

Main wares: *Crafts, paintings.*

To view Christopher Wren's St James's church is reason enough to flee the Piccadilly maelstrom for the relative tranquillity of this walled courtyard. But on five days a week there is the added draw of a market. The church – famed for its liberal leanings – was considered something of a ground-breaker when it allowed the market to be established here in the early 1980s. Indeed, St Martin-in-the-Fields (*see p.26*) followed suit a few years later. But the authorities were simply reviving a custom common in the Middle Ages, when traders would gather outside (or sometimes inside) a church porch each Sunday to wait for the congregation to emerge.

About 30 dealers set up stall outside St James's, selling a fair mix of imported goods from Third World countries,

Food, Drink and Shopping

The **Aroma** café chain has recently taken over the running of the café built on to St James's church. It is open all day, and has good coffee and adequate snacks. A posh but not too expensive alternative is to take tea (or breakfast, lunch, a snack or one of the fine choice of ice creams and sundaes) at the Fountain restaurant on the ground floor of **Fortnum & Mason** (181 Piccadilly).

For real indulgence, take tea at **The Ritz**, also on Piccadilly. Nearly next door at No.160 is the elegant and glamorous establishment favoured by London's fashion and media crowd and visiting celebrities: **The Wolseley** (t (020) 7499 6996). Set in an old bank, its double-height ceiling and Chinoiserie decor make it very grand. All meals are on offer, though brunch and tea are the best (you should book even for these though).

Shops around here are unfeasibly expensive, but it can be fun to window-shop along the Burlington and Piccadilly Arcades (both off Piccadilly) or down Savile Row. Watch out for old buffers straight out of a P. G. Wodehouse novel.

artwork, or Tibetan crafts at a stall run by broadly smiling Tibetans. There's an abundance of jewellery of every kind.

Several of the traders deal in second-hand and antique goods, and every Tuesday these dominate proceedings. One stocks old jewellery and watches; another, long-established, business sells wooden printers' blocks of elaborately adorned letters and numerals. **Fred Segal's** stall is equally unmistakable. His stock consists of a small collection of Roman coins, a more varied and colourful array of promotional phonecards and his own paintings of nudes and London landmarks. Nearby, a trader has an abundant range of old prints, mostly from the 19th century. They are ordered into sections and include many from *Punch* magazine, plus a good selection of buildings and landscapes from various counties of England. The 'London' section is particularly well stocked.

Cigarette lighters that glow in the dark, newly made tobacco pipes, furry hats and handmade glass cufflinks depicting the man in the moon – all can be netted on a quick trawl around the stalls. Prices tend to be high (this is, after all, one of London's poshest districts) and most traders are quiet, genteel types. However, charlatans aren't unknown; I listened to one seller of Chilean rainsticks (cactus sticks filled with small pebbles or such like, that sound like a downpour when up-ended; *see* p.26) claiming his wares helped cure tinnitus, dementia, autism and stress.

Wren built St James's, the only London church he constructed on an entirely new site, between 1676 and 1684. Though the church was badly damaged in the Second World War, it is still a fine building, with a modest and well-proportioned exterior and restrained classicism within. Don't

own-made artefacts and antiques. There's relatively little tourist junk on offer, and the variety and quality of the goods are higher than you'll find at St Martin's, although the stallholders are considerably grumpier! Most of the punters are, of course, tourists.

Highlights could include Chinese blouses in hand-finished silk, Russian dolls, chunky knitwear, serpentine stone carved into the busts of famous figures (by the Shona tribe of Zimbabwe), and handmade Venetian glass jewellery. You might also discover some original

Nearby Attractions

Buckingham Palace, *The Mall, ticket office* **t** *(020) 7766 7300, www. royalcollection.gov.uk;* ⊖ *St James's Park, Victoria, Hyde Park Corner;* **buses** *8, 9, 14, 19, 22, 38.* **Open** *26 July–24 Sept daily 9.45am–6pm, last entry 3.45pm;* **adm** *adults £14, children £8. Changing of the Guard May–Aug daily 11.30am, Sept–April alternate days 11.30am.* London's most famous family residence is open to the public for two months a year.

Royal Academy of Arts, *Burlington House, Piccadilly,* **t** *(020) 7300 8000, www.royalacademy.org.uk;* ⊖ *Piccadilly Circus, Green Park;* **buses** *8, 9, 14, 19, 22, 38.* **Open** *Sat–Thurs 10am–6pm, Fri 10am–10pm;* **adm** *on special exhibitions, permanent collection free.* Important exhibition venue. There are retrospectives of great artists throughout the year and the annual Summer Exhibition is a showcase for amateur British art.

miss the reredos (altar screen) carved in limewood by Grinling Gibbons. To the west of the building, a garden of remembrance commemorates the Londoners who died during the Blitz.

Further west on **Piccadilly**, every Sunday another market of sorts takes place when traders hang their wares and paintings onto the railings of Green Park. This is really an extension of the Bayswater Road market (*see* p.52), which takes place at the same time. Overpriced trinkets and pictures of beefeaters are the norm, though there might also be a few traders from the previous day's market at St James's. In addition to paintings and London souvenirs, there's a stall selling Egyptian gods and scarabs, a secondhand book stall, jewellery and pub signs.

STRUTTON GROUND

Strutton Ground, off Victoria Street, SW1.

Transport: ⊖ *St James's Park; buses 11, 24, 88, 148, 211, 507, C10.*

Open: *Mon–Fri 11.30am–3pm.*

Best time to go: *Midday Friday.*

Parking: *Difficult; within the congestion charge zone; try the (expensive) car park near the junction of Tufton Street with Great Peter Street.*

Main wares: *Clothes, umbrellas, fruit, household goods, electrical accessories, flowers, greetings cards.*

There's an evocative – but most likely false – tale that Strutton Ground gained its name from the strutting of peers of the realm, who sauntered along this little connecting street on their way to Parliament. Today the sauntering has given way to jostling, and the peers to plebeians, as every weekday hundreds of office workers emerge from the edifices of Victoria Street and pop round the corner in search of lunch. Few of the market stalls provide it. The traders don't try to compete with the many sandwich bars and snack joints on either

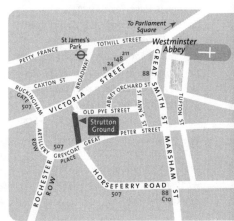

Food and Drink

Strutton Ground is crammed with sandwich bars, but if you fancy a sit-down meal try the **Laughing Halibut** at 38 Strutton Ground, a fish-and-chips café with seating in its clean, bright interior.

There are several good food shops along the street, including **Stiles** bakery (No.6), which has Eccles cakes and nougat sticks.

side of the street. All you'll find that's edible is provided by a seller of chocolates and sweets, a stall selling fried shellfish, and a couple of fruit and veg stalls with costers used to selling single apples or bananas to office juniors lunching on the hoof. Oh yes, there's also a deli stall which has stocks of olives, salad, olive oil and balsamic vinegar.

Most of the 20 or so barrows contain the type of goods snapped up as lunchtime impulse buys. Thus there's a good line in low-priced women's clothes and shoes. These range from simple tops to overcoats with mock-fur collars, via smart office

Nearby Attractions

Westminster Abbey, www.westminster-abbey.org; ⊖ Westminster; **buses** 11, 24, 88, 148, 211. You can enter free for services or prayers. Nave, Royal Chapels, Statesman's Aisle and Poets' Corner **open** Mon–Fri 9.30am–4.30pm, last adm 3.45pm, and Sat 9.20am–2.30pm, last adm 1.45pm; **adm** adults £10, 11–16s £6, family ticket £22. Cloisters **open** daily 8am–6pm. Chapter House, Pyx Chamber and Undercroft Museum **open** daily April–Sept 9.30am–5pm, Oct 10am–5pm, Nov–Mar 10am–4pm; **adm** included in ticket. The seat of the Anglican church in Britain, where monarchs are crowned and luminaries buried.

suits, scarves, underwear and gloves. Menswear is limited to silk ties, socks and underwear, plus a few shirts. A 'demmer' (see p.197) is also hoping to attract a few spur-of-the-moment purchases. He's good and attracts a knot of sandwich-munching punters as he tells them about the 'Eurotool' (a glorified Stanley knife): 'This knife will make a leg of lamb jump off the windowsill'.

A couple of stalls carry goods for use in the office. Buy a bunch of flowers at one barrow, and accompany it with a 'Sorry you're leaving' card from another. You can even buy the pen to write 'Best of luck finding a new job'. Some market traders are recession-proof.

One stall sells football scarves and umbrellas, while electrical bits and bobs (blank video tapes, indoor aerials, batteries and plugs) fill another. The CD seller has many of the latest albums and is also flogging Playstation games, 'clear 'em up, two for £30'. Near the north end of the market, the dealer in cheap watches has a new line in sales pitch: 'We're from St Helier, Jersey, so we don't pay the taxes' (uttered in broadest cockney).

This narrow bustling street, with its three-storeyed buildings, provides a relief from the monotony of the office blocks on Victoria Street. Though most of its present buildings are Victorian, Strutton Ground was first laid out during the 1670s, when the area was surrounded by market gardens. The market most likely started in the 18th century, with the produce of these gardens being sold to the citizens of Westminster. A hay market was once held in Broadway, to the north of Strutton Ground, but this was closed in the 1720s. A relic of that era survives around the corner in Caxton Street: the tiny brick Blewcoat School was built in 1709.

TACHBROOK STREET

Tachbrook Street, between Churton Street and Warwick Way, SW1.

Transport: ⊖ *Pimlico and Victoria;* ≷ *Victoria; buses 2, 11, 24, 36, 88, 148, 185, 211, 239, 360, 436, 507, C1, C10.*

Open: *Mon–Sat 9.30am–4.30pm.*

Best time to go: *Thursdays to Saturdays.*

Parking: *Difficult; within the congestion charge zone; try the multi-storey car park on Semley Place.*

Main wares: *Fruit and veg, fish, flowers, greetings cards, olives, bread, cakes.*

Specifics: *Antique furniture.*

Funny thing about Tachbrook Street: it has everything in place to be the centre of a thriving community, yet even on a Friday lunchtime customers only arrive in dribs and drabs, and the market is slowly shrinking. The dozen or so stalls are well stocked, but there's little passing trade, and at the beginning of the week only three or four traders turn up. While nearby Strutton Ground (*see p.45*) attracts battalions of office workers, Tachbrook Street is very much Pimlico's local market. It is surrounded by a wide mix of housing: well-kept Victorian terraces, home to affluent professionals, and low-rise council flats on the Longmore Gardens Estate. On weekdays, it is mostly old people from the flats who come to examine the stalls.

At least one business has been trading on the market virtually since it started in the mid-19th century. **Wright's** fish stall (Thurs–Sat) was established in 1876; the family's barrow is weighed down with a classy array of fish such as bass, salmon and monkfish, plus more lowly species such as whiting and mackerel. The Wrights also sell game birds in season, so there might be a mallard or pheasant up for grabs.

The three or four greengrocery stalls that remain have gradually started to stock a wider range of goods to suit their varied customers, so alongside the spuds and cabbages, apples and oranges you might find a bunch of flat-leaf parsley or some *pousse* (baby spinach leaves). There is also a bread and cakes stall (Wed–Sat), a

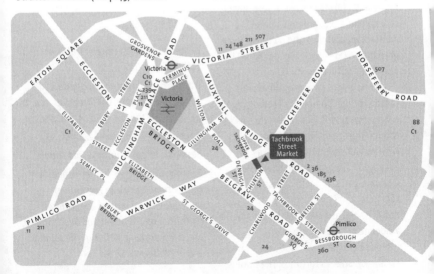

Food, Drink and Shopping

Back towards Victoria Station from the market, at 80–81 Wilton Road, is the **Seafresh Fish Restaurant**, the best fish-and-chip shop in the area.

There are two notable wine bars along Upper Tachbrook Street, both owned by Eldridge Pope the wine merchant. The **Pimlico Wine Vaults** (Nos.19–22) occupy underground cellars and have a daily changing menu plus a large range of wines by the glass; the **Reynier Wine Library** (No.16) offers a lunch buffet of nibbles along with the fruit of its cellars.

Both the small pedestrianized section of the street that holds the market and its northern neighbour, Upper Tachbrook Street, are peppered with fascinating small shops. Swoop in from the Vauxhall Bridge Road and you'll come upon **Rippon Cheese Stores** (No.26), a tiny cheese-monger's packed with British and foreign specimens, and **Cornucopia** (No.12) with its antique clothing for women.

stall selling fresh shellfish, and a trader with a stock of antique furniture. The usual socks, underwear, packaged food and sweets fill other stalls. A sole flower-seller, a stall selling mobile phone accessories, batteries and pictures, and a greetings-card vendor account for all but one of the remaining stalls.

The one bright phrase in the market's tale of decline is a new stall selling high-class provisions. It looks a picture – as though transplanted from Provence – with its half-dozen types of olives displayed in large wooden bowls. Pesto, vinegars, garlic and feta cheese are also sold here, and strings of red peppers are tied from the awnings. The trader also has a sideline in fancy soaps.

But one new stall will not turn around Tachbrook Street's fortunes. The traders seem to have little hope that their market will continue for long. They list several reasons for the decline. For a start, the market gets no help from Westminster Council, which has been known to impound traders' barrows left in the street overnight, charging owners £200 for their return. They also lament the reduction in the area's Spanish population, many of whom returned to their homeland during the last recession. 'They treat fruit as a staple, where the British treat it as a luxury.' The local Tesco – nearby, but not close enough to attract custom to the market – hasn't helped either.

The closure of Tachbrook Street's market would be a great pity, as central London has too few of these neighbourhood street markets, and the stalls complement the great collection of local independent shops. To cheer myself up, I gaze and drool at the **Bonne Bouche** bakery's display of pastries (at 38a Tachbrook Street), before plumping for an exploration of **Betabuy** delicatessen next door at No.38.

WHITECROSS STREET

Whitecross Street, between Old Street and Sutton's Way, EC1.

Transport: ⊖ *Barbican, Moorgate, Old Street;* ⇌ *Moorgate, Old Street; buses 4, 21, 43, 55, 56, 76, 100, 141, 153, 205, 214, 243, 271.*

Open: *Mon–Fri 10.30am–2.30pm.*

Best time to go: *Thursdays and Fridays.*

Parking: *Difficult; within the congestion charge zone; there's an (expensive) underground car park at the Barbican (entrances on Silk Street and Beech Street), and a few parking meters at the southern end of Whitecross Street.*

Main wares: *New clothing, shoes, watches, fruit.*

Specifics: *Women's wear.*

Whitecross Street is a narrow medieval thoroughfare that has long been home to a market. It used to run all the way to Fore Street at the edge of the City, but its southern half was destroyed by bombing in the Second World War and the Barbican Centre was built on the site.

The street was named in the 13th century after a white cross that stood near a house owned by the Holy Trinity Priory in Aldgate. Stow, writing in the 1590s, remarks that 'In White Crosse Street King Henry V built one fair house, and founded there a brotherhood of St Giles... the lands were given to the brotherhood for the relief of the poor.' But the street – sited just outside the jurisdiction of the City – became known for less charitable activities: a 17th-century ballad mentions it as the home of a famous brothel, and unlicensed street trading flourished. In the 1850s, Henry Mayhew counted 150 stalls here.

Over the years, Whitecross Street market has geared itself to the needs of local office workers. As soon as the main lunch break is over at 2pm, traders start packing up. Unfortunately, office relocations have slashed the number of workers in the area over the past decade, while those who remain tend to be chained to their desks by the 'lunch is for wimps' doctrine.

The market has shrunk noticeably as a result and there's evidence of development with lots of old shops under scaffolding being turned into...who knows. At the Old Street end of Whitecross Street there are a couple of shops heralding perhaps what is to come: **Elsie Habibi Flowers**, a smart florist, and next door **Bread & Honey** at No.205, an achingly hip clothes shop catering for both men and women and also stocking beauty products and the kind of trainers sporting brands no-one over the age of 25 has ever heard of.

Food and Drink

The **Cosy Supper Bar** (No.169), a fish-and-chip restaurant, is one of the most popular of the several cafés along Whitecross Street. The takeaway queue stretches out of the door on Fridays. High-class vegetarian food can be had at vegetarian **Carnevale** (No.135), which serves takeaway snacks and salads all day, though you might need to book (**t** (020) 7250 3452) for its excellent veggie Mediterranean lunches. **Alba** (No.107) is a good Italian, specializing in northern dishes, with a food store next door for stocking up on Italian essentials.

Market traders eat fry-ups and pizzas at **Elite Café** (No.187), while it is the stripy-shirted City brigade that frequents the **Trader** pub, opposite.

Though the market has lost some of its bustle, 50 or more stalls still take up pitches between Old Street and Dufferin Street. And there's still a fair number of customers parading up and down during their lunch hour.

The vast majority of stalls sell clothing. Although the stock changes with the season, it is mostly geared to women office workers, and might include smart jackets, pashminas, purple velvet tops, knitwear, lingerie, suits in black, white and bright red, gloves and skirts – the usual mass-produced stuff. One trader specializes in nighties, while another has a range of coats. There's also a cosmetics stand, a hair accessories stall, and a dealer in 'designer' handbags.

A couple of stalls stock women's shoes. The greetings-card stall (50p a card or three for £1.20) and the pitch full of men's shirts also attract office workers. Several customers eat their lunch while browsing, but only the adventurous risk their suits to eat freshly made Thai food while on the go. As well as the two stalls selling Thai food, there is Miss Dolly's Caribbean takeaway stall and the Mantra Indian Fusion food stall tempting office workers away from the cafés.

A few of the traders gear their stock to the inhabitants of the Peabody Estate, to the east of the market. There are stalls with fruit and veg, household goods and cosmetics, and a few selling children's wear, some dolls and a selection of learning-to-read books. Other stalls cater more for the office workers, selling gifts, oil burners, scented candles and oils. Videos, CDs and computer games are also on sale here, as well as a long stall selling all sorts of books – paperbacks are £2.

Apart from a stall displaying watches and nodding dogs, where you can get

Nearby Attractions

Barbican Arts Centre, *Silk Street*, *t (020) 7638 8891 (box office), www.barbican. org.uk;* ⊖ *Barbican;* **buses** *4, 56, 153*. This huge pile of concrete houses two theatres, two art galleries, three cinemas, a concert hall and a semi-tropical conservatory (*Level 3, t (020) 7638 4141; open 12pm–dusk*).

Bunhill Fields, *City Road*, ⊖ *Old Street;* **buses** *43, 76, 141, 205, 214, 271*. **Open** *April–Sept Mon–Fri 7.30am–7pm, Sat and Sun 9.30am–sunset; Oct–Mar Mon–Fri 7.30am–4pm, Sat and Sun 9.30am–4pm. See* main text, below.

Museum of London, *London Wall*, *t (020) 7600 3699, www.museumoflondon. org.uk;* ⊖ *Barbican, St Paul's;* **buses** *4, 56, 100*. **Open** *Mon–Sat 10am–5.50pm, Sun 12–5.50pm*. The story of London from prehistoric times to the present, with many artefacts.

watch straps and batteries fitted for free, that's about it. The pitches peter out near the junction with Dufferin Street. Fifty yards further south, however, the market makes a comeback under a block of flats outside a supermarket. On daft purpose-built stalls with cute little roofs you'll find bedlinen, socks, towels, posters, tennis balls, suitcases and bags, more women's clothes, and men's shirts and trousers. One suit stall even offers a seven-day money-back guarantee.

A short walk to the west of the market is **Bunhill Fields**, one of London's oldest burial grounds, much favoured by deceased nonconformists. The last burial took place here in 1854. Within are the graves of William Blake, John Bunyan and Daniel Defoe. It's a beautiful old place, with huge plane trees and well-worn flagstones, quite at odds with the busy roads and modern buildings around it.

West London

BAYSWATER ROAD

South side of Bayswater Road, from Clarendon Place to Queensway, W2.

Transport: ⊖ *Lancaster Gate, Queensway, Bayswater; buses 2, 6, 7, 10, 15, 16, 23, 27, 36, 70, 73, 74, 82, 94, 98, 137, 148, 204, 274, 390, 414, 436.*

Open: *Sun 9.30am–4pm.*

Best time to go: *Morning (early if looking for a parking space).*

Parking: *Plenty of places near Bayswater Road on a Sunday, but spaces are taken up quickly during the summer; try Lancaster Gate.*

Main wares: *New paintings, drawings, sculptures, etchings and crafts.*

Money has the art world firmly in its grip, but the brash commercialism of Bayswater Road's Sunday art market is almost refreshing compared to the haughty but equally venal commercial galleries of Mayfair's Cork Street. For almost a mile, the railings of Hyde Park are decked with oil paintings, watercolours, sketches and collages by undiscovered artists, would-be artists and con-artists from all over southern England. The quality of work varies enormously: a few are laughably inept, most are sentimental and dull, but very occasionally you might encounter something eye-catching.

The majority of traders have few pretensions. They are out for a quick buck (or yen, or euro), taking all major credit cards, and are well aware that they are hawking simple decorative pictures rather than serious works of art. They paint archetypal London scenes, with a reliably high beefeater count each week; mawkish horrors such as cuddly dogs, teddy bears and pussycats; or typically English landscapes (thatched houses, fields of wheat – you know the sort of thing). Spot the influence behind each picture – Monet, Constable and Renoir are the most slavishly copied, but Van Gogh, Lichtenstein and even L. S. Lowry and Beryl Cook have their imitators. Many traders display cards stating: 'All work displayed or offered for sale is entirely the original work of the licence-holder.' Take this with a large pinch of salt and gargle.

Nudes get a look in, and so do reproductions of Impressionist works, but there is also space for a few amateur enthusiasts who dream of selling their first painting. Some exhibit newspaper clippings, flaunting rave reviews from such organs as the *Bromley & Beckenham Times*. One artist, selling copper engravings of the

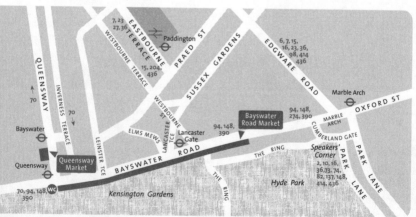

prophet Mohammed's last words, has an even greater endorsement: a photograph of himself standing next to Mohammed Ali taken in 1967. A few artists will draw your portrait while you wait. A brief head and shoulders sketch costs £8, a full-length sketch £20. I spotted one shameless individual charging £75 for a portrait of your favourite pet. Probably the cheapest original works you'll find are the tiny cartoons depicting aspects of London life: five for £10. Often the works are extravagantly framed and indeed the surrounds are often more desirable than the paintings themselves. Many of the artists will happily lower their prices a smidgen if you wish to take the painting home rolled up in a cardboard tube.

It's worth finding the work of painters who steer clear of immediately saleable themes. One specializes in military views, another in Native American portraits. (This last artist was asked by an American customer if he displayed any of his own work at home. 'No, my wife won't have them in the house', came the sad reply.) Perhaps the most interesting work is produced by the market's sculptors. John Spielman's graceful, curvaceous wooden figures have an ethereal quality, though they are rather pricey.

Increasing numbers of crafts traders now come to the market. Their stock varies from the amusingly novel (look for the colourful face masks depicting animal heads; there's a great one of a parrot with a huge red beak) to out-and-out tourist tosh. Several sell handmade jewellery and come to Bayswater after spending Friday and Saturday at St James's market in Piccadilly. On Sundays, paintings are also hung along the railings of Green Park on Piccadilly (see p.45). Embroidered bags, watch-part collages, painted table-mats,

Food and Drink

Across the Bayswater Road from the market, near the junction with Elms Mews, is the **Swan** pub, which dates from the 18th century. Despite the traffic, this is a good place to sit outside for a drink on a sunny day; pub food is sold.

There is a Thai restaurant, **Nipa**, on Lancaster Terrace. But my choice for Sunday lunch would be to walk down to Queensway, where some of London's best Chinese restaurants are situated. You can eat superb dim sum (inexpensive lunchtime snacks and filled dumplings) at **Royal China**, 13 Queensway. **Mandarin Kitchen**, at 14–16 Queensway, is another popular Chinese place, serving mainly Cantonese food, as does **Magic Wok** (No.100), which has the best crispy duck.

pub signs, fridge magnets and hand-painted coins can also be found. All too many traders sell cutesy olde-worlde tea shop and living-room window dioramas. Be careful before taking photos at the market, as many traders object to you sampling their works of art on the cheap.

Bayswater Road should be saved for a fine morning, but you shouldn't come here expecting a traditional London street market (head east to Brick Lane – see p.97 – for the best Sunday morning shindig). Rather, view it as part of an exploration of Hyde Park. Dappled sunlight streams through the plane trees onto the traders as you walk along one of London's oldest roads (Bayswater Road is part of the Roman Via Trinobantia). Only the unceasing traffic mars the peace. Glance across at 100 Bayswater Road, on the corner of Leinster Terrace. Sir James Barrie, the playwright, lived here from 1902 to 1909, during which time he wrote *Peter Pan*.

Nearby Attractions

Kensington Gardens, ⊖ *High Street Kensington, Queensway, Lancaster Gate;* **buses** *70. 94, 148, 390.* A large park divided from Hyde Park by the Serpentine lake, with a statue of Peter Pan, an art gallery and the Princess Diana memorial fountain.

Speakers' Corner, *Hyde Park;* ⊖ *Marble Arch;* **buses** *2, 10, 16, 36, 73, 74, 82, 137, 148, 414, 436.* Londoners have exercised their right to free speech on Sunday afternoons here since 1872. Speakers range from the Messianic to the downright dotty: legalization of cannabis, religion and world federalism are perennial topics. Some heroic characters even continue when no one is listening.

Queensway Market

23 and 25 Queensway. **Open** *Mon–Sat 10am–10pm; Sun 12–10pm; computer fair open Mon–Fri 11am–7.30pm, Sat 11am–6.30pm and Sun 12–5.30pm.*

At the south end of Queensway there is an indoor market with 100 shops which is worth a visit. Around the entrance are shops selling the usual tourist tat – London souvenirs, T-shirts, etc. Inside you'll come across Psychic Mews, built to look like an old London street, where clairvoyants, tarot card readers and palmists are gathered. Here help is offered for psychological or relationship problems, or you can have a crystal ball reading. To the right is a computer fair where you can buy computer equipment, books and old versions of computer software. In the main market look out for the Russian food shop next door to a shop selling Russian souvenirs, videos and CDs, and the **Rock Leather Shop**, a leather specialist which also sells Persian rugs, handmade pure wool kilims from £85 and sculptures.

PORTOBELLO

Portobello Road, Westbourne Grove, Acklam Road, Golborne Road, W10, W11; **t** *(020) 7727 7684; see individual markets for more details.*

Public transport: ⊖ *Notting Hill Gate, Ladbroke Grove, Westbourne Park; buses 27, 70, 94, 148, 390 (Notting Hill Gate); 23, 28, 31, 328 (Westbourne Park); 7, 23, 52, 70, 295, 302 (Ladbroke Grove).*

Open: *See individual markets for details.*

Best time to go: *Saturday morning.*

Parking: *Impossible at the antiques end; there are sometimes parking meter spaces along Chesterton Road, near Golborne Road.*

Main wares: *Antiques, food, new and secondhand clothes, bric-a-brac, crafts, household goods.*

Specifics: *Secondhand clothes under the Westway; junk bargains at the Golborne Road end of the market and on Acklam Road.*

Bermondsey might have the edge for antiques, Borough for food and Camden for clothing – but nowhere can compare to the Portobello for an all-in-one experience. Yet it's no homogenous mass: this Saturday celebration consists of five separate markets roughly stapled together, and it's easy to see the joins.

Portobello Road cuts through the neighbourhood like a cheese iron, taking a sample of all its constituents. The southern stretches, nearest to Notting Hill Gate tube, are opulent and genteel, while the northern tip is scruffy and verging on the lawless. The cutting edge of gentrification, currently just north of the Westway, is where to look for the trendiest stalls, shops and cafés. Going from south to north, the goods you'll find

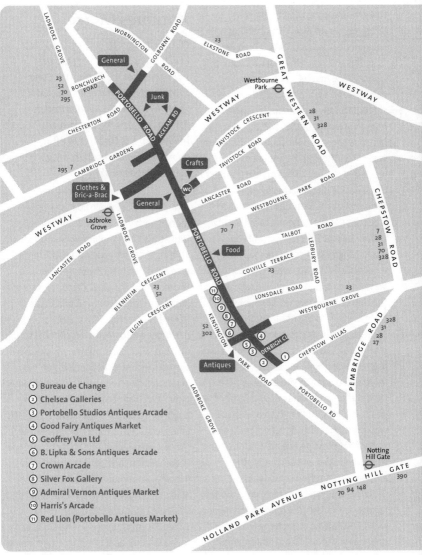

① Bureau de Change
② Chelsea Galleries
③ Portobello Studios Antiques Arcade
④ Good Fairy Antiques Market
⑤ Geoffrey Van Ltd
⑥ B. Lipka & Sons Antiques Arcade
⑦ Crown Arcade
⑧ Silver Fox Gallery
⑨ Admiral Vernon Antiques Market
⑩ Harris's Arcade
⑪ Red Lion (Portobello Antiques Market)

at the market are: antiques, food, household goods, clothes (new and secondhand), bric-a-brac and junk. The Golborne Road local market is tacked on to the northern end of Portobello Road.

Until the 19th century, Portobello Road was a track leading to Porto Bello farm, named to commemorate Admiral Vernon's 1737 capture of the Caribbean city Puerto Bello. By the 1860s, modest houses had

been built along much of its length; street trading arrived soon after. The market was at first limited to the northern stretch of the road, and most of its trade was in fruit and vegetables. Saturday has always been the busiest day. It wasn't until the late 1940s that antiques traders, displaced by the closure of the Caledonian market (*see* Bermondsey, p.150), started arriving here. During the 1950s and 60s the antiques trade mushroomed and Portobello's antiques market grew correspondingly. Today, well over 2,000 traders operate from this section of the market each week.

Such is the market's size, it would be exhausting to examine it all in detail on a single Saturday. Either saunter down the mile-long length of the road, dipping in here and there, or split your visit over two weeks, scrutinizing the antiques one week, and the rest of the market the next. If you decide on the latter, or want to miss the worst of the Saturday crowds and steer clear of the antiques, take the tube to Westbourne Park station and walk down Tavistock Crescent (perhaps dallying for a while at the Metropolitan pub on the way). The 10-minute stroll will take you to the centre of the market: to your left will be food stalls, to the right clothes.

If, however, you decide on the leisurely stroll along the length of the market, start at the Notting Hill Gate end on Saturday morning. As soon as you get out of the tube station and saunter down Pembridge Road, you'll notice that everyone else is walking in the same direction. You'll also notice that most people are tourists. But there's a greater age range here than among the Camden market-goers.

There is no grand entrance to Portobello Road at its southern end; nor are there any stalls. The narrow street bends round and goes down the hill. Follow the crowds.

At present the market starts just after Portobello Road's junction with Chepstow Villas, but such is its popularity that you might well come across stalls muscling in on the territory further south. These tend to sell the most predictable sort of tourist codswallop, but you might also encounter one of Portobello's many buskers, perhaps a steel drummer or a Peruvian band playing Andean pipe music.

Antiques Market

*Portobello Road, from Chepstow Villas to Elgin Crescent (including the west side of Westbourne Grove), W11. **Open** Sat 7am–3pm. For more details contact The Portobello Road Antique Dealers Association, 223a Portobello Road, London W11 1LU, **t** (020) 7229 8354, info@portobelloroad.co.uk, www. portobelloroad.co.uk.*

Tens of thousands of visitors are attracted to Portobello Road's antiques market each week. But even if you balk at tourist tosh and a multinational scrum of punters, it's worth paying a visit. The trick is to avoid the main thoroughfares and the most obvious sites. Rather, explore the edges, the basements and first floors of the many premises that have been partitioned into tiny trading booths where scores of traders set out their wares. Here the stall rents are cheaper and you'll find genuine enthusiasts keen to chat about their collecting obsessions. True, you'll rarely find a bargain, but if you're a fanatic and need just one more perfume bottle, military medal, cigarette card or Dinky toy to complete a collection, then you'll find friendly, like-minded folk who might be able to help you. Outside these premises, stalls are crammed either side of the street. An empty space on this stretch of the road is unheard of – pitches are highly prized at the Portobello; in summer casuals turn up as early as 5.30am to try to bag a pitch.

One of the first sights that comes into view after the junction with Chepstow Villas is a bureau de change (there are several along the upper portion of the Portobello). This gives more than an inkling of what to expect; most traders are thoroughly geared up for foreign visitors and raise their prices accordingly. (There are also bureaux de change inside **The Crown Arcade** at No.119, **The Admiral Vernon Arcade** at Nos.141–9, **The World Famous Market** at No.177 and **The Antiques Gallery** at 288–96 Westbourne Grove – all boast no commission with repeated exclamation marks.) Many stalls accept credit cards, and some operate the export scheme whereby visitors from outside the EU can have VAT returned on the goods they purchase (ask for a form).

Silver cutlery, pot dogs and magnifying glasses fight for space on one of the first stalls. Next to it, a trader is selling a collection of printer's woodcuts. Denbigh Close, a quaint cobbled mews cluttered with BMW cars, provides an overflow for a clutch of stalls filled with old clocks, a varied collection of antique cameras, Victorian glass bottles and elderly typewriters. One trader has marked her wares with price tags that give an address on Bermondsey Street, SE1. Several Bermondsey Street traders make the journey northwest every weekend; hundreds of goods that change hands at Bermondsey (*see* p.150) on a Friday morning go up for sale at Portobello on the Saturday – often with a hefty mark-up.

Directly opposite Denbigh Close are the **Chelsea Galleries** at 67–9 and 73 Portobello Road, the first of the indoor concourses of traders. Antique jewellery forms the bulk of their stock: necklaces, old gold rings and elaborate brooches. You will also find silver, old tools and linen. Upstairs is a café.

Back on the street, there's what looks like a boxful of rubble. On closer examination it turns out to be a collection of fossils, going for £5 each. More expensive, mounted fossils (a pair of pre-Cambrian fish will set you back £140,

a polished ammonite six inches in diameter £225) can be found at No.88, while at **Atlam** at No.77, in among a sea of brass and silver plate, is a horde of antique cameras. Fly-traders fill in every inch between the legitimate stalls, selling their usual collection of cigarette lighters and novelty goods.

Portobello Studios Antiques Arcade (at Nos.101–3) is another gallery filled with traders and bursting with punters. Again, jewellery is the most common commodity, but you'll also find carved ivory, small ornaments, candlesticks, beautiful old pocket watches, silverware and Hornby train sets. Upstairs is another cluster of traders dealing in small furniture, decorative objects, antique dolls and old glass display jars. The highlight for me is a business named **Old Father Time**. Its varied collection includes a 1941 clock from an RAF operations room, grandfather clocks and a number of early 20th-century Planimeters: marvellous old gizmos that look like something removed from the dashboard of an H. G. Wells rocket. Their various dials and discs can tell you the time, the month, the stages of the lunar cycle and the visible constellations. There's also a small café here, with filled bagels, pastries and home-made soup. Most of the crowds that jam downstairs seem unaware of the first-floor stalls, so you can have a jostle-free browse.

At 105 Portobello Road is **Geoffrey Van Ltd**, which has yet more traders inside, including **Manor House Antiques** with its folk art. The **Good Fairy Antiques Market**, opposite Geoffrey Van, is one of the largest groupings of stalls on the Portobello. About 50 traders are packed into the semi-permanent, covered structure set just off the street. Hundreds of customers block the tiny corridors. Most traders specialize in antique jewellery, but others concentrate on old watches, woodwork tools (well-weathered chisels, lead plumbs), silverware, cutlery (some with ivory handles) and 19th-century prints. One young chap has a collection of old fountain pens going back to 1910, the oldest selling for £150. Nearby is a stall selling a variety of antique phones: for £350 you can pick up a 1920s model set in a mahogany cabinet with a separate toothglass-shaped earpiece; £50 will buy you a nice bright red Art Deco number or a stern black War Office version, while for £750 you can have an imported American coin-operated model from the 1930s (of the type much used by Jimmy Cagney, apparently), converted to accept British currency and work on the British telephone network.

There are more stalls in the arcades at No.109 (including the **Portobello Print Rooms**, with prints, maps and engravings) and No.113. The latter premises go back quite a way, and lead to a large room at the rear where there is more space to wander among the stalls. Many of the traders here sell antiquarian books, though their collections are small and somewhat disparate. One woman has a selection of embroidered cloths bearing religious homilies. Old glass or pottery bottles, candelabras and light shades can also be found.

The market spills into Westbourne Grove, which bisects Portobello Road. On the east side there are four or five stalls selling new clothes; on the west section there are more antiques stalls out in the street (right up to the junction with Kensington Park Road), plus additional traders housed in indoor arcades. At 282–90 Westbourne Grove is the **B. Lipka & Sons Antiques Arcade**, containing clocks, crockery, collectibles and glassware. Your best bet is to head for No.290. In the basement, you'll usually be able to escape the crowds and have plenty of time to peruse the traders' goods. Many of these folk are inveterate enthusiasts. Take a look at the magnificent collection of cigarette cards, depicting anything from military uniforms to golf. Should you want to buy a set of 'The Mysteries of the Bunker' or similar (costing £50 framed), you'll usually have to interrupt the stallholder's conversation with another avid (and often wheezing) collector. He also has a display of old cigarette packets and tobacco tins featuring various brands you've never heard of: Rich Uncle, Harris's All Gay, Thunder Clouds, Golden Bud, Ogden's Cobnut Sliced (as well as the renowned Ogden's Impi Twist), Three Nuns and Walkürë. Also in this basement is a stall full of rare records (blues, jazz, 1960s). The top of the stall is decorated with a fringe of 45s stuck to a board. A woman asks the stallholder for music to accompany her ballroom dancing team; he duly rummages in his Latin collection.

This basement leads into the next-door premises. Here you'll find more collectors' stalls. One majors in military clothes and medals, another in old radios, a third has sheaves of magazine adverts. There's also a jewellery repairer who offers a bead restringing service, and a man selling ancient and rather alarming looking pieces of 19th-century medical equipment. Model trains and Dinky toys are also sold down here.

Back on the Portobello Road, north of Westbourne Grove, the antiques stalls continue to dominate the market on each side of the street. Pewter tankards, old mah-jong sets, brass candelabras, farmyard animal models, kitchenware, magnifying glasses, old pistols and cigarette lighters might all be on view. Coins, stamps and old postcards attract a fair few customers to one stall. The **Crown Arcade**, occupying 119 Portobello Road, has a back entrance down Vernon Yard. Just inside, one trader displays his cherished collection of corkscrews. Next door, at No.121, the **Silver Fox Gallery** is mostly full of jewellery traders.

Opposite the junction with Lonsdale Road is the **Admiral Vernon Antiques Market** ('120 traders plus a bureau de change' reads the sign), which takes up indoor space between 139 and 151 Portobello Road. Pewterware is sold outside No.151, which is also the entrance to the Lower Market Hall. Jewellery and polished wooden jewellery boxes account for many of the goods, but one dealer specializes in gramophones, stocking models dating back to the days of wax cylinders. Pottery, lace doilies, cameras, pens, oriental porcelain and Art Deco ornaments and furniture are also displayed. There is a café downstairs.

Further north, outdoors on Portobello Road, is a stall chock-a-block with telescopes and binoculars; another trader's stock is based around military headgear, including wartime tin helmets and gas masks. At Nos.161–3 is **Harris's Arcade**. Inside, there's a dealer with a fascination for drink. His collection includes a cocktail shaker from Asprey's (the Bond Street store for the dangerously wealthy) and silver wine-bottle holders.

At 165–9 Portobello Road is the oldest of the street's indoor antiques markets, the **Red Lion**. Here Susan Garth 'launched London's first antiques market making the Portobello Road an international institution', according to the blue plaque on the outside of the building. In fact, this indoor market is not now among the more popular sites, and some of the pitches remain unlet. Silverware, crockery and jewellery are among the antiques traded; more out of the ordinary are the lace and cotton nightdresses, plus the collection of old tiles. In front of No.171 is a stall selling pewter plates and tankards; once you've made your purchase, take it to be filled up in the **Portobello Star** pub which lies behind. Yet another indoor market – '**The World Famous Portobello Market**' – can be found at No.177, including books and a stall full of old teddy bears, a stall selling Russian dolls and several traders selling paintings. By now you're probably suffering antique-fatigue, and my list of synonyms for 'old' has been exhausted. Fear not: the antiques market finally comes to an end at Portobello Road's junction with Elgin Crescent and Colville Terrace.

Food Market

*Portobello Road, from Colville Terrace to Lancaster Road, W11. **Open** Mon–Wed 8am–6.30pm, Thurs 8am–1pm, Fri and Sat 8am–6.30pm; **organic market** (under the Westway) Thurs 11am–6pm.*

Yes, food is what's wanted now, and food is what we get. The food market takes up most of the space on the right-hand side of the street (as you walk northwards), between here and just before the Westway flyover. But the first fresh produce you find is a big vibrant stall of fresh cut flowers, selling sunflowers even in winter. Next is a traditional fruit and veg pitch with really low prices (20p for 1lb of bananas, 3lbs of grapes for £1.50). Further along, fresh fruit and nuts are sold by a venerable lady sporting pearl earrings, black beret, smart gaberdine and a pink neckscarf. 'Mind how you go, dear', she greets a regular.

This is the longest established section of the market, and some stallholders have been here for years. I heard tell of a man who invited one of the costermongers to his wedding; when he returned to the area 40 years later, the trader still had a stall at the market. Despite the large number of tourists who visit the antiques market, the food traders have kept their prices down; locals make good use of the food stalls, both during the week and on Saturdays. What has changed is the number of fast-food sellers catering for the Saturday crowds. Bratwürsts, Thai fried noodles and curries, kebabs, goat curries and Afro-Caribbean takeaway food might all make an appearance. The latter is a reminder that Notting Hill was a centre of London's Afro-Caribbean population. Unfortunately, this community's presence has become less noticeable since the area's gentrification in the late 1980s, but Afro-Caribbeans are still the heart and soul of that huge annual knees-up, the Notting Hill Carnival, held on the last Sunday and Monday of August.

There's little in the way of tropical produce at the food market – nothing more exotic than a box of mangoes. But you will find the self-proclaimed 'tomato and banana king', and a butcher who might have quail and pheasants (in season) alongside a row of strung-up chickens and a plastic bag full of pigs' feet. The occasional new-clothes stall has managed to get a pitch on this stretch of the market, but most traders sell inexpensive comestibles such as sweets, packaged food, eggs and traditional salad ingredients. About 15 years ago there was also a cheese stall where I bought a particularly ripe Gruyère as my contribution to a family meal. It wasn't until we saw a battalion of maggots shuffling towards the candlelight that we realized something was amiss. By that time, half the cheese had been eaten. Sadly that stall has gone.

Instead, there are traders selling baked goods such as focaccia, pastries and muffins, and some of these also sell sandwiches. Other stalls sell cheese, honey, dried fruit and nuts, olives and dried herbs. **The Cool Chili Company** offers dried chillies and sauces. Interspersed among the food stalls are traders selling batteries, plugs, masking tape, household goods, socks and gloves.

Near the Westbourne Park Road junction there's a fishmonger's barrow with a fair choice of seafood and fish (squid, smoked salmon and haddock, mackerel, crabs and mussels). **J. H. Smith**, the shop at No.208, also does a good line in crab and skate.

At this point we must interrupt this Saturday excursion for a word about Thursdays under the Westway (just 100 yards further north from the daily food stalls). From 11am to 6pm each week, a small market devoted to organic food takes place. Here you'll usually find a large, well-stocked fruit and veg stall (with squash, yams, cabbages, apples, oranges and even organic Brussels sprouts in season); an enticing and varied bread stall (soda bread, sourdough and sun-dried tomato focaccia); a meat caravan run by Longwood Farm (an organic farm in Suffolk), which displays a few organic cheeses, butter and free-range eggs, as well as all the usual cuts of organic meat; and finally a stall selling an enticing array of organic dried fruit and nuts: cranberries, papaya, blueberries, cashews, pistachios and Brazils.

Back to Saturdays, when the market undergoes another transformation after the junction with Lancaster Road.

Clothes, Crafts and Bric-a-brac Market

Under the Westway, from Portobello Road to Ladbroke Grove, W11; Acklam Road, W10; Portobello Road, from the Westway to Bonchurch Road, W10; t (020) 7229 6898. **Open** *Fri 7am–4pm, Sat 8am–5pm, Sun 9am–4pm.*

From Lancaster Road to the Westway, stalls contain everyday goods such as haberdashery, new bags, electrical goods, fabrics, crockery, kitchenware (enamel breadbins, cheese graters), leather belts, shirts, hair-care stuff, children's wear, lingerie, make-up and tops, as well as cheap trainers (£15 a pair) made by such well-known companies as Ascot, Mercury and Salvador (who?). Every Saturday there's a small crafts market on the pedestrianized section of Tavistock Road, just off Portobello Road, where on a dozen or so stalls people show off increasingly sophisticated crafty wares: leopard-skin cushions, a medley of candleholders, mirrors framed with beads, and jewellery.

In the gloom beneath the motorway flyover, the atmosphere changes palpably, becoming more like that of Camden. Almost hidden between stalls and huge bins before you get to the flyover is the stooped old man who plays his fiddle with no regard to the chaos around him, rain or shine. Under the motorway you will find soul and funk music stalls selling records and CDs, hippyish jewellery, brassware, candlesticks, or silk ties and shirts. Songs from Bob Marley's *Natty Dread* album compete with the latest dance offerings and *The Girl from Ipanema*, and mix with the hum of overhead traffic and the echoing hubbub of the market crowds. Spicy aromas emanate from the Makan Malaysian takeaway under the bridge.

On Fridays, when retro fashions (1960s clothes, old Levi's and the like) are sold in this area, there's a distinctly relaxed feel to the place; on Saturdays, however, business is brisk and the crowds are much bigger.

Hip flasks, candelabras, jewellery, Art Deco ornaments, framed portraits of dogs, sunglasses, coffee percolators, glassware, clocks and old 78s are gathered together in the area outside the **Portobello Green Arcade** every Saturday. Here, sheltered under a huge curvaceous tarpaulin, you can find the market's best clothes stalls: reproduction camouflage trousers, tweed jackets, Indian print T-shirts, leather, suede and sheepskin coats, silver lamé bodies. Each stall sells something different and many feature their own designs; many well-known fashion designers have started out here. Pick up some tie-dye baby clothes from **Baby Planet** or a velvet basque from **Identity**, a stall selling Vivienne Westwood designer lines. As at Camden and Greenwich, several stalls specialize in secondhand jeans; an old pair of Levi's can go for as much as £45.

The **Portobello Arcade** itself is home to women's fashion shops, including 2 Tuff and Rohan Clarke, and a couple of cafés.

Follow the Westway westwards and the Camdenesque nature of the market becomes even more apparent. Sheltering under the roadway are a mixture of crafts, cassette tape and bric-a-brac stalls, together with more new and secondhand clothes. Further along, the stalls sell aromatherapy oils, coins made into pendants, collections of old glass bottles, secondhand books and dance mixes on tape. One dealer jams along with a tambourine to his mix of jazz-funk. Nearby is a fabulous collection of buttons, from toggles to great black discs 2 inches in diameter. Here kitsch is chic: why not buy a telephone coated in Astroturf or a 3D portrait of the Virgin Mary? Designer mirrors also make an appearance; one has a furry fringe with the words 'Miaow, sex kitten' written on it.

This narrow alleyway of stalls wends its way as far as Ladbroke Grove, and on Saturdays the inevitable bottlenecks will give you plenty of time to peruse each stall's wares in depth. As you make your slow, halting progress you'll encounter bootleg tapes and rock videos, a dealer specializing in Brazilian music and football shirts, ethnic jewellery, second-hand records (Pink Floyd albums 50p), and a stall full of pastries (croissants 40p). There are a handful of takeaway stalls, one selling Indian food – *sag aloo* (spinach and potato curry) and *keema* (minced lamb curry), for instance – the other with West Indian dishes (salt fish, jerk chicken, fried plantain, and peanut cake for afters). Burning joss sticks further flavour the air.

To discover the rest of the market you need to retrace your steps back to Portobello Road (which on a Saturday afternoon could take you a good 20 minutes). Cross the street and you arrive at Acklam Road, where a small tarmaced area is home to about 30 more stalls. Here the market's character changes into something more like the poorer areas of Brick Lane: one trader sells old TVs and hi-fis, another has dog-eared secondhand books (both hardback and paperback), a third sells vacuum cleaner bags. A suitcase without an obvious owner lies open to view. Within is a display that no pop-artist could have imagined: a frying pan, the hand-set of a telephone and an empty tin of Cadbury's Smash. One stall has boxes of old records going for £1 each, or four for £3; a couple of avid collectors expertly flick through them. Next to it, a trader is selling

new and secondhand work overalls. On a rug on the floor is a pile of old remote controls and bootleg videos. Around the edges of the tarmac, forlorn piles of clothing are laid on the ground next to a sign reading '30p each'. Another trader sells old guitars, golf clubs, cricket bats and lacrosse sticks. You might also come across CDs, new and secondhand clothes (including a vintage clothing stall), secondhand videos and electronic goods, furniture and mobile phone accessories.

Back on Portobello Road (heading northwards), the standard of goods and the prices are noticeably higher. There's a couple of good secondhand record pitches with well-ordered stock, and a book stall with old copies of Iris Murdoch novels. The gentrification process has spread up the Portobello as far as the Golborne Road – witness the achingly trendy Simon Finch Art at No.319 with its gallery and rare books in a new-built contemporary space. **Visible**, a bar and lounge serving global dishes with a Lebanese twist at No.299, is typical of the kind of trendy spots that have sprung up since the mid-1990s.

There are a couple more designer clothes pitches on the stretch up to Oxford Gardens (one selling hats), but from here northwards the market becomes more raggedy, the piles of goods less ordered, and the prices lower. Along with Acklam Road, this is the one section of the market where you might still find a bargain. Secondhand clothes, hung on rails further down the road, are now piled on tables willy-nilly. North of here, they might be dumped on the pavement or sold from car boots. Stallholders and their stock change every week, but there's plenty of wheat among the chaff. Perhaps you'll find some traditional West African jewellery, some fire-grates or a haberdashery stall. I met a

Food, Drink and Shopping
Cafés and Fast Food

Sausage and Mash Café (286 Portobello Road), just under the Westway, is trendy and cheap, serving a variety of delicious sausages with mash. **Galicia** at No.323 dishes up authentic tapas and Spanish food. On Tavistock Road, just off the Portobello near the Westway, are **Mika**, a pleasant and reasonable sushi bar, and the **Gallery**, a vegetarian snack bar with dishes such as vegetarian moussaka and pasta. You'll often find some of Portobello's liveliest buskers performing nearby. More Italian food can be found at **Café Bellini** at 199 Portobello Road. The **Electric Brasserie** at 191 Portobello Road is one of the funkiest Portobello venues, with its all-day restaurant, de luxe cinema featuring sofas and champagne and private members' club.

Golborne Road's Moroccan community meets and eats at the **Marrakesh Café** (91 Golborne Road), which serves meals such as dried bean soup and vegetable couscous; next door is a Lebanese restaurant. The Portuguese have the **Lisboa Delicatessen** (54 Golborne Road), with its stocks of salt cod, *choriço* and Portuguese wines, and the **Lisboa Patisserie** (No.57), which has seats outside and is great for a coffee and a *bolo de nata* (custard cream).

Pubs

The **Portobello Star**, at 171 Portobello Road, is a cosy old pub popular with traders. It serves pub food such as chilli con carne (£5.50). **Portobello Gold**, Nos.95–7, serves excellent food and cocktails. **Golborne House** (36 Golborne Road) is a stylish gastropub. On the walk back to Notting Hill Gate tube station you can stop off at **The Sun in Splendour** pub on the southern end of Portobello Road, to rest your legs, have a drink and wonder at the logic that led you to make your purchases.

Shops

Anyone interested in food should make a pilgrimage to **Books for Cooks** at 4 Blenheim Crescent, just off Portobello Road's food market. It has London's best collection of new and secondhand books about food. Cookery demonstrations often take place at the back of the shop on Saturdays, with the food served in a tiny café. **The Travel Bookshop** at 13–15 Blenheim Crescent is popular with tourists seeking Hugh Grant, but is still one of the best places to browse all genres of travel literature.

trader trying to rid herself of a box-load of false fingernails, and a chap attempting to flog a Harrods mink coat for £150 – 'It would cost £3,000 new.' One stall had a half-empty bottle of Cinzano for sale.

About 20 yards up the road, a punter has found a bargain. She gleefully clutches her purchase, a 50-year-old pressure cooker that looks more like a First World War mine. 'I'm going to try and sell this to the Design Museum.' If you're an inveterate rummager, it's almost impossible to escape this section of the market empty-handed.

Just before the junction with Golborne Road, there's an argument at one stall. Does the used CD player work? A nearby trader with a few old batteries steps in to solve the dispute. A few traders take pitches north of Golborne Road at the northernmost end of Portobello Road. One stallholder has secondhand books and a top hat; another hopes to get rid of a radiogram and a typewriter. The next stall has a stock of old postcards, sold by a trader who couldn't get, or couldn't afford, a pitch at the antiques end of the market.

Golborne Road

Golborne Road, between Portobello Road and Wornington Road, W10. Open Mon–Sat 9am–5pm.

Golborne Road is, in effect, a separate local market with a self-contained set of about 30 stalls that complement the small shops and cafés along the street. It is open during the week, though best on Saturdays, and serves the community that lives in the nearby tower blocks and terraces. The area is markedly less moneyed than the southern stretches of Portobello Road. Here most of the weekly essentials are sold: vegetables from **E. Price's** stall, a traditional barrow 'noted for potatoes' that stands outside the Prices' greengrocer's shop (96–8 Golborne Road); new clothes and training shoes; toiletries; a variety of household goods from disinfectants to cheese graters or crockery; cakes and sweets; fruit and salad food. At the Afro-Caribbean food stall there's a fair selection of tropical fruit and vegetables, including green coconuts, red sorrel and yellow peppers.

The small secondhand section of the market carries on the theme already established on the northern reaches of the Portobello. Rickety chairs are placed out on the south side of the street, and occasionally there's a pitch full of well-worn tools and a hodgepodge of electrical components such as old radio valves. Books and secondhand clothes are also to be found here, while nearby a Moroccan stall sells tagines.

Gentrification is spreading to Golborne Road. Already, two new antiques shops have opened up (**Antiques & Decorative** at No.80 and **Bazar** at No.82), chef Antony Worrall Thompson has set up a Mediterranean restaurant on the street

(**La Poissonnerie du Pêcheur**, at No.46), and fashion designer Stella McCartney has converted a house into her studio and showroom – you won't miss it, it sticks out a mile. But for now locals still buy their fish at **Golborne Fisheries** (No.77), and the **Lisboa Patisserie** (No.57) remains a centre of the area's Portuguese population.

SHEPHERD'S BUSH

East side of railway viaduct between Uxbridge Road and Goldhawk Road, W12, t (020) 8743 5089.

Transport: ⊖ Shepherd's Bush, Goldhawk Road; buses 49, 72, 94, 95, 207, 220, 237, 260, 283, 295, 607.

Open: Tues, Wed, Fri and Sat 8.30am–6pm; Thurs 8.30am–1pm.

Best time to go: Friday or Saturday morning.

Parking: Try finding a parking meter on the side streets to the west of the market, between the Uxbridge and Goldhawk Roads.

Main wares: Fruit and veg, household goods, clothing, electrical goods.

Specifics: Afro-Caribbean foods, fish, pots and pans, men's suits, fabrics.

I once asked a Brazilian chef where in London he could find the ingredients to make his wonderful Bahian stews. His reply, of course, was Shepherd's Bush market. Along with Brixton in the south and Ridley Road in the east, Shepherd's Bush is the epitome of cosmopolitan London. Here you'll find Afro-Caribbeans selling to Arabs, Bangladeshis selling to the Irish and Africans selling to Brazilians.

Like much of Brixton, the market clings to a Victorian railway viaduct. It runs between Uxbridge Road and Goldhawk

Road, about a quarter of a mile, occupying land originally intended to be an access road to the Underground station. Shops inhabit premises under the arches, temporary stalls are constructed down the middle, while wooden lock-ups with awnings have been built along the eastern side. Towards the Uxbridge Road end, the stalls become semi-permanent structures and the alleyways narrow and dark, adding to the exotic appeal of the place.

Trading started here in the summer of 1914, but did not go on for long. During the First World War the market had to make way for the army, which billeted troops and stabled horses under the arches. After the war the market resumed, gaining in popularity and spreading to the west of the railway (this site was closed and redeveloped in 1969). When the area was badly bombed in the Second World War the market was threatened with closure, but the costermongers helped to clear the rubble and trading resumed within days.

Today, the first stall you encounter from the Goldhawk Road end sells a large but atypically staid choice of fruit and veg: potatoes, onions and broccoli; oranges, grapefruit and apples. The record shack next to it is more in tune with the market. Its range includes ex-chart bands, Irish music, gospel tunes and reggae records, plus videos of African and reggae bands. There is another CD stall further along which sells soca, steel band and calypso music. All manner of household goods can be found at the market: fly spray, bin bags, umbrellas, leather purses, briefcases, bags, and plenty of toiletries, bed linen and cosmetics. New householders should head for the lock-up with a vast collection of crockery and china, and a nearby business with scores of stainless steel pots and pans from little milk pans to huge cauldrons,

plus gargantuan Thermos flasks, ladles and baking trays. Shepherd's Bush is also a magnet for dressmakers, with its haberdashery, lace and colourful textile stalls. Fabrics, rugs and linoleum can also be found in the lock-ups, along with pillows, fancy quilted bedspreads, cushions and 'West London's largest DIY foam centre' with its bags of kapok and EPS beads outside. Toys, pet food, jewellery, perfume, feather boas, mobile phones, watches and small electrical bits and bobs (from plugs to secondhand TVs) fill other stalls. One business deals in secondhand computer games ('buy, sell, exchange'), another specializes in woolly hats emblazoned with the names of football clubs.

The market is a good source of clothing. As well as the usual children's wear, lingerie, cheap shirts (three for £10), leather jackets, women's dresses and tops, there are beautifully embroidered African tunics and clothes and beaded hats. Towards the Uxbridge Road end, the thoroughfare forks. Both prongs continue (each with lock-ups and stalls) until they reach the Uxbridge Road. Take the left prong under the railway and you'll find an excellent-value men's tailor – **Danny's Men's Suits** – selling a large stock of new coats and jackets, plus suits from £40 upwards.

The spirit of the market is to be found in its ethnic diversity. Take a look at the Asian-run businesses selling incense sticks, decorated tool boxes, plastic flowers and pictures that are also clocks. Or the Afro-Caribbean hair-care lock-ups with their collection of wigs. Several Arab traders also take stalls here, and women in yashmaks can often be spotted among their customers. There are two falafel vans here. At one, **Oasis**, various dips are sold to accompany the chick-pea snacks, and there's ice-cream for pudding. Outside, a couple of Middle Eastern gents are chewing the cud with the owner.

Nowhere in west London can match Shepherd's Bush market for Afro-Caribbean and African foodstuffs. One large fruit and veg stall sells three types of mangoes; another has about 10 varieties of sweet potato, including Ghana yam, cassava and eddoes. Then there are green plantains, green bananas and strange produce called garden eggs (yellow aubergines, about the size of a chicken's egg). Asian and cockney traders cater for West Indian customers, so the halal meat lock-up sells fresh goat's meat, while at the fishmonger's, **W. H. Roe's** (great name, great stall), you might find red bream, blue runners, grouper and live crabs.

The Caribbean feel of the market is most intense at its northwest corner, near the Uxbridge Road exit. Several traders, as well as customers, hail from the West Indies. Singed cow's feet, mobee bark tonic (whatever that is), dandelion root tea and lots of dried fish are sold under the corrugated shelters. At **Webster's Records** shack, soca holds sway.

Nigerian videos are sold nearby, and at least one stall in this section sells Nigerian-brewed Guinness. There are also several fast food stalls: snatch a quick

Food, Drink and Shopping
Cafés and Restaurants

If you're not tempted by the market cafés, try **A. Cooke's**, round the corner from the market (48 Goldhawk Road), a west London outpost for traditional pie and mash. **Blah Blah Blah** (78 Goldhawk Road) is a popular restaurant serving vegetarian food from around the world. **The Patio** (No.5) is an excellent-value, welcoming Polish restaurant. At the top end of the market on Uxbridge Road, **Esarn Kheaw** (No.314) is a very reasonable, high-quality Thai restaurant.

Shops

The permanent shops by the stalls don't quite qualify as part of the market, but several are worth exploring. Take a look in **International Cash & Carry** (160 Shepherd's Bush Market), with its alluring collection of food and drink: a wide choice of rum (with names like Wray & Nephew and Conquering Lion Overproof Rum), Jamaican syrup, dragon stout, sorrel (not the green-leafed plant, but a drink made from the pink flower-heads of a type of hibiscus) and sarsaparilla. **Moon Foods Cash & Carry** (No.183) has huge bags of rice, enormous tins of vegetable oil, and bags of spices and nuts.

curry, or sample some fried flying fish or goat roti. The less adventurous diner is also catered for; a couple of traditional caffs occupy lock-ups on the market, with tables and chairs outside. Breakfasts and fry-ups account for most of their menus.

Even if you fail to buy any mobee bark here, you're likely to find Shepherd's Bush market a tonic. Walk along its length and, for a moment, you're out of London, out of Europe even. A blast of celebratory soca sends you on your way. Can shopping really be this much fun?

North London

CAMDEN

Camden Lock, Buck Street, Electric Ballroom, Chalk Farm Road, Camden High Street, NW1 (see individual markets), www.camdenlock.net.

Transport: ⊖ *Camden Town, Chalk Farm;* ⇌ *Camden Road; buses 24, 27, 29, 31, 46, 88, 134, 168, 214, 253, 274, C2.*

Open: *See individual markets for details.*

Best time to go: *About 10am on Sunday.*

Parking: *Try the side streets north of the Chalk Farm Road, but expect a long walk.*

Main wares: *Secondhand clothes, designer clothes and jewellery, antiques, books, crafts, furniture.*

Specifics: *Street fashion and accessories.*

If you arrive at Camden tube never having visited the market before, it won't take you long to get your bearings – everyone is walking in the same direction. Some smell of joss sticks and have spangly trousers; many have the fast, urgent walk of those who don't want to miss anything. You are heading for London's biggest weekly street festival. Along Camden High Street, north of the tube station, there's a carnival atmosphere. The road is jammed with traffic as crowds overflow from the pavements. Shops and cafés join in the street life by placing their wares outside, and hawkers use any available space to milk the passing throng.

Camden market first opened in 1974 at a disused timber wharf beside the Regent's Canal. At first it consisted of craftsworkers who had colonized the Victorian waterside warehouses, selling their goods in the old cobbled yard. Since then it has grown alarmingly, sprouting new shoots at half a dozen sites around Camden. It now vies with Petticoat Lane and Portobello Road for the title of London's most famous market. And for popularity Camden wins hands down, attracting hundreds of thousands of people each week. The market came into being after the British institutions of churchgoing and Sunday lunch had crumbled, so, unlike the older East End Sunday markets, it continues into the afternoons and reaches a zenith at 2pm when its clubbing regulars have woken up and are ready for the day. Camden may be smartening up its act, but it's the one market in London where you will find a few Londoners rubbing shoulders with the tourists, and it's also the place to go if you need any proof that the goth, punk and other alternative movements still thrive, even if most of the practitioners have come from abroad.

The traditional fruit and veg market of Inverness Street is also in the centre of Camden. It is quite different in character from the weekend clothes and crafts market, so is listed separately (*see* p.84).

Electric Ballroom

Camden High Street, south of junction with Dewsbury Terrace, NW1, **t** *(020) 7485 9006.* **Open** *Sat–Sun 10am–5pm.*

The Electric Ballroom, just north of Camden tube, is a deeply dark nightclub that opens its doors on weekends for clothes trading. The atmosphere here is still pretty traditional Camden: one of the first stalls you see sells T-shirts emblazoned with band names such as Motorhead and ACDC, and there is still plenty of evidence of the counter-culture that took Sid Vicious and Che Guevara as its heroes. However, it is not all 1980s angst and gothic gloom – there are plenty of stalls selling fun jewellery and high-street fashion at very reasonable prices.

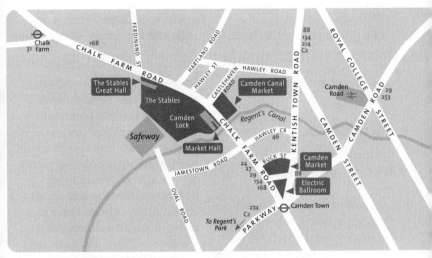

Plus the secondhand stalls are all the rage these days when 'vintage' is such a buzz word. You can buy a faux-leather coat for £5 and a glitzy dress will set you back £15. At the entrance there is a bureau de change, and inside is a man selling a wonderfully sparkly selection of handmade jewellery.

There are lots of stalls run by entre-preneurs who trawl the jumble sales and charity shops of England for 1950s stilettos, 1960s zoot suits and 1970s skinny-ribbed sweaters – anything retro, in fact. One stall has been here for years, selling entire men's outfits: suits, shirts and ties, ranging from early 1960s FBI-style black suits to late 1960s lounge-lizard velvet jackets. You can even get genuine fur coats for a song, if that's what you are into (£29 for a fox fur jacket).

Modern clothing is also sold, including coats, bags and skirts in the latest high-street styles. Diversions from clothes shopping are provided by DJs selling club-mix CDs, and record stalls pumping out dance music at a volume that is guaranteed to wake you up.

Camden Market

Camden High Street, NW1, **t** *(020) 7485 3459.* **Open** *daily 9am–5.30pm.*

This is one of the most crowded parts of the market, and it can get quite claustrophobic in the narrow alleyways between the stalls. It is still worth heading into the den, though, if you're after clothing or jewellery. But be warned: the Carnaby Street process is well under way here, turning street cred into straight crud.

Some of the prices are plain daft: secondhand flared jeans cost as much as £35. There are also the wax coats, Doc Marten boots (£39.99), cheap jewellery (one man will give you a 'special price' for body-piercing jewellery) and watches, and the leather belts, popular with heavy metal fans, that can all be found at many London markets for a good deal less. If you're prepared to squeeze yourself through the crush, though, you might discover a few gems: jolly handbags and hats made from recycled clothes; secondhand boots and shoes; secondhand suede jackets for only £15; old leather and velvet jackets at £10 each. As well as fashion-wear, there's a bunch of stalls displaying hippyish artefacts, record stalls, and a trader specializing in music videos. There's also a burger stall in the middle of the crush.

Camden Lock

Camden Lock Place, off Chalk Farm Road, NW1, t (020) 7485 7963. Open daily 10am–6pm.

This is where Camden market started in 1974. If you arrive early on a fine day, it's still a place of great charm. Longboats chug down the canal watched by couples relaxing on the banks; traders lay out their wares on stalls in the cobbled yard; and buskers play a few chords before the crowds arrive. By midday, however, the lock is choked with people and its layout, confusing at the best of times, takes on an almost labyrinthine quality.

The Lock market was started by craftsworkers selling their handmade goods, and nowadays artisans are staging a bit of a comeback among the 400 or so traders. New clothes as well as old are sold, and many traders in Andean, Asian or African artefacts and clothes seem to be professional importers. Yet there are stalls still worth finding: don't miss the pitch full of percussion instruments, from African talking drums to Irish bodhráns, or the hand-crafted ocarinas (pot flutes), and there's always lots of new handmade jewellery to be examined.

As you walk north along Camden High Street, the first part of the market to come into view, overlooking the canal, is the **East Yard**, where you will find the complex's highest concentration of basic tat. Patchwork flares, CDs, model cars and bicycles made out of drinks cans,

soapstone buddhas, leather bags and cheap silver jewellery are among the more inspiring items.

Moving northward, you enter the **Market Hall**, an impressive building with elaborate wrought-ironwork, tiled floors and stalls on each of its three floors. The East Yard is level with the first floor, where you will find crafts from around the world, bought cheap and sold dear: Indonesian batik, stone sculptures from Africa, cassette tapes from Latin America. Local craftsworkers get a look-in here as well, with hand-painted plant pots, jewellery and glassware. There's also a stall selling custom-made soaps of various technicolour designs by the slice and handmade stationery at **Leatherbound**, where a leather photo album costs £20.

Upstairs is what could be termed the interactive section. Here you can get tarot readings, alternative therapy, henna tattoos and piercings, as well as an array of crystals.

On the ground floor is a fairly good bookstall selling new fiction, a man selling blow-up see-through plastic furniture, and his friend whose stock consists entirely of lacquered backgammon boards. Check out the bright little House of Guadalupe, a riot of Mexican colour and motifs, looking like an installation that Frida Kahlo would have made. Part of this hall leads to **Dingwalls Gallery**, where there's a toilet and a shop where you can buy jewellery, old pub optics, teddy bears and Indian cushions. Shops line the outside of the market hall; all of these, as well as many of the indoor businesses, trade through the week.

Moving west from Dingwalls Gallery, you come to the **Middle Yard**, the largest of the three yards and the one with the greatest range of goods. Toy boats, painted lightbulbs, didgeridoos, back massagers and hammocks can all be found in among the rows of stalls, as can new clothes from young designers (bright mini-skirts, tops in unbleached fabrics), designer jewellery, furry leopardskin beanbags, knitwear, kinky leatherwear, pink furry handcuffs and multicultural fast food.

Further west, across a small stretch of canal, is the final part of the market, the **West Yard**. This area has seen the most benefit from the recent facelift and there is now a permanent selection of multicultural food stalls at the back of the yard, which is in turn lined by new cafés and restaurants. The first stalls you'll encounter sell ocarinas and rainsticks. After that it's art prints, furry bags, Indian crafts, bongo drums, mosaic mirrors, bean bags, jewellery, clothes, Afghan and Turkman rugs...

Camden Canal Market

*Off Chalk Farm Road, south of junction with Castlehaven Road, NW1, **t** (020) 7485 8355. **Open** daily 9.30am–6.30pm.*

This outcrop of the market is reached down a sloping covered walkway opposite Camden Lock. The dawdling crowd peruses the clothes, electrical goods, jewellery and reggae stalls on either side of the walkway. One trader has a serene expression and a stock of pot-pipes.

At the end of this corridor there's an outside courtyard that is filled with stalls. There are some secondhand clothes, but most garments – including colourful shirts and Latin American knitwear – are new. One trader even sells wax jackets and green wellies – symbols of the landed elite, here in Alternative Camden.

Off the courtyard, an indoor section contains dozens of stalls full of all manner of secondhand goods, plus a few tacky new things. In unsung parts of Camden like this, you can still happen upon a goldmine. Lovers of old Western books will find a stall dedicated to their passion (look out for the Hopalong Cassidy series). And, if you agree that Britain's prime contribution to world culture is the public house, head for **Pub Paraphernalia**, a stall packed with genuine artefacts from British boozers – such as tankards and Guinness water jugs – as opposed to the bogus pub signs found at some tourist markets. There's even a stall selling a few secondhand Levi's for £15: the lowest price in Camden.

There are coats for £15, wig and hair extensions and a stall selling bizarre underwear. **Madame Anita** offers clairvoyance, palmistry, crystal gazing and tarot card readings. A large aromatherapy stall contains oil burners, essential oils and pot-pourri at not-so-knockdown prices. One trader specializes in Chinese opium pipes, while another has a large stock of New Age books, and a third is selling his collection of pipes and cigarette lighters. Several display household artefacts from the 1920s to the 1970s of the type that can also be found at the Stables (*see* below). Look out for the collection of old sewing machines. If you're desperate for currency, visit the bureau de change at this market.

Camden market used to have many secondhand record stalls, but in these post-vinyl days they are dying out. One of the best remaining ones is to be found here, with LPs and singles well ordered by genre. Punk, indie and 1960s bands are especially well represented.

The Stables

Off Chalk Farm Road, opposite junction with Hartland Road, NW1, **t** *(020) 7485 5511.* **Open** *daily 10am–6pm.*

The Stables is without doubt the most vital of Camden's markets and the recent redevelopment has not dimmed its vigour. The intention is to turn this area into the largest commercial complex in London and, though still not complete at time of writing, the Triangle Site (the section adjacent to Camden Lock) is finished and so far looks good. There's a covered food section at the start of the yard, with different food stalls and trestle tables where you can sit and eat. Then the market spreads out in every possible direction, full of colour and noise and always crowded. Rave music, mixed with indie tunes and reggae, is never out of earshot. Trading takes place both outdoors on cobbled thoroughfares and any available piece of land. There's a lot of cutting-edge fashion here, as well as more regular high-street style and plenty of old-time Camden favourites such as skin-tight PVC catsuits and crushed velvet for the goths. Retro clothing is also big here and there are lots of unusual ways to decorate your home. If you go left into the Stables Block you will find the antiques section: the Horse Hospital is the place for vintage clothing, hugely popular with rummaging crowds.

Camden is very different from the established antiques markets such as Portobello Road or Camden Passage. Many of the traders are young and hip, which means they may let an unfashionable hunk of Victoriana through their grasp without realizing its worth. But when it comes to 20th-century fashions, which account for most of their stock, these traders are totally clued-up. Where else would a pair of tarnished 1950s cats'-eyes sunglasses cost £12.50, or old BOAC bags be sold as fashion accessories?

Camden fashion doesn't stop at clothing. Many of the market's teenage customers of the 1970s and 80s now have their own flats to furnish, so there's plenty of stripped pine furniture about, some of it rather roughly painted in Mediterranean turquoise. Antique pieces can be found in the Stables **Great Hall**. This large Victorian structure, once a hospital for horses, also contains old kitchenware, cigarette tins, books and various household goods from the 1920s to the 1970s.

Outside the Great Hall, secondhand street fashions are interspersed with traders selling bootleg tapes of live gigs, concert videos and army-surplus gear. You might also encounter club DJs selling cassettes of their rare groove, samba or techno mixes: it's near impossible to avoid moving to the beat.

Outside **Piazza** and **Antiques Passage** (both converted railway arches) are stalls displaying African crafts, CDs, clothes, luggage and video cameras. You'll find **Kalimantan Creations** here, which sells African wooden ornaments and instruments as well as handmade chairs and toys. There's also a trader selling old guitars and a collection of 1960s records. In an old building opposite the arches is a room full of American gear: US licence plates, workwear from the 1930s to the 1950s, and reproduction posters from Jimi Hendrix concerts. Under the arches along Antiques Passage is the **Millennium Art Gallery**, a shop selling modern furniture from the 1950s onwards and a selection of designer shades, garden ornaments, Art Deco furniture, leopardskin furniture, boxes and cushions, and restored antique furniture. CO_2, which sells modern designer 20th-century furniture, features a sofa in the shape of a baseball mitt in homage to Joe Di Maggio (it costs £2,200).

Walk into **Objets d'Arch**, under one of the railway arches, and wonder why you ever bothered to bring back souvenirs from your travels – it's all here, including African masks, shields and spears, and multifarious crafts and glassware. Next to it, **Collectors' Arch** has old cutlery, silverware and crockery. Others contain stalls selling old Dinky toys, 1950s children's annuals, 'carefully used' American clothing (some of the leather jackets on offer are bargains, around £10–15), woodcarving tools, a set of working traffic lights, and 'reclaimed' stripped pine furniture.

Camden is not without its shysters: one notice reads 'Did you know that your quartz watch emits harmful electro-magnetic radiation? Have it neutralized here, £1 only.' Another trader is trying to sell a rock, describing it as masonry dislodged from St Paul's Cathedral during the Blitz – yours for £40.

Stalls with 'cyber' prefixes seem particularly popular of late at the Stables. There is a **Cybercafé**, where you can get internet access and which has a separate eating area. There's also **Cyberdog**, a shop which quite obviously imagines itself to be inhabiting some *Blade Runner*-type futuristic dystopia. A spacecraft sculpture is suspended at the entrance.

Further into this labyrinth, named the **Catacombs**, are some of Camden's most colourful traders. Clothes from the 1950s are sold by a chap with bright orange and yellow hair who demands a tip if you photograph him; another trader seems in a trance in his dimly lit dungeon, which is decked out in shawls and strewn with

Food and Drink

Cafés and Fast Food

Many of the varied fast-food joints in the market itself are mentioned in the text, but if you want to escape the crowds, try **John's Café** (39 Chalk Farm Road). The trendy goings-on down the road seem to have passed by this basic caff.

Pubs

If you want to tune in to upbeat Camden, order a cocktail at **WKD** (18 Kentish Town Road), one of the funkiest venues for a drink and a snack, or have a semi-quiet pint in the **Caernarvon Castle** at 7–8 Chalk Farm Road. **Lush** on Jamestown Road is a modern converted pub which is not just hip, but also features leather sofas great for lounging in with that Bloody Mary.

Restaurants

There are plenty of good restaurants in Camden. **Cheng Du** (9 Parkway) is a quiet place serving spicy Szechuan cooking, while **Café Delancey** (3 Delancey Street) is a French brasserie which also does snacks and soups. For good Greek food, try **Andy's Taverna** (81 Bayham Street). Heading north, **Mango Room** (10 Kentish Town Road), is a very cool bar-restaurant with modern London-Caribbean cooking and a great range of cocktails. For some grown-up food, head to the **Camden Brasserie** (9–11 Jamestown Road), a light and airy modern European brasserie that is great for a serious brunch. Next door is the ever-popular **Wagamama** with its canteen-like shared tables and menu of uncomplicated oriental dishes and soups, perfect for refuelling after a few hours at the market.

strange ornaments. In other arches you might find restored carriage clocks, old musical instruments, wooden carvings, and Indonesian or Indian woodwork and

Nearby Attractions

Regent's Park, ✆ *Baker Street, Regent's Park, Great Portland Street, Mornington Crescent, Camden Town, St John's Wood;* **buses** *2, 13, 18, 27, 30, 74, 82, 113, 138, 189, 274, 453, C2.* **Open** *daily 5am–sunset.* One of London's loveliest parks, with zoo (*see below*), rose garden, boating lake, open-air theatre and the London Central Mosque.

London Zoo, *Outer Circle, Regent's Park,* **t** *(020) 7722 3333, www.londonzoo.com;* ✆ *Camden Town, St John's Wood;* **bus** *274, C2.* **Open** *March–23 Oct daily 10am–5.30pm, Oct–11 Feb 10am–4pm, Feb–5 March 10am–4.30pm;* **adm** *adults £13.50, children £11.* London's famous menagerie has thousands of animals. The emphasis now is on conservation and education, though the zoo still offers traditional attractions such as Feeding Time.

artefacts. One section, **Raven Iron Art**, specializes in beautiful, theatrical wrought-iron furniture: a kidney-shaped sofa covered with purple faux fur and adorned with zebra-skin cushions stands next to a glass table, its legs and sides entwined with iron ivy. Many of the goods for sale in the Catacombs are quirky and postmodern, yet all are highly polished and professionally produced. The traders in these sprawling caverns display a marked air of superiority over the rough 'n' ready types outside; high-quality business cards are brandished at every opportunity and the snazzy sound systems help to create an atmosphere akin to a subterranean shopping precinct. A nearby café specializes in East African curries.

All the above can be found to the left of the main entrance to the Stables. If, however, you turn right, you come across more old buildings filled with antiques stalls, where you might find anything

from a 1920s accordion to a silver cutlery set. Farther along, the **Long Stable** advertises its wares above its entrance: '40s 50s 60s & 70s Vintage Clothing & Collectibles'. The stalls inside are crammed with paraphernalia, some predictable, like Elvis key rings and Beatles magazines, and some rather more unusual: Bettie Page cufflinks, Jayne Mansfield transfers and a painted Dirk Bogarde cardboard mask. There are swathes of retro clothes, many from the 1960s and, appropriately, the Velvet Underground blares out from the huge CD record and tape stall that spans almost half of the building.

On a fine day, the benches outside the Long Stable make a good stopping point to rest and watch the crowds pass by (if you can get a seat). Fast food huts supply the nourishment, from the traditional pie and mash to ultra-exotic Burmese cuisine, and cater for vegetarian tastes with falafels and vegetarian pizzas.

CAMDEN PASSAGE

Camden Passage, off Islington High Street, N1, **t** *07960 877035.*

Transport: ✆ *Angel;* buses *4, 17, 19, 30, 38, 43, 56, 73, 91, 153, 259, 274, 341, 476.*

Open: *Antiques and bric-a-brac Wed 7am–2pm and Sat 8am–4pm; books Thurs 7am–4pm.*

Best time to go: *Wednesday.*

Parking: *There are parking meters on the side streets east of Camden Passage.*

Main wares: *Antiques.*

Specifics: *Old cutlery, military clothing and artefacts (Sat only), crockery, glassware, jewellery.*

Don't confuse this with the kerfuffle at Camden Town (*see* p.68). Camden Passage is in the heart of Islington, where old goods are sold to the nouveaux riches; where quaintness is quantified in quids; and where collectors fork out for silver spoons. The narrow, flagstoned walkway was once called Cumberland Row, but was renamed in 1876 after the Earl of Camden, who owned the land. Despite the venerable surroundings, the antiques market is a relatively new affair, dating from 1960. The timing was spot on. In 1960, Islington was just starting to become fashionable again, with middle-class couples moving into the area and renovating its beautiful Georgian and early Victorian houses. This, coupled with the increasing popularity of antiques, ensured the market's success.

Get yourself in the mood by walking through the **Mall** antiques arcade, which occupies a renovated tramshed to the south of the Passage. Bijou shops packed with *objets d'art* line a central walkway. Exquisite china, wooden sailing boats, 19th-century paintings, pristine glassware – most stuff is in impeccable condition and seriously expensive. Take heart: the market proper is not quite as exclusive.

There are 32 stalls in the **Gateway** antique market between Upper Street and Islington High Street, and apart from a couple of restaurants virtually every shop on the northern stretch of Islington High Street and Camden Passage now sells antiques. Every inch of space is used.

Take the **Angel Arcade** (near the northernmost end of Islington High Street), which occupies only part of one terraced house yet contains 20 antiques shops. China, Victorian ornaments and old brassware are everywhere, but on Saturdays (from 8am to 2pm) the most fascinating events take place in the basement, which hosts the **London**

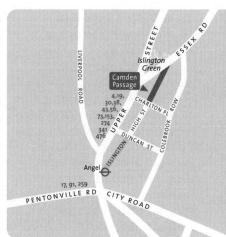

Military Market. Descend the staircase on that day and you'll find this market with its plethora of belts, buckles, badges, bayonets, uniforms and medals. Smell the odour of khaki encrusted with ancient sweat as you pass the old uniforms.

It's a relief to climb the stairs again and reach the open air. Turn right, continuing northwards, and you soon reach Camden Passage. In every available space, trestle tables are set up in clutches between buildings, most covered by translucent shelters. The first batch of stalls is just off the Passage on **Pierrepont Row**. Silver cutlery and tableware, jewellery, glassware, china and old coins are ten-a-penny, but there are also collections of magnifying glasses and early cameras. Further down this tiny cul-de-sac is a collection of small antiques shops, single-roomed cubby holes packed with elderly artefacts. One has a notable collection of old Rolex watches, going back to 1914.

The fleamarket arcade at the end of Pierrepont Row contains two small floors of antiques stalls. Silver tableware is much in evidence; you'll also find carriage clocks, Victorian prints, silverware, glass bottles, buttons, baubles and general bric-a-brac.

The next outcrop of the market occurs at the junction with Charlton Place. On Thursdays a small book market takes place here (mostly paperback fiction, though also some hardback reference books), but on Wednesdays and Saturdays half a dozen more antiques traders set up their trestle tables. Among their stock you might find antique lace, writing cases, crockery, old spectacle frames and a collection of faded rugs. 'Genuine Arabian dust here,' remarks one trader as a rug slips off its perch, sending a powdery cloud over the proceedings.

Farther along Camden Passage, a few of the antiques shops put wares out onto the walkway. Near to the Camden Head pub (worth popping into for refreshment), the Passage widens and several traders exhibit their stock on the pavement or from car boots. This is the cheapest but also the dodgiest part of the market, and there's a fair amount of junk: cigarette cases and souvenirs of the Silver Jubilee. In the main, though, traders along the Passage are a genteel bunch, and a good number of their customers are from North America.

Opposite the Camden Head is a more official part of the market, also under shelter. About half a dozen traders try to sell a wide variety of goods: jewellery, crockery, wooden boxes with inlay work. The largest part of the market is but a few steps on from this outcrop.

Opposite Islington Green, at the end of Camden Passage, there are about 30 stalls under cover. Again there's a good choice of jewellery, silver cutlery, candlesticks and tableware, but also clothes brushes and tools. Roman coins and brooches might go for as little as £5. Most wares are well presented, though one stall boasted a jumble of broken watches surrounded

by a knot of necklaces. As with virtually every other object at Camden Passage, you'll be able to get a substantially lower price by haggling.

The **Georgian Village** is yet another indoor antiques market, just off the outdoor section described above. The basement is taken up by antique furniture and the café (*see* above). There are 14 shops on the ground floor selling dolls, clocks, antique tiles and china. Among the 20 or so traders on the first floor you can find Victorian kitchen utensils, vintage clothes, British collectibles and jewellery.

Food and Drink

Cafés

In the basement of the **Georgian Village** there is a very basic but cheap café selling hot drinks and sandwiches.

Pubs

Upper Street has some of the area's best pubs, including the **King's Head** (a 10-minute walk up Upper Street).

Restaurants

Islington is full of great eating and drinking places. A cheap lunch can be had at the **New Culture Revolution** (42 Duncan Street, just off Islington High Street), a Chinese dumplings and noodle bar with an emphasis on healthy, meal-in-one dishes. Other nearby places are: **Metrogusto** (11–13 Theberton Street), serving cool, simple but sophisticated modern Italian food; and the cheaper **Le Mercury** (140a Upper Street), a delightful French restaurant serving delicious and surprisingly ambitious food at rock bottom prices. **Gallipoli** at 102 Upper Street is a fun Turkish restaurant with an exotic interior and good, reasonable food.

CHAPEL MARKET

Chapel Market, N1.

Transport: ⊖ *Angel; buses 4, 17, 19, 30, 38, 43, 56, 73, 291, 153, 74, 341, 476.*

Open: *Tues, Wed, Fri and Sat 9am–4pm; Thurs and Sun 9am–1pm.*

Best time to go: *Saturday and Sunday.*

Parking: *Try looking for parking meters on the side streets off Liverpool Road to the north of the market.*

Main wares: *Fresh food, clothes, household goods.*

Specifics: *Fruit and veg, women's clothes.*

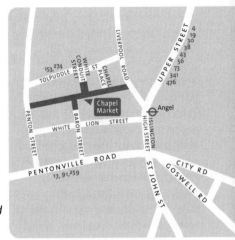

Islington has been linked with London's markets since its medieval beginnings as a village on the main road north of the city. For centuries, drovers used the place as a final stop-off point before guiding their livestock to Smithfield market. Even today you can see the high pavements of Upper Street, built to prevent mud and dung from the road splashing pedestrians.

Chapel Street was built in 1790 (the writer Charles Lamb was one of the first residents), but the market probably dates from the 1860s. By then, Islington contained two distinct strata of society living in close proximity. Gentry from the beautiful squares of Barnsbury (north of the market) would have steered clear of the mayhem of Chapel Street, which catered for the new working-class communities of Pentonville and Angel. The market gained official recognition in 1879, and in 1936 Chapel Street was renamed Chapel Market.

Today, Islington still contains a fascinating social mix. In the 1960s and 70s its larger houses were rediscovered by prosperous folk and it became fashionable among centre-left-leaning professionals – it's no coincidence that the current Prime Minister, Tony Blair, used to have a house here. At Camden Passage (*see* p.74), the residents of exquisite Victorian terraces can be seen browsing for their antiques.

Chapel Market, on the other hand, continues to provide basic foodstuffs, clothing and household goods. Despite the proximity of several supermarkets (Sainsbury's has had a store on Liverpool Street for more than a century), street trading thrives and Chapel Market remains one of London's best.

In the week, stalls are concentrated at the Liverpool Road end, but at the weekend they stretch over 200 yards to Penton Street. A large stall selling greetings cards and party goods (streamers, balloons and, from November, Christmas decorations) seems to be a fixture at the Liverpool Street junction. There are several fruit and veg stalls, well stocked and varied: fennel bulbs and mooli alongside spuds, apples and pears. One trader does a good line in fresh herbs, selling thyme, sage and dill even in winter; catch him before he gets into deep discussion with his neighbouring stallholder (who sells dried fruits and nuts) about that night's Arsenal game. The next stall sells herb and fruit teas.

The clothes stalls dotted along the street supply all age groups: frilly clothes for toddlers, sensible frocks for women (sensible jumpers in winter), not-so-sensible party gear for the packs of teenage girls that roam through here on their school lunch breaks, shoes, boots and slippers, T-shirts, tracksuit bottoms, coats, gloves, jeans, socks, underwear and lingerie.

A small stall selling yams and plantains often appears, but otherwise little is geared to Asian or Afro-Caribbean shoppers, though among the stalls selling hot food there's a Caribbean one, as well as Thai, Indian, pies and bangers, a Turkish stall selling stuffed vine leaves, good feta and olives, and sandwiches made to order. A fishmonger usually arrives on Saturdays, with enticing displays of Dover sole, mullet and cod, and there's a fresh fish stall selling salmon, Dover sole and jellied eels. For jackfish and snappers, take a 10-minute ride on the no.30 bus to Ridley Road market (see p.114).

A couple of stalls veer away from the norm: one displays the candles and aromatherapy oils that have become popular on London's markets; the other, **Bass Rhythms**, is run by an effortlessly cool bloke who sells dance records. The rest of the traders stock everyday goods for locals: kitchenware, cut flowers, cosmetics, secondhand paperbacks (mostly romantic fiction), toys, electrical goods (from watches and batteries to radios and toasters), mobile phone accessories, pet foods and accessories, leather bags, and household goods such as dusters, freezer bags and clingfilm. There are duvets and bed linen to be found on a couple of stalls and blankets on another. There's also a key-cutter and a trader who will cut net curtains to order for you.

> ## Food and Drink
>
> **L. Manze**'s pie and mash shop at 74 Chapel Market is an unyieldingly traditional place, right down to the marble-topped tables and wooden benches worn smooth by generations of costermongers' buttocks. There are plenty of decent restaurants and pubs along Upper Street (see Camden Passage, p.76), but **Indian Veg** at 92 Chapel Market offers a less expensive option, with a cheap all-you-can-eat buffet.

At weekends, a few traders take up pitches in neighbouring side streets. On Chapel Place you'll find handbags, curtain material and perhaps a candlestick stall; White Conduit Street has a large cut-flower and plant stall. But Baron Street has the best entertainment. Here, outside antediluvian premises (marked 'Wm Yearley') that are used as a lock-up, a couple of weathered old traders sell extremely cheap tinned food, biscuits, chocolates and nuts. This is old-style Islington, where French loaves are 'bagwets' and three tins of ham cost a nicker. No one minds that the 'best before' date is fast approaching, if not gone. A huddle of elderly locals surrounds the stall, bantering with the traders. The best show is saved for new, fancy lines:

Trader: *'Ever tried a drop of fruit tea?'*

Customer: *'Not likely, have you?'*

Trader: *'No, of course I haven't. I don't like the bleedin' stuff.'*

Customer: *'What d'you want it for then? Give it away.'*

Trader: *'Well, it's no good if you don't like it, is it?'*

Allow yourself a secret smile: half a mile away, the burghers of Barnsbury will be paying through the nose for fruit tea at their wholefood shops.

CHURCH STREET AND BELL STREET

Church Street, W2 and NW8 (Alfie's Antiques Market, 13–25 Church Street); Bell Street, between Edgware Road and Lisson Street, NW1; t (020) 7723 6066.

Transport: ⊖ *Edgware Road; buses 6, 16, 18, 98, 139, 189, 414.*

Open: *Church Street Tues–Sat 9am–5pm (Alfie's Antiques Market Tues–Sat 10–6); Bell Street Sat 9–5.*

Best time to go: *Saturday.*

Parking: *Try the side streets off the Edgware Road to the north of Church Street (it's free at the parking meters on Saturdays).*

Main wares: *Church Street – fruit and vegetables (Tues–Fri); antiques, clothes, household goods, plants and flowers, fruit and veg, meat, fish (Fri and Sat). Bell Street – general junk, secondhand clothes.*

Specifics: *Antique jewellery, packaged food, fruit and veg, old clothes.*

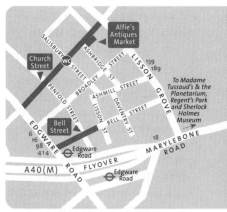

Barely outside the West End, the markets of Church Street and Bell Street offer a wealth of junk, antiques and traditional street-market clobber every Saturday. Though Madame Tussaud's is little over half a mile away, few tourists come here. The markets are mostly left to a cosmopolitan band of local shoppers: lads from the nearby council flats, tweedy antiques collectors and Arab women wearing yashmaks.

Bell Street is the poor relation of the two. On weekdays, only a couple of traders take pitches at its Edgware Road end. One stall sells hundreds of useful bits and bobs: razor blades, shoe laces, padlocks and batteries. On Saturdays, it is joined by a couple of dozen junk stalls that straggle along the road as far as Lisson Street, plus an assortment of fly-traders who simply throw their junk onto the pavement – the market is informal in the extreme.

Old petrol cans, door handles and a pair of Wellington boots could grace one stall; another might have a wartime ARP warden's helmet atop an old coal scuttle. Pass down the road and you're likely to encounter some intriguing conversations. A man is trying to sell a midi hi-fi: 'no sound comes out of the CD or radio, but the tape works'. Another old hopeful is proffering a plastic bag full of Barbie dolls: 'Who'll give me 20 quid for six of them?'

Among the forlorn display of crumpled clothes, old video tapes and solitary shoes you might come across a bargain. One trader who turns up most weeks has a collection of old electrical equipment, including an ancient amplifier and equally antediluvian counting machine; nearby, an old train set and a Box Brownie camera might be up for grabs. In the main, though, Bell Street is best simply for offering a glance into the strange contents of other people's attics.

Few cars venture down Bell Street, so the market is perfect for a peaceful potter, before taking one of the side streets north and walking the hundred or so yards towards the tumult of **Church Street**.

Church Street market can be traced back to 1830, when the Portman market began trading in meat, fruit and vegetables near Lisson Grove. At the turn of the 20th century, plans to provide indoor premises near Marylebone Station faltered, so the market moved to its present location in 1906. From Tuesday to Thursday Church Street is little more than a minor local fruit and veg market, with the occasional household goods and clothes stall, all bunched up near the Edgware Road. But, on Fridays and especially Saturdays, upwards of 200 stalls crowd both sides of the street right up to the junction with Lisson Grove.

Most fruit and veg stalls cluster at the Edgware Road end. A few of these costermongers are well over 70, but they still turn up every week. One trader always wears a suit and tie to serve his spuds; another puts up notices like 'Have a bit of good and cheap, for the doctor,' over his tomatoes. Though there's the occasional experiment with mangoes or lychees, most produce is run-of-the-mill. Prices are reasonable on Saturday, but higher early in the week.

On Saturdays there are also clothes stalls stocked with leather jackets, children's and babies' garments, new shoes, men's trousers, low-priced shirts (£3.99 each, four for £10), women's smart jackets, jeans, pyjamas, silk blouses, silk ties (£3.99 each, two for £5), women's jumpers (also £3.99 each), overcoats, underwear and even leather trousers.

An old stall by the junction with Penfold Street has been a Church Street regular since 1968. The trader looks as if he might be the son of the ruddy-faced woman who ran the stall 10 years ago. The bucolic-looking range of stock is the same, though: eggs, home-made marmalade and Eccles cakes.

There are two cheap food stalls on Church Street that have traded here for years; they usually have a similar stock of tins, packets, biscuits and chocolates. Both sell in bulk (three bags of peanuts for £1, say); they only trade here on Fridays and Saturdays, and tend to sell out by the early afternoon. The stall on the north side of the street also sells a range of household cleaners and pet foods; extra virgin olive oil might be next to the Kit-e-Kat and not far from the bleach. There is also a Greek specialities stall which sells olives and feta cheese.

Close to this stall, at the junction with Salisbury Street, is an oddity worth exploring. The small mock-Tudor building houses spotlessly clean, award-winning public toilets. In the gents is a tiled mural depicting the market outside.

Across the street from here, a glorious fish stall occupies a pitch on Fridays and Saturdays. Live crabs wave their claws in the air, and raw jumbo prawns are sold at low prices. Cuttlefish, carp and St Peter fish stare bleakly at proceedings. Nearby, a falafel van provides market-goers with fast food.

At one stall, several veiled Arab women are laughing, chatting and rifling through heaps of clothing in old bread baskets marked 'only £1 each'. Duvets, towels, pet food, saucepans, plant pots, handbags, suitcases and cut flowers can also be found in this middle section of the market. One trader sells umbrellas, kitchen bowls and roasting trays. He calls across to a butcher at the Meat Market shop across the pavement: 'Had a day off, Dick? How was it?' 'Ten' is the enigmatic reply.

On Saturdays there's space for specialist stalls: one just selling watches; another with nothing but umbrellas; a large fabrics stall; a hat stall selling felt and lace creations; haberdashery and net curtains. In summer, the plant and herb stall and the gardening pitch draw a crowd. The cosmetics and perfumes stall, with a man spraying testers on passing women, and the one selling hair accessories are popular all year round. The butcher's has chickens, gammon and suckling pig. There's also a shellfish stand with crabs, roll-mop herrings and mussels; occasionally the trader will cook king prawns in a huge pan and sell them in fives, hot, with a wedge of lemon. Nearby, a wholefood stall has bags of dried herbs, cereals, pulses and dried fruit and the guy selling handmade herbal soaps is doing a roaring trade.

After the Salisbury Street junction, the shops on either side of the street undergo a noticeable change. The butchers, bakers and caffs occupying postwar buildings are replaced by antiques shops trading from well-kept 19th-century terraces. The market takes some time to catch up with this change, and for a while the women's clothes (smart jackets, fashionable bodies, lingerie), cheap jewellery, shoes and electrical goods continue. But from the junction of Ashbridge Street, there are two lines of stalls on the south side. The second line is gathered on the pavement outside **Alfie's Antiques Market**. The outside stalls have a mixture of old crockery, jewellery and cutlery – rather like stands at a car-boot sale. One specializes in old toys, Duplo bricks and tatty Dinky toys; another has a mishmash of pottery.

Alfie's itself takes up all the Victorian terraced premises between 13 and 25 Church Street. Up to 370 dealers occupy

Food and Drink

On a fine day, an outside seat at **The Rooftop Restaurant** in Alfie's Antiques Market is the best bet. Breakfasts, salads, bagels and inexpensive lunches are all served here.

Edgware Road boasts plenty of cheap cafés. The **Regent Milk Bar** at No.362 has fried breakfasts, ice creams and sundaes, plus an original 1950s interior. Traders tend to eat at the **Market Grill** on Church Street, near the junction with Salisbury Street, which sells fried breakfasts and sandwiches. They drink at the **Traders Inn** opposite. Arguably the best fish and chips in town can be had at **Sea Shell** (49–51 Lisson Grove), which also has fine home-made fish cakes and tartare sauce.

A 15-minute walk south on the Edgware Road will bring you to a collection of Lebanese restaurants; try the **Ranoush Juice Bar** for fresh fruit juices and cheap Middle Eastern snacks.

the 35,000-square-ft space, which includes a basement and three floors plus a roof-top café. There is a bureau de change, and tax-free shopping can be arranged. Silverware, old jewellery, furniture, Victorian prints and ceramics make up the majority of the exhibits, though you are also likely to find picture frames, leather armchairs, carriage clocks, toy cars, toy soldiers, antiquarian books, old sewing machines, football club cards, postcards of 1940s pin-ups (£5 each), record players and wooden writing cases. Highlights include vintage clothes at **Persiflage**; and **Tin Tin Collectibles**, which stocks Victorian to 1970s clothes and luggage from the Victorian era to the 1960s. Check out their gentlemen's top hats.

It's worth spending some time wandering around Alfie's. In one corner

Nearby Attractions

Madame Tussaud's, *Marylebone Road,* **t** *0870 999 0046, credit card hotline* **t** *0870 400 3000, www.madame-tussauds.com;* ⊖ *Baker Street;* **buses** *13, 18, 27, 30, 74, 82, 113, 139, 159, 274.* **Madame Tussaud's open** *Mon–Fri 9.30am–5.30pm, Sat–Sun 9am–6pm;* **adm** *adults £20.99, 5–15s £16.99, seniors £17.99.* The world's most famous waxworks museum, with film and pop stars, politicians, royalty and famous villains. Be prepared to queue for hours if you haven't booked in advance. The Planetarium recently closed to make way for a 'celebrity experience'.

Regent's Park, ⊖ *Baker Street, Regent's Park, Great Portland Street, Mornington Crescent, Camden Town, St John's Wood;* **buses** *2, 13, 18, 27, 30, 74, 82, 113, 139, 189, 274, 453, C2.* **Open** *daily 5am–sunset.* One of London's loveliest parks (*see p.74*).

Sherlock Holmes Museum, *239 Baker Street,* **t** *(020) 7935 8866, www.sherlock-holmes.co.uk;* ⊖ *Baker Street;* **buses** *13, 18, 27, 30, 74, 82, 113, 159, 274.* **Open** *daily 9.30am–6pm;* **adm** *adults £6, children £4.* Tour round the famous sleuth's residence.

the crowds are thin at Alfie's and browsing is painless. And though traders are experts and know the value of their stock they are often willing to lower their prices.

Together, Church Street, Bell Street and Alfie's reveal something of the scope of street trading in London. If you've little time in the city, come here on Saturday and spend a morning joining in the bustle.

HAMPSTEAD COMMUNITY MARKET

78 Hampstead High Street, NW3, **t** *(020) 7794 8313.*

Transport: ⊖ *Hampstead;* ≥ *Hampstead Heath;* **buses** *46, 268, 603.*

Open: *Sat 10am–6pm; permanent stalls Tues–Sat.*

Best time to go: *Saturday.*

Parking: *Try the side streets south of Hampstead, but expect a long walk.*

Main wares: *Crafts, books, fruit and veg, wholefood, fish.*

Specifics: *Hot snacks, fish, secondhand books.*

you'll encounter an evocative collection of gardening artefacts, including old metal watering cans and wooden vegetable baskets. Another well-established business is in the basement, where antique kitchen equipment (pots, pans, milk jugs and enamel storage jars) is displayed on shelves as though part of a 19th-century scullery. **Ian Broughton's** stall also conjures up the domestic past, with household kitsch from the 1930s–60s including record players, radios and even picnic sets and fabrics. Stock includes Bakelite items such as door fittings which are quite rare. Stock is quirky and lovingly collected. Compared to Portobello Road,

Ever since Alexander Pope came with his friend John Gay to take the waters at Hampstead Wells, this borough-cum-village has attracted the literati. These days the place has fallen victim to its beauty, and only rich literati can afford to live here; behind the door of every 18th-century cottage lurks a corpulent novelist or a millionaire literary agent. But Hampstead's beauty is undeniable; to wander its streets (especially away from the busy main roads) is to immerse yourself in sophistication and gentility.

To Kenwood House

Hampstead Heath

HEATH STREET

268 603

CHRISTCHURCH HILL

WELL RD

NEW END

WELL WALK

EAST HEATH ROAD

WILLOW ROAD

Hampstead

GAYTON ROAD

WILLOUGHBY ROAD

DOWNSHIRE HILL

KEATS GROVE

Hampstead Heath

HAMPSTEAD HIGH ST

Keats' House

ST CRISPIN'S CLOSE

Hampstead Community Market

46 268 603

ROSSLYN HILL

POND STREET

Keats' House (*see* 'Nearby Attractions', p.84) attracts many visitors to the area, while a stroll on **Hampstead Heath** is *de rigueur* for both visitors and locals on fine weekends.

As a rule, affluent areas do not have thriving street markets, and the rule is obeyed here. The folk who fortify their monstrous mansions on Bishop's Avenue, north of the Heath, would as likely frequent a fruit and veg mart as campaign for an equal distribution of wealth. Yet Hampstead Community Market, though small, does have a certain Women's Institute-style charm. It is held indoors in a building akin to a village hall. Notices are displayed near the entrance advertising local events, and there's a collection of paintings by under-5s around a serving hatch. Tea, coffee, soft drinks, sandwiches, cakes and biscuits (but no hot food) are served on trestle tables near the entrance. A notice on the wall politely requests that, as a courtesy to other customers, you spend no more than 30 minutes on your refreshments.

There are numerous crafts traders around the hall, selling hats, home-made jewellery (prices range from £5 for a pair of earrings to £160 for a studded choker),

cushion covers, fresco-style tiles, handmade cards, pashminas (£58), handblown Eastern European glassware and handmade lace. Clothing stalls display Chinese-style garments, leather coats, cashmere jumpers and scarves. An aromatherapy stall has incense, oils and soaps. Several stalls sell prints depicting aspects of Hampstead's history, including some of the market itself. As you'd expect in Hampstead, there's at least one book stall, stocked with weighty biographies, old Ordnance Survey maps and highbrow novels. Most are secondhand and in good condition; prices start at £1.50.

Next door to the Community Centre, three permanent wooden stalls sell food. The first is well stocked with fruit and vegetables; the second, **Greggs**, sells wholefood (cereals, nuts, dried fruits and

Food and Drink

Cafés

Hampstead is awash with tea rooms and cafés, though tweeness is a recurrent problem. **Louis Pâtisserie** (32 Heath Street) serves Hungarian-style cakes and pastries, while **The Coffee Cup** (74 Hampstead High Street) has red leatherette banquettes, a small outdoor terrace and a splendid menu, including delicious raisin toast.

Pubs

Of Hampstead's many old pubs, try the **Holly Bush** (22 Holly Mount), a cosy old place serving standard pub grub. A bit further afield, at the northwest edge of Hampstead Heath, is the **Spaniards Inn**, a 16th-century inn frequented by highwayman Dick Turpin.

Restaurants

Giraffe (46 Rosslyn Hill) offers a lively modern global menu with a Middle Eastern slant, and is open all day.

Nearby Attractions

Keats' House, *Keats Grove, t (020) 7435 2062, www.keatshouse.org.uk;* ⊖ *Hampstead; buses 46, 268, 603.* **Open** *Tues–Sun 1–5pm;* **adm** *adults £3.50, under-16s free.* The house and garden where Keats wrote some of his best work, including *Ode to a Nightingale.*

Kenwood House, *Hampstead Lane, t (020) 8348 1286;* ⊖ *Highgate, then bus 215, or walk across the Heath.* **House open** *April–Oct daily 11am–5pm, Nov–March daily 11am–4pm.* **Grounds open** *summer daily 8am–8pm, winter daily 8am–4pm.* An elegant stately home on the edge of Hampstead Heath, with lovely gardens, breathtaking views over London and a fine collection of paintings including a Rembrandt and a Vermeer.

pulses); while the third has a wealth of seafood and fish geared to local tastes and pockets (wild salmon when in season, sea bass, Dover sole, Tiger Bay prawns). But, all in all, prices at the food stalls aren't as high as you'd expect for the area. Hampstead Community Centre, which established the market in the mid-1970s, should be praised for ensuring that some basic commodities are provided. The food stalls are a godsend in an area that could easily be swamped by antiques shops.

INVERNESS STREET

Inverness Street, NW1.

Transport: ⊖ *Camden Town; buses 24, 27, 29, 31, 88, 134, 168, 214, 253, 274, C2.*

Open: *Mon–Wed, Fri and Sat 9am–5pm; Thurs 9am–1pm.*

Best time to go: *Friday and Saturday.*

Parking: *Try the streets north of the Chalk Farm Road, but be prepared for a long walk.*

Main wares: *Fresh food, household goods.*

Specifics: *Fruit and veg.*

Camden Town sprang up in the 1840s, in the wake of the railways. Workshops and factories clustered along the lines running north out of London, and workers' housing followed. Until the 1970s, Camden remained a largely working-class district; then, helped by the opening of Camden Lock market (*see* p.70), it became one of London's most fashionable areas.

Inverness Street is a survivor from earlier times, a small street market that supplies local people with very cheap fruit and veg. Even on Saturday there are only about 20 stalls. At the junction with the High Street, the worst of them try to divert crowds heading for the more famous weekend markets. One sells cheap jeans; another flogs bags, suitcases, sunglasses and pashminas (three for £20). But as you proceed down Inverness Street the market gets back to basics, with lots of fresh food.

During the week, the market has sadly declined in the past few years. There might be only fruit and veg stalls operating, but

Food, Drink and Shopping

Bar Gansa, at 2 Inverness Street, is the nearest place for a bite, open from 10am and serving breakfasts, Spanish tapas, good coffee and Spanish wines and beers. The **Good Mixer** (No.30) is a run-down pub with an excellent jukebox that attracts fashionable types. The street also has an interesting independent record and CD store, **Shakedown**, at No.24. *See also* Camden, p.73.

these are worth investigating. In addition to the staples (apples, onions, potatoes, oranges), you can often find more exotic stuff. Mooli, fennel, coriander and Turkish dates and figs were all displayed in winter. Prices are keen: 3lbs of tomatoes for £1, for instance. Another trader who usually makes an appearance through the week is the flower seller, his stall crammed with blooms, even in the depths of winter.

To view other stalls, it's best to visit on a Saturday. A cheese seller, a butcher and a fishmonger have all been spotted on that day, when crowds teem past Inverness Street on their way to Camden Lock. At the westerly end of the market, a chap sometimes arrives with a lorry-load of household goods to sell: from cheap coloured candles to tablecloths and napkins. Other pitches on a Saturday hold clothes stalls and a luggage stall; and you can also buy jewellery, cards and socks.

Local competition from both Safeway and Sainsbury's seems to be taking a toll on Inverness Street market. Yet still the fruit and veg traders soldier on, selling produce at a fraction of supermarket prices. Next time you visit Camden Lock market on a Saturday, make a detour and grab yourself a bag-load of bargains.

For nearby attractions, *see* Camden Market, p.74.

KILBURN SQUARE

West side of Kilburn High Road, opposite Quex Road, NW6.

Transport: ⊖ *Kilburn Park;* ⇌ *Kilburn High Road; buses 16, 31, 32, 98, 139, 189, 206, 316, 328.*

Open: *Thurs–Sat 9am–5.30pm; Sun 11am–5pm.*

Best time to go: *Saturday.*

Parking: *Try the side streets to the west of Kilburn High Road.*

Main wares: *Clothing, pet food, household goods, cassettes and CDs.*

Specifics: *Pet food, tropical fish.*

These days, Kilburn Square market looks neat and new, but a little too well ordered. A blue and grey security fence was put up in 1994 and stallholders were given permanent lock-ups. The market was nothing special when temporary stalls were set up on this dreary concrete square, but now some premises are empty or closed even on a Saturday.

Many of the 30 or so traders sell clothing and other goods of the type common at London's street markets: jeans, women's jackets, tawdry nightclubwear, string vests, baby clothes, socks, shoes, greetings

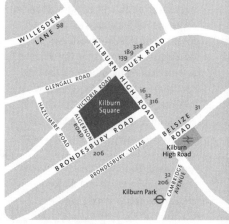

cards, leather bags and suitcases. But a few stalls are worth closer inspection. **Paul's Aquatic World** stocks tropical fish together with all the accompanying gubbins (and guppies); take a look inside at the terrapins, neons and metallic gold barb fish, darting about in large tanks. Nearby, the **One-Stop Pet Food** stall deals in dog baskets and bird cages; **Rainbow Fabrics** stocks a wide range of haber-dashery (and also sells net curtains); and **Dave's Linen** does a good line in colourful bed sheets.

There's also a cut-flowers pitch where big bouquets go for a fiver, and one traditional fruit and veg stall where the barrow boys flaunt their seedless navels. Not far away, **Serwaa Enterprise** has boxes of yams and coconuts outside. Other basics are sold by the household goods stall.

Although Kilburn is home to Irish and Antipodean communities, there's little to remind you of this at the market. However, you can get some idea of the cosmopolitan make-up of the area in **Kabul John Café**. Inside, an old cockney geezer with a fag sits beneath a huge poster of Bob Marley smoking a spliff. Fried breakfasts vie for attention with Jamaican patties on the menu. Two other businesses are also run by Afro-Caribbean Kilburnites. At **Supernails** ('Special rates for senior citizens', 'Yes, we do ear piercing') two women sit in the window, one manicuring the other. And **Top That** specializes in felt hats and umbrellas.

At junctions up and down the Kilburn High Road solitary vendors set out their wares. In December Christmas trees are sold outside the **Cock** public house, 50 yards north of the market. Across the road is a fruit and veg stall. It's hardly enough to make a market, but these

---

Food, Drink and Shopping

Kilburn High Road is a busy main street with many of the usual chainstores, but it does contain the occasional gem. Watch out for Irish white pudding at the butchers, soda bread at the bakeries and Irish stew at the caffs (take a trek north on the High Road to find all three). Kilburn is now as much a centre of the Antipodean community as the Irish – try the **Southern K** pub, at the junction with Willesden Lane.

---

hawkers seem more in keeping with the unfettered traditions of London street trading than the enclosed stallholders of Kilburn Square.

NAG'S HEAD AND GRAFTON SCHOOL

Nag's Head, Seven Sisters Road, southwest of junction with Hertslet Road, N7, t (020) 7607 3527; Grafton School, off Hercules Place, N7.

Transport: ⊖ *Holloway Road; buses 4, 17, 29, 43, 91, 153, 253, 254, 259, 271, 279.*

Open: *Nag's Head: general Mon, Tues and Thurs 8am–5pm; secondhand and antiques Wed 8am–5pm; new goods Fri 8am–5pm, Sat 8am–5.30pm; flea market Sun 8am–2pm; Grafton School market Sat 8am–4.30pm.*

Parking: *Try the side streets to the north of the Seven Sisters Road.*

Main wares: *Bric-a-brac, new and secondhand clothes, household goods, fruit and vegetables, fish, secondhand CDs and videos.*

Until the late 1980s, the **Nag's Head** market occupied a patch of wasteland near the pub that has given its name to the busy junction of Holloway Road and

Seven Sisters Road. However, developers planned to build a Safeway store there. After a battle involving locals, stallholders, the developers and the council, a compromise was reached. Extra shops were built, but the market was granted a permanent, if smaller, site close to its original position.

It's now a compact, somewhat sanitized affair occupying a hangar-like structure. Lock-up shops line the building, and there's space for 40 or so trestle table traders in the middle. Outside the shopping centre and the market, people sell cigarettes from cartons. There's a public toilet at the back of the shopping centre.

As was always the case, the market varies greatly through the week. On mixed market days (Mondays, Tuesdays and Thursdays), you'll find a satisfying blend of old and new commodities: secondhand clothes, bric-a-brac and electrical equipment; new clothes, fresh food and household goods.

On Wednesdays, all the temporary stalls sell secondhand goods. Again, there's plenty of bric-a-brac, but also cheap clothing, shoes (including some great thigh-length leather boots) and well-worn household goods. There is a fruit and veg stall and a fishmonger's at the Seven Sisters Road exit.

On Fridays and Saturdays, only new goods are sold, and consequently the market is relatively bland. There are a couple of big fruit and veg lock-ups, but the variety and prices aren't exceptional. The fish lock-up is better; along with North Sea regulars, it stocks milk fish, snappers and saltfish (popular with the Afro-Caribbean locals). One firm sells a decent range of babies' and children's wear; another specializes in haberdashery and the vibrantly coloured material used to make saris – the glittering collection in golds, purples and turquoise costs from 50p a yard. Electrical bits and bobs, the aptly named Cushion World UK, a key-cutter, a butcher's van (from Thursdays to Saturdays) and Sharon's Household toiletries complete the picture.

Every Sunday the market changes character yet again. Though a few new goods are sold, secondhand clothes and bric-a-brac are to the fore, giving a flea-market feel to the place. As Holloway isn't on the tourist map, and competition from Camden and the East End markets is fierce, you're likely to find bargains among the crockery, ornaments and glassware if you're prepared to root around.

There are some stalls at the bottom of Eburne Road, off Seven Sisters Road, selling clothes and household goods, but nothing particularly inspiring.

Holloway's other market is more like the Nag's Head of old. It is held in the tarmac playground of **Grafton School**, down Hercules Place (a walkway off the Seven Sisters Road, opposite the new Nag's Head market). A total of 70 or more stalls congregate here every Saturday, selling all manner of new and old goods.

Police were clearing away fly-traders from Hercules Place last time I visited – a sure sign of a thriving market. There are always plenty of car-boot-style stalls within the playground, where homely junk is placed on trestle tables. Many of the professional traders also deal in secondhand wares: leather and sheepskin jackets; Levi's jeans from £10 (cheaper than Camden); old TVs, telephones and cameras; well-used power tools (Black & Decker and the like); and a large number of secondhand CDs (from reggae or gospel music to a stall full of French, Italian and Spanish titles).

As at Hackney (see p.104), some of the goods are of questionable provenance or legality. One trader offers punters nips from his stock of vodka and rum; another is selling computer software for £10 or less; and there's a large business in secondhand computer games. The breadth of wares displayed on some stalls is astonishing: barbed wire, a 1970s computer and a toaster; or eggs, buttons and condoms. Old cookers, comfy chairs and electric heaters give one pitch the feel of an open-air bedsit. New goods include stationery, household cleaners, fruit and veg (just the one stall), handbags, cheap jewellery, cosmetics, pots and pans, bedlinen, joss sticks, haberdashery, lingerie and electrical

goods. One 'demmer' is selling toys, another likely lad is flogging woolly tops: '£10 yer polar fleeces, you can't be looking'. A burger van offers sustenance of a type to the frenetic crowd.

Despite its ramshackle and fly-by-night appearance, the ad hoc get-together outside Grafton School has continued for a good few years now, attracting more Holloway punters than the relatively orderly Nag's Head market. Proof positive that authorities mess with markets at their peril.

QUEEN'S CRESCENT

Queen's Crescent, between Grafton and Malden Roads, NW5.

Transport: ⊖ *Chalk Farm, Kentish Town;* ⇌ *Kentish Town, Kentish Town West; buses 24, 31, 46, 134, 168, 214, C2.*

Open: *Thurs 9am–1.30pm, Sat 9am–5pm.*

Best time to go: *Saturday before 3pm.*

Parking: *Try Queen's Crescent south of Malden Road where parking is free at weekends.*

Main wares: *Women's clothes, household goods, plants and flowers, fruit and veg, meat, fish.*

Specifics: *New and secondhand clothes for women.*

Queen's Crescent is the sort of place where knots of locals, some of them Cypriots, gather to chat about the week's events. Trading has taken place on this street for a century and a quarter, but most Londoners from outside the district remain ignorant of its existence. The market is now suffering from this anomaly and plans are afoot to

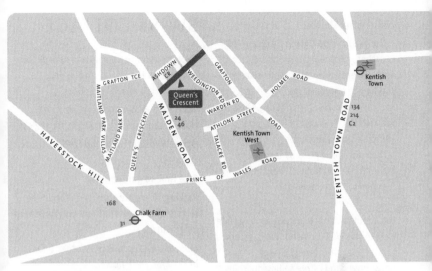

regenerate it, with various possibilities being touted; these include attracting new stallholders with more specialist goods to sell, and signposting the market from Camden Town in order to draw in passers-by.

Already there are a few stalls selling Italian foods, a fresh fishmonger, the market's first hot-food stall and even some handmade jewellery. Special market festivals are now a feature a few times a year, with a continental market festival planned as well as an Asian market. Money is being spent on jazzing up the stalls and there are plans to have special lighting decorations not just for Christmas but also for other ethnic festivals such as Diwali. There are new hanging baskets, the street has more efficient cleaning and shop fronts are also being spruced up, a laudable effort from the local council who really understand the value of this local market.

Queen's Crescent, located roughly midway between Kentish Town and Chalk Farm, is a usually quiet Victorian street filled with small butchers and bakeries, caffs and junk shops. On Thursday

mornings and Saturdays, however, stalls are set up along its northern stretch and scores of people from nearby flats and houses take to the streets to shop, browse and chat.

About 60–70 traders come here on Saturdays, about 50 or so on Thursdays. On both days the street is barred to traffic. There's a good range on offer, with all the basics supplied. The scattering of fruit and veg stalls sell the usual bananas, apples, watercress and potatoes at fair prices, and might have the odd mango or pumpkin in season. The butcher has an old-fashioned barrow full of big joints of gammon, and (less appetizing) chicken in breadcrumbs. Two other food stalls are worth noting: one sells a traditional assortment of seafood and fish (smoked haddock, cod, whelks and mussels); the other (at the Malden Street end) is full of cheap tinned food, as well as cakes, eggs and biscuits.

The market also supplies useful household items, including haberdashery, hot-water bottles, kettle de-furrers, masking tape, cleaning fluids and stationery. Some shops put their wares on

Food and Drink

The **Gossip Stop Café** at 88 Queen's Crescent is appropriately named, clean and modern. It serves all-day breakfasts, sandwiches, pastries, and lunch specials such as lamb stew for under £3. The **Blue Sea Fish Bar** (No.143) is a traditional chippie on the Crescent.

There are three pubs by the market, including the **Sir Robert Peel** at the junction with Malden Road.

the street to attract custom, among them **Hole in the Wall** (on Ashdown Crescent, just off the main street), a large household goods store selling dustbins, mops and the like.

But although Queen's Crescent also has the usual selection of street market clobber – electrical goods (from plugs to answerphones), greetings cards, toys, net curtains, bedlinen, cut flowers, pot plants, watches, mobile-phone holders and handbags – clothes are its forte. Women are best catered for, and prices are low. Cardboard boxes full of warm tops are ripe to be rifled through by eager punters. One long-serving trader specializes in larger-sized clothes for women, from size 16 to 36. Unfortunately, the selection of big jumpers, tracksuit bottoms and button-through dresses is hardly alluring. Football towels are on sale for £14.

Camden's trendiness hasn't spread this far. Few clothes here could be described as fashionable – pastel-hued frocks, stretchy slacks and suits favoured by middle-aged women are the norm – but there's a fair choice of socks, knitwear, coats, underwear, shoes and T-shirts, plus a small selection of children's clothes and men's shirts. Out-of-season garments sell at knock-down prices, so come in December for your skimpy tops (£5) and hot pants (£2.99).

SWISS COTTAGE

By Swiss Cottage tube station outside the Hampstead Theatre, at start of Eton Avenue, NW3, t (020) 7974 6917.

Transport: ⊖ *Swiss Cottage;* ⇌ *South Hampstead; buses 13, 31, 46, 82, 113, 187, C11.*

Open: *Wed 8am–4pm and Fri–Sat 8am–5pm.*

Best time to go: *Saturday.*

Parking: *There are parking meters in the surrounding streets but you may be in for a long search.*

Main wares: *Secondhand clothes, books, bric-a-brac, fresh flowers.*

There has hardly been a moment since its birth in the 1970s that Swiss Cottage market hasn't faced an uncertain future. It used to occupy a concrete square away from the Finchley Road traffic, near a community centre. But finally it is safely installed on its own site in Eton Avenue, very close to the tube station.

It would be a pity if the market were to disappear, as it provides a pleasingly well-balanced mix of stalls. The market on Wednesday is a farmers' market (see page xx). On Saturdays the traditional street market boasts about 40 traders, less on a

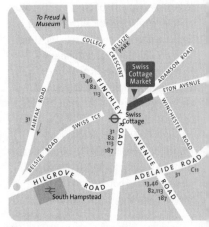

Food and Drink

Pubs

The **Swiss Cottage** pub (by the tube) looks like a chalet, but feels more like a ship, surrounded by a tumultuous sea of traffic.

Restaurants

The Gate (72 Belsize Lane) is a cool, minimalist space serving excellent vegetarian dishes and a good range of snacks all day. Slightly pricier is **Wakaba** (122a Finchley Road), one of the first Japanese restaurants in London and still one of the best.

Zuccato (top floor, O2 Complex, 225 Finchley Road) is a chic yet inexpensive Italian place with very good food.

Friday. Some stalls are run by local amateurs, selling bric-a-brac, secondhand books or perhaps (having switched to CDs) their record and tape collections. These are discerning folk, and the quality of their goods is often high: secondhand books are a deal more highbrow than the norm (a biography of Byron, say). There are antiquarian books on offer too for collectors. A couple of stalls have all manner of collectibles, with odd bits and pieces from the Edwardian and Victorian eras. There are also craft and jewellery stalls selling crystals and Indian artefacts such as bronze gods and buddhas. Along with all this interesting old stuff,

Nearby Attractions

Freud Museum, 20 Maresfield Gardens, t (020) 7435 2002, www.freud.org.uk; ⊖ Finchley Road, Swiss Cottage; buses 13, 82, 113. Open Wed–Sun noon–5pm; adm adults £5, children £3. The house where Freud set up his last home in 1938. The consulting room contains the couch on which his patients lay during sessions.

the market also provides a fair selection of new goods. These can range from toys to kitsch pottery. The fish stall brings fresh fish direct from Looe in Cornwall and there are olives from Italy, Spain and Greece. Pastries and cakes are all organic and home-baked, while the green-fingered can buy plants direct from the nursery with plenty of advice on offer.

In addition, you might find a van selling sweet and savoury crêpes, and there's plenty of artisan bread and local and speciality cheeses to taste at the cheese stall. The fruit and veg here also have local pedigrees, while cut flowers are sold around the year by one trader. Fashion for both men and women is offered by a handful of stalls, and there's also a lot of jewellery to be had: new, vintage and antique.

WEMBLEY

Stadium Way, Wembley, Middlesex, t (01895) 632221.

Transport: ⊖ *Wembley Park;* ⇌ *Wembley Stadium; buses 79, 83, 92, 182, 204, 223, 224, 297, PR2.*

Open: *Sun 9am–3pm.*

Best time to go: *9am Sunday to avoid the crowds.*

Parking: *There's a car park to the west of the market with lots of space, or try the industrial estate and DIY superstores off Fulton Road and Rutherford Way.*

Main wares: *Clothing, household goods, electrical goods.*

Specifics: *Cheap leather jackets, coats, men's shoes, football strips, hats.*

Northwest London's attempt at an East End Sunday market certainly brings the hordes down Olympic Way, in the shadow

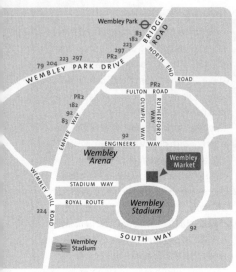

patterns, twee frills for toddlers or – fittingly, given the location – football strips in Premiership team colours for schoolkids (also sold in men's sizes – a West Ham top is £25 while, typically, a Man Utd top goes for £35). Children's football boots start at around £10.

Men can also snap up three shirts for £7.99, three pairs of Calvin Klein boxer shorts for £5, new worsted suits for £49.99 (advertised as 'Cheaper than stolen goods, honestly'), or 'work jeans' (i.e. with unknown brand names) for £7.99. One stall has a vast array of trousers, ranging from grey flannels for schoolboys to tent-like togs with 50-inch waists. Jumpers, T-shirts, underwear and socks suit both sexes and most sizes. There are a couple of discount jeans stalls, selling Pepe and Levi seconds.

Wembley is not primarily a food market. There are only two fruit and veg stalls, but both are large and the traders sell their stocks of mostly standard produce at low prices and with hearty voices: 'No man goes like a mango goes,' yells one lad, proffering his most exotic fruit. The bread and cake stall does a good trade in iced doughnuts, and there are also a couple of sweets stalls, a butcher's lorry and various tables piled high with soft drinks and chocolate (five Bounties for £1). A Greek specialities stall sells olives, feta cheese and marinated garlic. Where fast food is concerned, though, the market really comes into its own. There's a seated area in the centre of the market fringed with takeaway vans; as well as the ubiquitous hot-dog lorries and jacket potato sellers, there's a Chinese takeaway stall with stir-fries cooked in a wok before your eyes. You'll also find Indian *seikh kebabs* cooked over charcoal, hot pancakes and Brazilian-style sausage doughnuts.

of the vast construction that is the new Wembley Stadium. Coachloads of hefty shoppers shuffle and muscle their way along the wide avenues that separate the acres of stalls. Many have come miles down the M1 from the north; most have come for the cheap clothes and household goods. But anyone who enjoys snuffling around in mounds of old junk will be disappointed; junk there may be, but it is all spanking new.

This is a big market with big stalls – over 450 of them. The entrance is framed by a florist's (the only one on the market) and a newsagent selling papers and cigarettes. Then you're among the clothes. Wembley is one of London's best markets for cheap leather coats and jackets. The leatherwear stalls have garments in scores of styles, from pink miniskirts to bulky suede jackets; prices start around £50.

Men, women and children have a wide vista of clothes to choose from. Women's wear ranges from high-street fashions (Lycra leggings, smart suits, woollen skirts) to lingerie and nightclub wear. Children's clothes come in swirly

Food and Drink

There is nothing worth visiting in the immediate vicinity of Wembley Stadium, so you'd be better off eating at one of the fast-food stands in the market. If, however, you have a car and fancy some fabulous, no-frills Punjabi food, head for **Karahi King**, a 10-minute drive away at 213 East Land, north Wembley.

A major attraction of the market is the range of household goods offered, from electrical gadgets for the kitchen (kettles, toasters, liquidizers) to gnomes, motor mowers, ironing-board covers, keys (cut while you wait), tissues (18 packets for £1.50) and garden furniture. At many markets you can buy leather handbags, bath towels, toys, rugs, tools, net curtains, duvets, watches, mobile phone accessories, plants and shrubs, country tapes and CDs, net curtains, gold jewellery, videos, haberdashery, dress material, radio-cassette players and sunglasses. Here, there's more choice of all of these goods, plus several specialist stalls. Tablecloths and napery, car phones, office stationery (including Tippex, cashboxes and reams of paper), mountain bikes (prices start at around £60), amplifiers and speakers, video games, car accessories (from chamois leathers to hub caps and personalized number-plates), wooden furniture, Indian bedspreads and even AA membership can be bought at Wembley.

A couple of large stalls sell men's shoes at very low prices: brogues with leather uppers going for under £15. One stall has a pair of size 14 monstrosities on display. Another highlight is the hat stall. A huge variety of headgear is in stock: panamas, frilly things for babies, wedding hats and trilbies. A middle-aged woman is trying on a particularly flamboyant model and her daughter is howling with laughter. The stallholder desperately tries to reassure his customer: 'It looks all right, that'.

You can hear all the wide-boy patter at any one of up to half a dozen lorry auction sales: 'Versprung Durk Technik, that's German for very good...all I can say is, these retail in IKEA for £29.99 but it's me birthday, so I'll tell you what I'll do... Forget £30 and £25, don't worry about £20, £15 is below cost...tenner the lot, who's first?... I'm not working next year, so it's all got to go... Where else can you get a microwave set like that for 50p a piece?' (where indeed?)...'If for some reason you're not satisfied, bring it back and I'll buy the polish back off you, but I'll tell you this, I've never in my life had to buy back some polish.'

To see all of the market is something of an endurance test. As you leave Wembley, you might feel like you've played 90 minutes plus extra time in a cup final. In the distance you hear a man at the crockery stall, still trying his darnedest to sell an ugly white china bread bin. 'Tell you what I'll do...'

WILLESDEN

Church Road car park off the High Road, Willesden, NW10.

Transport: ⊖ *Dollis Hill, Neasden; buses 52, 98, 226, 260, 266, 297, 302, 460.*

Open: *Wed and Sat 9am–5.30pm.*

Best time to go: *Saturday.*

Parking: *Parking is reasonably easy and there are no meters around here.*

Main wares: *Household goods, clothing, fresh food.*

Specifics: *Haberdashery and material, Caribbean produce.*

Neasden

DUDDEN HILL LANE

DENZIL ROAD

Dollis Hill

BRENTHURST RD

CHAPTER RD

226
302

NEASDEN LANE

COLIN ROAD

MEYRICK ROAD

Willesden Market

297

HIGH ROAD

52, 98, 260, 266,
297, 302, 460

WHITE HART LANE

CHURCH ROAD

ILEX ROAD

ROUNDWOOD RD

CONLEY RD

Willesden's bi-weekly sale is a fine example of a local urban market: compact, well balanced and with a healthy multicultural mix of customers and traders. It has also recently been the subject of a heated battle between the local community and the local authority. Championed by the local newspaper, the campaign to save the market ensured that, even when the market lost its original site, a new temporary site was found round the corner; it will remain at its present site for a year or two. It will most likely have to move again and the long-term site is as yet undecided, but, with the amount of vehement public support that the market has received, it will definitely survive, probably somewhere very near by. On both Wednesdays and Saturdays about 40 stalls squeeze into the market's present space.

There are two sizeable fruit and veg stalls, one specializing in Caribbean produce: yams, plantains and also hot pepper sauces and bottles of 'Baldwin's Original Sarsaparilla'. The other is packed with more run-of-the-mill stock (apples,

oranges, broccoli, spuds), but come here at knocking-out time on a Saturday (5pm in summer, earlier in winter) and you might snap up some astonishing bargains. Local Asian women have their weekly haggle with the costermongers at this time – it's all good-natured stuff. A butcher's lorry (selling bacon joints, hunks of meat and the odd bit of cheese), a fishmonger's (spotted grouper, gleaming milk fish and a tray of salmon heads were prize exhibits on a Wednesday) and a large stall of biscuits, chocolates, cakes and bread also provide Willesdeners with their victuals.

The traders here supply most of the usual market goods – greetings cards, cheap jewellery, toys, tools, CDs and cosmetics, plus a varied choice of toiletries and household goods – and even cater for a couple of more specialist interests. The haberdashery stall is well frequented by local dressmakers, who also have a lace stall and a barrow of material to peruse.

The remaining stalls concentrate on clothing. Again, all the basics are present: underwear, T-shirts, tops, children's wear, shirts, shoes and training shoes. But there are also a few intriguing oddities, like the hat stall with its straw trilbies for men and colourful felt wedding titfers for women; or the pitch specializing in glittering creations to be worn in Cricklewood nightclubs.

Food and Drink

The **Hamburger Bar and Café** at 222 Church Road sells sandwiches and fried breakfasts. **Saravanas**, at 77–79 Dudden Hill Lane, is a south Indian restaurant open through the day. **Shish** at 2 Station Parade is a large Silk Road restaurant with great food and a lively bar upstairs.

East London

BETHNAL GREEN

South side of Bethnal Green Road, from
Wilmot Street to Vallance Road, E2,
t (020) 7377 8963.

Transport: ⊖/≷ *Bethnal Green; buses*
8, 309, 388, 903, D3, D6.

Open: *Mon–Wed, Fri and Sat 9am–5pm;*
Thurs 9am–4pm.

Best time to go: *Friday and Saturday.*

Parking: *Try the backstreets north and*
south of Bethnal Green Road.

Main wares: *Fruit and veg, household*
goods, women's clothes.

Bethnal Green market is the heart of
the East End. Take a look at some of the
fruit and veg stalls – they're as traditional
as they come. The barrows are of the old
wooden-wheeled variety, many of them
made locally by an old firm called Hillier's.
Some of the costermongers, gnarled
and tough, look as though they've spent
their entire lives planted on the Bethnal
Green Road, while many of the other stalls
are run by Asian families.

Few London markets have managed to
survive on main roads, but the stallholders
at Bethnal Green soldier on amid the
fumes and noise of the A1209. The market

Food and Drink

There's a fine choice of pie and mash
shops in the vicinity: try **G. Kelly** at
414 Bethnal Green Road, or **S. & R. Kelly's
& Sons** at No.284. At No.332 is **E. Pellicci**,
which has traditional caff grub: meat
pudding with potatoes and veg, roast
beef, etc. In the 1960s, Ronnie Kray, the
gang leader, was a regular. Now Pellicci's is
a favourite meeting place for local young
artists as well as an eclectic mix of locals.

Roman Road, a few minutes' walk away,
also has food outlets (*see* p.116).

has been held here since the early 19th
century, and has remained true to its
locals, providing clothes, staple foodstuffs
and household goods. Henry Mayhew
records that 100 costermongers usually
attended in the 1850s, while Mary
Benedetta notes that in 1936 it traded
seven days a week, and included furniture
and junk stalls. These days it tends to
straggle during the week, with no more
than 20 or so of the 76 pitches taken, but
a good enough show is made on Fridays
and Saturdays.

Most of the weekly shop can be done
here: soap, bin bags and kitchen scourers
(20 for £1) at the household goods stalls;
children's pyjamas and mittens at a
clothes pitch; crisps and tins of spaghetti
hoops at the cut-price food stall, as well
as exotic fruit juices from the Middle East.
A regular trader sells Afro-Caribbean
produce; as well as yams and plantains, he
stocks imported soft drinks, banana chips
and some fresh herbs. There's ample
opportunity to buy cheap women's
clothing as well, with high-street fashion
on show: a bright red suit, right on trend, is
£25. Other stalls sell pet accessories, shoes,
handbags, sequinned Indian slippers of all
colours, Bollywood DVDs, luggage, toys,

Nearby Attractions

Bethnal Green Museum of Childhood, *Cambridge Heath Road, t (020) 8980 2415; ⊖ Bethnal Green; buses 8, 309, 903, D6. Open Sat–Thurs 10am–5.50pm. Take plenty of 20p pieces to work the old-fashioned automated machines.* Fantastic collection of toys, games, dolls and train sets. *Closed until Nov 2006.*

mobile phones and accessories, bed linen and embroidered quilts from Pakistan, and towels and net curtains.

Bethnal Green tube station was the site of London's worst civilian disaster of the Second World War. Fearing that the Germans were dropping gas bombs, a crowd fled down the steps to shelter in the Underground. Someone fell, and over a hundred people were crushed to death. A plaque commemorates the spot. A less sobering local landmark, the Bethnal Green Museum of Childhood, is just around the corner from the market (*see* above).

BRICK LANE (CLUB ROW)

Brick Lane (north of railway bridge), Cygnet Street, Sclater Street, E1; Bacon Street, Cheshire Street, E2; t (020) 7377 8963.
Transport: ⊖ *Aldgate East, Shoreditch, Bethnal Green, Liverpool St; ⇌ Liverpool St; buses 8, 26, 35, 47, 48, 67, 78, 149, 242, 388.*
Open: *Sun 6am–1pm.*
Best time to go: *As early as possible.*
Parking: *Try the side streets to the north of Bethnal Green Road; there are parking meters (free on Sundays) on Boundary Street.*
Main wares: *Secondhand goods (from books to furniture), tools, tapes and CDs, leatherwear, tinned food, pet foods and batteries.*
Specifics: *Look out for secondhand bargains.*

It's 6.40am on a dark Sunday morning. Outside the caff at the junction of Shoreditch High Street and Commercial Road, a forlorn-looking gent stands by a fully extended fishing rod which overhangs the road. He's getting few bites, but his rod marks the beginning of Brick Lane market.

Of all London markets, Brick Lane comes closest to the mayhem of the pre-20th-century marts: lawless, sprawling and splendid; never the same two weeks running, it always attracts thousands of locals (but few tourists) onto the streets.

Trading began here in the 18th century, half a mile from the City of London to escape the taxes imposed by the City authorities. The district has provided a home for a succession of refugees, from Huguenot silk-weavers in the 18th century, to East European Jews fleeing the pogroms of the late 19th century, to the present-day population of Bangladeshis. Unfortunately, the Bangladeshi influence on today's market is small, limited to a few stalls selling leather jackets made locally.

Rooted alongside the rundown Victorian terraces in and around Brick Lane, the market also flourishes on nearby wasteland, in warehouses and under railway arches. In the late 1980s and early 1990s parts of the market were sectioned off for redevelopment. As the bicycle sale on Granby Street followed the Chilton Street traders into obsolescence, it began to seem inevitable that the City's ivy-like insinuation into the area would kill off the street trading. Happily, this has not occurred and the market continues to

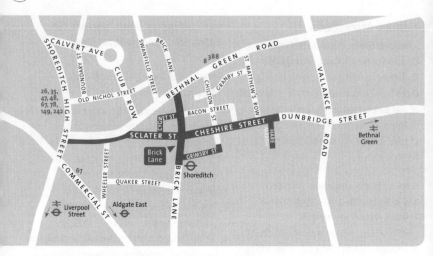

enjoy very rude health. The City's encroachment has, for the time being, abated and, despite the council's attempts to apply cosmetic flourishes, much of the market still resembles a bomb site – not a particularly attractive bomb site, at that, but nonetheless one where you can indulge every Sunday in one of the most lively, intoxicating shopping experiences in all London.

Many locals still know the market as Club Row, but this stub of a street off Bethnal Green Road no longer has any stalls on it. Club Row used to be famous for selling birds, ornamental fish and small animals of all kinds, but in 1982 Tower Hamlets Council, under pressure from animal welfare groups, banned the sale of live animals. Hydra-like, Brick Lane accommodated the change and grew in other directions.

The following street-by-street guide should be seen as a snapshot taken one Sunday morning. Though Brick Lane, Cheshire Street and Sclater Street are the heart of the market, half the fun lies in exploring its gloriously frayed edges: the backstreets, lock-ups and cubbyholes where transient traders sell a variety of dodgy wares.

Bethnal Green Road

On Bethnal Green Road, from Shoreditch High Street to Sclater Street, unlicensed traders line up with their backs to an old brick wall and try to sell the contents of someone else's broom cupboard; the poverty is palpable. Competition for pitches is fierce and a first come, first served system applies, so you'll find life here at unearthly times of the morning. There are no stalls on the first hundred yards of Bethnal Green Road; instead goods are 'displayed' on blankets or bin liners laid flat on the pavement. One entrepreneur's stock consists only of shirt buttons, two fishing reels and a Harry Belafonte record. Nearby is a pile of car radios and a mountain bike. Elsewhere you can find the constituent parts of a bike, yards of hosepipe and boxes of orphaned TV remote controls – all seemingly as useless as each other and yet still attracting attention. As if in protest at these mysteriously acquired goods, a burglar alarm whines unceasingly somewhere off Great Eastern Street.

Makeshift clothes lines – lengths of string hung between rusty nails banged into the wall – display crumpled suits and corduroys of uncertain ancestry. Two old men haggle over the price of a broken watch. Surreal combinations of wares are proffered: a septuagenarian woman sells old spectacles and egg whisks. An anxious young man jostles between two traders and opens a grubby case full of pirate porn movies with German titles. Rugs, mobile phones and even a secondhand fish tank might also come to light here. Yet despite the Dickensian sleaze, the market rarely feels threatening.

Further along the Bethnal Green Road, the brick wall rises to become a Victorian railway bridge. A few lock-ups are incorporated in its structure. A couple are well-ordered: one contains secondhand books (1970s football annuals and the like), the other wallpaper. Yet another has an incredible collection of junk, some of it still in Rentacrates, while rusty office furniture fills a fourth.

Sclater Street

Trading takes place on a more legitimate footing in Sclater Street. This used to be the centre of the animal trade; now only a few pet food stalls remain. At the Bethnal Green end of the street electrical goods and tools stalls, full of spanner sets, pliers, saws and other DIY paraphernalia, dominate. There's also a video stall, a jellied eel stall and a stall with 50 or so red plastic tubs full of merchandise. A large felt-tipped 'everything £1' sign is displayed on each bin, but this doesn't stop every third customer from asking the price of the goods. Further up, there are stalls selling cheap tins of food and cakes. Two old traders are grumbling about the size of the crowd: 'They don't come down here like they used to early morning.'

Sclater Street eventually joins Brick Lane, but, before it does so, a large area of wasteland opens to the left, followed by a yard; to the right are two more yards. The one on the left sells old junk and office furniture. The smaller of the two on the right has tools and fuses, cardboard boxes of fruit and veg and Heinz soup, as well as the ubiquitous plastic tubs full of hairspray. Towards the end of the market, boxes of veg go for £1, 'nanas for £2. Tower Hamlets Council has recently tried to beautify the yards to little effect. It will take more than some green gates and a 'Welcome' sign to hide the blemishes on this earthy, semi-lawless fizzog.

The land to the left of Sclater Street incorporates Cygnet Street and a car park. This is where to find the best of the bantering stallholders. **L&J Meats**, the butcher's, is having a show. 'Cut the bugger in half, mate,' roars the frontman, as his assistant, cleaver held high, takes a lunge at a pork joint. 'Loverley great English pork. You couldn't see less fat on a banana.' The gags flow with practised ease: 'You want joints, luv? The ones you smoke or the ones you eat?' Nearby, a frozen-food seller who arrives every week is instructing his audience: 'Today we've got chicken Kiev and chicken cordon bleu, but we'll call them Kevin and Gordon in case you can't get your mouth round the fancy French words. Who'll give me two quid for Kevin, two quid for Gordon?' Competing with them, a man selling TVs and video recorders shouts into his microphone: 'Where do you usually do your shopping, then, or do you steal it?' Anything is possible in this market.

Miked-up wideboys conduct 'clearance' sales literally off the back of lorries (which should be warning enough) with all the aplomb and crowd control of seasoned performers, which is exactly what they are. 'I'm not going to charge you £20,

I'm not going to charge you £18, I'm not going to charge you £15, I'm not even going to charge you £10, no put it away madam...' – the punters know the routine as well as the traders; it's as familiar as pantomime and just as seductive. Be warned, though, it's not advisable to buy anything here, no matter how attractive the prices. During the early stages of the sale the patter master will indeed serve up several bargains – a black bin liner containing a remote-control car, a clock, a box of Belgian chocolates and a video three-pack for £15 – which are rapidly snapped up by the crowd whose faith and fervour will begin to grow. Hands will shoot up with increased rapidity to claim the latest cut-price offerings. Little by little, the prices will begin to rise. Starting with toys for £1, the crowd will then be offered video games for £5, Walkmans for £10, CD players for £20. Soon people are paying £50-plus for a brand new Sony hi-fi that's nothing of the sort. Make any attempt to protest and several rather burly members of the audience, who up until that moment seemed to be as involved in the morning's entertainment as anyone else, will quickly persuade you otherwise.

Also occupying the car park are a bike seller with scores of good-value new and secondhand models, a vacuum cleaner spare parts stall, bread and cakes, coats and jumpers, more tools stalls, watches, a cheese stall, fruit and veg, stationery, bicycle and car accessories including wheel trims, and a man selling incense sticks.

Bacon Street

Tucked away behind all this is Bacon Street, a relatively quiet road running parallel to Sclater Street where you can find a gloomy lock-up full of mouldy furniture and cheap new household goods, and some more goods laid out on the street.

Brick Lane

Brick Lane itself is perhaps the most mundane part of the market. Most of the goods for sale are new clothes: socks, leather jackets and bags, and children's wear. One stallholder comments on the disappearance of a few other traders since the arrival of the police. There are also a couple of shellfish stands where prawns, jellied eels and whelks are spooned down greedily by traders having an 11am lunch. Nearby, a man stands on the corner of Cheshire Street selling peacock feathers: seven for £1.

The market takes up the stretch of Brick Lane north of the railway bridge. Only a couple of traders occupy the southern part, selling secondhand books and duvet covers. It is still well worth a trip southwards as this is where you will find most of the Lane's famous curry houses. After the market ends at 1pm, head this way for lunch.

Under the railway bridge you'll come across one of the market's most atmospheric lock-ups, a dank, dark Fagin's cave with a cobbled stone floor and grimy brick roof. It contains about 20 stalls full of secondhand and quasi-antique goods: musty books, gramophones, festering old clothes, printer's blocks, golf bags, leather suitcases, furniture, old radios, and disparate bric-a-brac, including several mangles.

Across the road on Grimsby Street, but still under the railway arches, is a newer, brighter lock-up. This lock-up, which spreads out its wares under a series of linked archways, houses a secondhand bookstall (worth checking for bargains),

Food, Drink and Shopping

Cafés and Fast Food

If it's too early for jellied eels, walk up to the **Brick Lane Bakery** (open 24 hours at No.159) for a salmon and cream cheese bagel, or stop off at the **Evering Bakery** at No.155 for a salt beef sandwich. **Sweet & Spicy** (40 Brick Lane) is one of the cheapest and best of the curry caffs that proliferate on the southern stretches of Brick Lane. For a great coffee, stop at either one of the two **Coffee @** organic cafés on Brick Lane.

Le Taj (No.134) offers more attractively presented food and surroundings, but is also good value.

Pubs

The Carpenters Arms on Cheshire Street is very much a locals' pub, and buzzes with life on a Sunday lunchtime. Non-East Enders might feel a little out of place, but it's worth popping in for a surreptitious pint as long as you keep a low profile and don't disturb the regulars. **Pride of Spitalfields**, at 3 Heneage Street, is also a good locals' pub.

Shops

Many of Brick Lane's leatherwear shops are open on Sunday morning; prices are among the lowest in London. **Truman Brewery**, on Brick Lane, now has a new lease of life as a collection of trendy shops and boutiques and **Rockit** is the capital's best vintage clothes shop.

as well as secondhand clothes, jewellery and records. Further up is the Old Truman Brewery which has been smartened up and now houses businesses. On Sundays, though, there are two halls that become the **Sunday Upmarket** (t (020) 7770 6100). The Upmarket has taken in many of the traders that were pushed out of Spitalfields by price rises and is the hub

of new and young design in both fashion and accessories. Of the two spaces, the one on the right (as you head southwards towards the curry houses) is the most vibrant. As you enter from Brick Lane you first come upon the food stalls; again trestle tables allow you to sit and eat before you check out the rest of the stalls. At this end there is an astrologer and clairvoyant, and a back-massage stall, but here the hippy stuff ends and the rest of the stalls are a delight if you are after hip fashion and edgy design. The atmosphere is much more raw than at Spitalfields and stallholders more ready to strike a bargain. Choose between Lucy's handmade chocolates, a Rajasthani saddle bag, Teah Wilson's handmade jewellery or beautiful chiffon and silk beaded dresses from Neetam. There are record and CD stalls offering rare grooves and funk, the sounds of which provide the rhythm of the market, and a whole range of delightfully odd handprinted T-shirts, cards and art. Fashion includes both new and secondhand and prices are more reasonable than in nearby Spitalfields. At the Commercial Street end, the market is rounded off by a delicious fresh fish sandwich stall (try a grilled fresh sea bass sandwich for £2).

Cheshire Street

It's now best to retrace your steps along Brick Lane, past the fruit and veg stall and perhaps an eccentric busker, and turn right up Cheshire Street. On the corner there is a long stand where you can buy Indian beaded slippers in every colour of the rainbow. Just make sure you haggle. New goods are interspersed with old. Opposite a stall with cheap videos is a man selling old stamps (many Victorian), coins, banknotes and postcards. Further up the street are stalls of new tools, spray paints for cars, radios and cassette players, kitchenware, stationery, socks, hats, gloves, jeans, underwear and shirts ('any shirt, any colour £3, three for £5'). On the left at 23–25 Cheshire Street, a yard offers bits of refrigerators, radiators and doors for inspection. Outside you can pick up a sheepskin rug. Further on are the quality secondhand goods stalls and shops. Here a bookshop keeps a stall of early Penguins outside; another trader has a collection of 19th-century prints. To the left, at 78–90 Cheshire Street, is a warehouse used as an indoor bric-a-brac market where you can often spot serious antiques dealers examining pieces with a magnifying glass. There are fireplaces round the entrances. The highlights here are the antiques stalls specializing in jewellery, war medals, coins, banknotes, Dinky toys, tools, collectible stamps (showing, for example, Marilyn Monroe) and cigarette lighters. Upstairs, there is a toilet.

Past the warehouse, the market returns to the shabbiness of the Bethnal Green Road. Down Haremarsh, a cobbled prong of a street going down to the railway, disconsolate men stand by small piles of broken electrical goods, taps, battered saucepans and mildewed clothes. This is the East End described by Henry Mayhew, Dickens and Jack London – it still flourishes in the early years of the 21st century. At this end of Cheshire Street, you might also encounter odd pieces of masonry or fireplaces, liberated from houses in (official or otherwise) architectural salvage operations.

By 1.30pm the market is coming to a close. Only a few would-be traders remain on the streets, cramming discarded clothing and broken hair dryers into shabby shopping baskets. They will be back to try to sell them next week.

COLUMBIA ROAD

Columbia Road, from Ravenscroft Street to Barnet Grove, E2, **t** *(020) 7364 1717.*

Transport: ⊖ *Shoreditch, Old Street; buses 8, 26, 35, 43, 47, 48, 55, 67, 78, 149, 242, 388.*

Open: *Sun 8am–2pm.*

Best time to go: *Busiest in spring and the weeks leading up to Christmas.*

Parking: *Try the side streets north of the Hackney Road.*

Main wares: *Pot plants, shrubs, bulbs, flowers and garden accessories.*

Specifics: *Bulk buys of shrubs and herbs; garden ornaments; Christmas trees and evergreens in winter.*

The Luftwaffe spared this stretch of Columbia Road during the Blitz, as did the developers in later years. While the surrounding district is covered by stark 1960s flats and houses, the short span of road that entertains the market is flanked by quaint Victorian terraces and diminutive shops – a fitting setting for London's best weekly flower show.

From the start of the market at the junction with Ravenscroft Street, both sides of the narrow road are packed with

Food, Drink and Shopping
Cafés and Fast Food

Despite recent change (*see* Restaurants, below), old-school cuisine still has its representatives, notably **Lee's Seafoods** at No.134, which provides the London market-goer's traditional snacks of jellied eels and whelks, and **Val's Store** at No.108, where either Val or one of her capable assistants will make you a sandwich while you wait. Ready-made smoked salmon and cream cheese bagels are available at **Café Colombia** at No.138. **The Blue Orange** at No.65 is a great café with a delicious selection of cakes and pastries and an outdoor courtyard for the summer. On Ezra Street, you'll come across the **Jones Dairy Café** where fashionable Islingtonians drink freshly ground coffee.

Pubs

The local traders are more likely to continue past the Jones Dairy Café and through the passageway to drink at the **Nelson's Head** on Horatio Street.

Restaurants

The upwardly mobile nature of Columbia Road can best be seen in a visit to No.110. Formerly George's Café, a no-nonsense market stalwart serving fry-ups and bagels, it has been transformed into the **Perennial Restaurant and Wine Bar**, where you can tuck into a bowl of chestnut soup laced with Madeira for £5.95.

Shops

The ornament and gift shops along Columbia Road are open while the market is in progress. In December they sell Christmas decorations.

plants, shrubs, cut flowers, cacti and herbs. Prices are enticingly low, particularly if you're buying in bulk. They tend to drop still further towards the close of the market. What's on offer changes with the season, but even in winter there's a scrum of customers jostling for a look at the evergreens. During December the great metal funnel Christmas tree wrapping machines are in almost constant operation. A medium-sized spruce costs between £10 and £15, a larger Trafalgar Square-esque model £20–£30, while a small, live tree in a pot is about £5. Holly, mistletoe and bright red 'points' (poinsettia – two pots for £10) are also in evidence at this time of year. Kangaroo vines, pots of chrysanths, fuchsias, rose bushes, dried flowers, dwarf conifers, various house plants and bundles of twisted willow might be on sale at the 20 or so stalls in autumn. In spring, it can take a quarter of an hour to negotiate the hundred yards of the market as a rustling

herd of foliage-bearing punters fights through the jungle. Special bags, known as 'Columbia Carriers' are sold to help you get your colourful purchases home with the foliage more or less intact.

Flower trading started here in the 1920s, but there was a large fruit and veg market in the neighbourhood during the 19th century. The costermongers were housed in a huge neo-Gothic edifice called Columbia Market, which opened in 1869 and was financed by a £200,000 donation from the philanthropist Baroness Burdett-Coutts. Resembling St Pancras railway station in its preposterous grandeur, Columbia Market never really took off; the costermongers preferred the streets. By the First World War the building had fallen into disrepair, and in 1958 it was finally demolished to make way for council flats.

During the last decade, Columbia Road has undergone some gentrification. **Fred Bare**, the trendy hat store, has opened a branch here at No.118, and there's a smattering of expensive ornament and gift stores. But the poshing-up process isn't complete, so you'll still find a couple of basic caffs in among the wine bars and bistros.

This mix of cultures is reflected in the market. Some traders are East Enders who've been coming here for decades; others seem to hail from bijou north London flower shops. It all helps to generate an exciting tension. The Camden market feel is especially evident down Ezra Street, off Columbia Road, where, to a soundtrack provided by some buskers, you can find old garden tools, garden ornaments and a variety of pots in a variety of cubbyholes and alleyways. The backyard of the **Royal Oak** pub is often given over to collections of interesting pots and wrought-iron garden adornments. Another patch of land has a few stalls selling rustic-looking clothing, secondhand jewellery and bric-a-brac, ferns, olives, bonsai trees and hippyish robes. Given the market's increasing popularity, the trade in 'garden accessories' looks set to expand.

HACKNEY STADIUM

Off Waterden Road, E15.

Transport: ⇌ *Hackney Wick; buses 26, 30, 236, 276, 308, S2.*

Open: *Sun 6am–3pm.*

Best time to go: *Before midday.*

Parking: *Along Waterden Road.*

Main wares: *Secondhand goods (particularly video games and computer software), new clothes, electrical and household goods.*

Specifics: *Electrical goods, computer software; look out for secondhand bargains.*

The dividing line between a market and a car boot sale is sometimes flimsy. Many see the weekly jamboree around the car park of Hackney's dog track as a car booter, but the event's longevity and the large number of professional traders selling new goods make it feel more like a market.

Everyone seems to come here by car, and every Sunday large numbers of vehicles are parked on the roads surrounding the stadium. It's easy to find the entrances: just follow the crowd. As you approach the entrance, there are stalls displaying videos and CDs, and people selling cigarettes and tobacco out of plastic carrier bags. At the gates you will see a gathering of muscular gents. These are the bouncers – sorry, the stewards. Hackney Stadium market is like that: a bit dicey. Look at what's on offer at some of the stalls. A naked Sindy doll, a length of piping and six old hub caps are among one trader's merchandise; pirate software, Playstation and Nintendo games are major lines; bootleg videos are not unknown and there are always plentiful supplies of last year's 'must-have' toys.

Food and Drink

There are a couple of fast food stands at the market, but otherwise not much in the locality. However, **Frocks** (95 Lauriston Road, E9, **t** (020) 8986 3161), only a short car ride away, is a homely British restaurant that does a superb Sunday brunch (starting at 11am). Book to be sure of a seat.

The hint of lawlessness brings out the crowds. Thousands of punters and hundreds of traders arrive every week. New goods on sale include: a vast array of electrical equipment, from cordless phones and electric ovens to TVs and CD players; clothing (men's, women's and children's) including jeans, leather jackets and work clothes (boiler suits for £5); haberdashery; discounted seeds, crockery, towels and bed sheets; carpets; stationery; leather bags and purses; fruit and veg; decorative toilet seats; DIY materials; pet food; cosmetics; and (a nice touch of irony, this) security floodlights. You might even be lucky enough to discover a local Afro-Caribbean woman who occasionally comes here to sell her West Indian coconut bread.

The secondhand goods are of an even greater variety: 'warehouse-returned phones, sold as seen, no refunds', water pumps for fish aquariums, old dishwashers and washing machines ('with three months' guarantee'), LPs, golf clubs, spectacle frames, Black & Decker power tools, furniture, old shoes, fishing rods, vacuum cleaners, quite a few old books of varying quality, musty piles of clothing, rails of jackets, as well as stacks of that most legitimate of all secondhand goods, the car radio. I even spotted a rather taciturn chap selling his old wedding photos. But it is the high-tech

secondhand goods that attract most attention: satellite dishes, vast collections of disks, computer programs with and without manuals, though only the odd bit of hardware. There's also a good trade in Asian film music CDs and DVDs. One stall is devoted to all things African and Afro-Caribbean – from home-made herbal potions sold in old squash bottles to reggae records.

It's this preponderance of amateur traders, out to grab a few bob on a Sunday, that gives Hackney market its flavour.

HOXTON STREET

Hoxton Street, N1, from Crondall Street to Ivy Street.

Transport: ⊖ *Old Street; buses 55, 67, 76, 141, 149, 242, 243, 271, 394.*

Open: *Mon–Sat 9am–5pm.*

Best time to go: *Saturday.*

Parking: *There are often spaces on Pitfield Street, which runs parallel to Hoxton Street to the west. Park near the junction with Crondall Street then walk down it to the start of the market.*

Main wares: *Clothes, household goods, fruit and veg.*

Specifics: *Cheap clothing (Saturday), gifts.*

Forget the north London postcode – Hoxton is part of the East End, and in recent years at the vanguard of London's most happening art scene. The availability of cheap studios drew artists east in the 1990s and, with the arrival of White Cube – London's coolest gallery – in 2002, the area's hip credentials were confirmed. A host of bars, clubs and restaurants have sprung up around this scene, which is rooted in Hoxton Square. Step outside the square, though, and Hoxton Street can seem bleak and unpromising from Monday to Thursday, despite the odd fashionable shop that can be spotted on the upper reaches towards Old Street. Dismal postwar council flats spread out to the west (though most of the main street is Victorian), and the market is desultory. On Fridays a few more traders turn up, and there's usually a large stall full of cheap tinned and packaged food. On Saturdays, though, the market and the entire area come to life.

There has been a market here for donkey's years; it goes back at least to Tudor times, when Hoxton was a country village. Though the district lies less than a mile north of the City of London, the City authorities didn't invoke their charter to ban the market, as it had little effect on their trade. Until 1820 trading took place in what is still called Hoxton Market (the now achingly trendy artists' hangout, just off Boot Street to the southwest of Hoxton Street). But by that time the district had been covered by workers' housing and the market had become so popular that it outgrew the site. After a spell on Pitfield Street it moved to Hoxton Street in 1840. The original site was

Food, Drink and Shopping

There are several basic cafés along Hoxton Street. **F. Cooke's** pie and mash shop at No.150 even does a vegetarian pie for £1.10. **The Real Greek** at 15 Hoxton Market is a fashionable restaurant, featured in the film *Bridget Jones' Diary*.

The pubs on Hoxton Street are very much for locals and can seem intimidating; in the 1960s, Hoxton was part of the Kray gang's manor. **Bluu** is a relaxed bar at 1 Hoxton Square, and at No. 2, **Hoxton Square Bar and Kitchen**, there are plenty of sofas to lounge in after traipsing round the market.

The hip **Cube & Star** (39a Hoxton Square) is a smart restaurant and bar with black velvet padded walls setting off the giant black and white photos covering the walls and ceilings. The food is nuevo Latino, a fusion of South American and Caribbean food that is set to be the next big thing. Downstairs in the lounge bar there is live music most nights and cocktails aplenty.

On Old Street itself is an outpost of **Shish** (Nos.313–19), the modern take on 'Silk Road' cuisine with a huge, open interior and very good grills and kebabs. Another sign of the times is **Favela Shop** (Nos.12–18). The unpromising location next to the Job Centre does nothing to diminish the glamour of this Brazilian bikini and lingerie shop, selling its brightly coloured triangles of fabric for high prices.

deserted for years, but has now been redeveloped into desirable flats.

Hoxton became a centre for working-class entertainment, and in the 19th century there were several music halls and theatres along the main street. But away from the brash jollity of the market Hoxton was a desperate place. Local

Nearby Attractions

Geffrye Museum, *Kingsland Road, E2, t (020) 7739 9893, www.geffrye-museum.org.uk;* ⊖ *Liverpool St, then bus 149 or 242;* ⇌ *Dalston Kingsland (on North London Line, two stops from Highbury and Islington).* **Open** *Tues–Sat 10am–5pm, Sun 12–5pm.* Excellent displays of house interiors from various periods in England's history.

Hoxton Hall, *130 Hoxton Street, t (020) 7684 0060, www.hoxtonhall.co.uk;* ⊖ *Old Street (exit 2);* ⇌ *Dalston Kingsland (then bus), Old Street, Liverpool Street (then bus);* **buses** *67, 149, 242, 243.* A rare example of a surviving Victorian music hall, with a varied programme of shows and classes.

resident A. S. Jasper wrote about his childhood here in the early years of the 20th century. He lived with his family of seven in a two-room hovel. Life was full of petty theft, infant mortality, pub brawls and mother scraping a living by selling home-made clothes at the market. Sunday tea was a pint of winkles and some watercress.

It's still possible to buy winkles and watercress at Hoxton Street market, but only on Saturday. **Ron's Wetfish** supplies the seafood (along with pickles, whelks, jellied eels, prawns, kippers, smoked haddock, cockles and mussels), while the **Swinton** family, who run a traditional fruit and veg stall, are 'noted for the finest-grown celery and watercress'. The other food sellers at the Saturday market include a scattering of fruit and veg coster-mongers (prices are average), a woman selling eggs, a doughnut and pancake stall, plus various trestle tables piled high with cash 'n' carry goodies: biscuits, soft drinks, chocolate bars and the like.

But most of the 50 or more Saturday traders deal in clothes, and you won't find many places cheaper; there are literally dozens of 'reduced to clear' racks. Near the southern end of the street, a big crowd of women are grappling for secondhand (or are they new?) clothes tipped out of bin bags. One of the stallholders stands on a stool, to make sure her stock isn't pilfered. Another stall has a huge collection of tights and stockings. Unattractively screwed up, most of them look second-hand. Nearby, a trader has all his wares in old cardboard boxes. On one is scrawled 'M&S boxers £1'. Secondhand raincoats and children's clothes, school uniforms (£1, or three pieces for £3), new shoes, lingerie, skirts and dresses 'for the larger lady' (sizes 16–30), and more chainstore seconds are all sold for bargain prices.

Other stalls stock all kinds of household goods: Palmolive soap, Blue Loos, Bic razors, a bumper bottle of Cif for £1; you'll also find pet food, duvet sets (a single for £5), cosmetics, greetings cards, net curtains, toys, fancy-dress costumes, jewellery, records and CDs, gloves, mobile phone cases, videos, crockery, saucepans and electrical goods. The Saturday market is big enough to attract likely lads trying to flog the latest 'bargains' and grizzled old traders proffering the latest toys. They're surprisingly adept at 'walking the dog' and the 'cradle', putting many of their younger customers to shame. Further highlights include curtain material, sold at 50p a yard ('ay ay, it's all cheap today, the guvnor's gone on holiday'); a good plant and flower stall; and gift stalls where you can buy incense holders, candlesticks, scented candles and bath bombs.

There's little traffic on Hoxton Street, as it's not a major thoroughfare and only local shops have their premises here. This adds to the tightly knit feel of the place – though everyone will tell you 'It's not what it was'. On a fine Saturday, groups of old Hoxtonians stand between the stalls, chewing over their memories. But, though there's plenty of cheery shouting, it's impossible to get sentimental about chirpy cockneys here. There were no good old days, and the present is almost as bad. Locals are streetwise and tough; the market has been in decline for years; and, all too obviously, money is tight, as illustrated by the following cheery notice from Hackney council pasted on every second lamp-post: 'Our final rent demand is impossible to ignore. We evict four families a week. Pay your rent.'

KINGSLAND WASTE

Kingsland Road, between Middleton and Forest Roads, E8.

Transport: ≥ *Dalston Kingsland; buses 30, 38, 56, 67, 76, 149, 242, 243, 277.*

Open: *Sat 9am–5pm.*

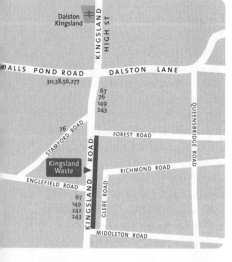

Food and Drink

This is a good area for Turkish food, be it for takeaways (try the kebabs at **Yuvam Barbecue**, 398a Kingsland Road), or a lavish but inexpensive sit-down meal (**Istanbul Işkembecisi** – *see* p.114).

Viet Hoa Café, 70–2 Kingsland Road, serves delicious Vietnamese food.

For traditional grub or a cup of tea, try **Faulkners** fish restaurant (424–6 Kingsland Road).

Parking: *Try the backstreets to the south of Middleton Road.*

Main wares: *Secondhand clothes, bric-a-brac, tools and electrical goods.*

Specifics: *Tools, hardware.*

Disrepute works wonders to bolster a market's popularity. Perhaps it's the air of immorality, the feeling you might be dealing with 'fences', the enticement of sharing in the booty by getting an outrageous bargain.

Whatever it is, Kingsland Waste seems to thrive on it. You might have trouble tracing the history of some of the articles up for grabs, but the wide pavements and cobbled street that run alongside the A10 Kingsland Road are packed with stalls (and cardboard boxes, and bin bags, and plastic washing-up tubs, and trestle tables – almost anything, in fact, that could conceivably hold merchandise) and customers every Saturday.

Both new and secondhand goods are on display, sometimes jumbled together on the same stall. However, the north end of the market consists mainly of stalls selling new goods, with the secondhand stalls predominating at the southern end. Tools and hardware, plus electrical and mechanical components, are the market's strengths. The Waste has been a noted supplier of artisans, DIYers and bodgers since the market was first held in the mid-19th century. Now you can find anything from door knockers and plumbing pipes to toilet seats and plungers. Some of the tools are of high quality, others are shoddy. A few seem archaic: little interest was being taken in two great scythes up for sale – Hackney not being noted for its hay meadows.

But, even if you've no DIY talent, there's plenty to rifle through among the three long lines of stalls. You never know what's coming up next. There are traders selling secondhand hi-fis, car radios, TVs, cameras, video machines and Walkmans – from unblemished consumer durables (but who knows if they work?) to hollow shells; from the faintly suspect to the downright dodgy; from the mundane to the bizarre, such as the clear plastic toilet seats with decorative sea shells stuck in them, or the slightly incongruous stall selling Egyptian souvenirs.

New and secondhand clothes get more than a look-in. Old boots and shoes come newly polished. You'll also find leather belts, children's coats, jumpers, bundles of shirts, trousers and jackets, even long-johns – many at bargain prices.

Food takes second place here: you'd be better taking the 10-minute walk to Ridley Road (see p.114) for your fresh provisions. However, there are some fruit and veg stalls, plus a couple of popular pitches selling tinned goods, cakes and sweets at very low prices. Whether all the food is within its sell-by date is another matter. Crockery and basic household goods also attract locals out for their weekly shop.

Only Brick Lane and Westmoreland Road can compete with the bizarre conglomeration of junk displayed at some stalls. Beneath a tarpaulin propped up with a couple of old skis, one trader is trying to sell two fluffy pink pigs. Another flogs used video tapes and sachets of Bisto. Yet another boasts a selection of secondhand, half-empty bottles of perfume. You can take your pick from a selection of toys, CDs, videos, old records and tapes. The pavement is lined with old fridges, furniture, washing machines and cookers – the spoils of house clearances.

A brisk walk from the market, down Kingsland Road towards the City, is the Geffrye Museum (see p.107).

PETTICOAT LANE

Middlesex Street, Goulston Street, New Goulston Street, Toynbee Street, Wentworth Street, Bell Lane, Cobb Street, Leyden Street, Strype Street, Old Castle Street, E19, t (020) 7377 8963.

Transport: ⊖ *Aldgate, Aldgate East, Liverpool Street;* ⇌ *Liverpool Street; buses 8, 15, 25, 26, 35, 40, 42, 47, 48, 67, 78, 100, 149, 205, 242, 254, 344, 388.*

Open: *Sun 9am–2pm;* **Wentworth Street** *Mon–Fri 10am–2.30pm, Sun 9am–2pm.*

Best time to go: *9am on Sunday, before the crowds get too bad.*

Parking: *You might find spaces on the side streets north of Middlesex Street; otherwise try the side streets south of the Whitechapel Road.*

Main wares: *New clothes, souvenirs, household goods, electrical goods.*

Specifics: *Leather jackets.*

We will survey the suburbs and make forth our salleys,
Down Petticoat Lane and up the smock alleys.

When the playwright Ben Jonson was writing in 1616, Petticoat Lane had already gained a reputation for clothing. Today, it

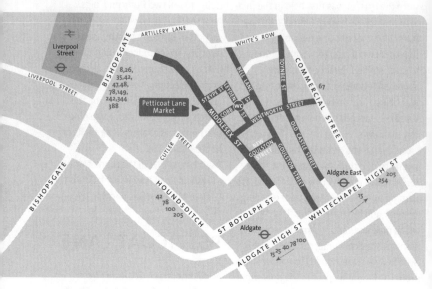

is one of London's most famous markets. Tens of thousands of Londoners and tourists swarm through these streets every Sunday, but sadly the Lane has become tarnished by its success, losing some of its verve and much of its variety along the way.

In the early 16th century, Whitechapel was known for its piggeries, but by Jonson's time it had become a desirable area. 'Some gentlemen of the court,' observed John Stow in the 1590s, 'built their houses here for the air.' Perhaps it was this gentrification, as much as the link with clothing, that caused Hog Lane to be renamed Petticoat Lane around the start of the 1600s. But the clean air and aristocratic inhabitants didn't last. The plague of 1665 hit the East End badly. All the wealthier householders fled, leaving Whitechapel to successive waves of immigrants and refugees: French Protestant Huguenots, East European Jews and, most recently, Bangladeshis.

Jews have been associated with the market from its inception. Thousands arrived from Central and Eastern Europe in the 18th and 19th centuries. Many entered the rag trade, selling old clothes and hats. Sunday became the main day for trading; the area was – and still is – largely deserted on Saturday, the Jewish sabbath. London's oldest surviving synagogue (1700) is nearby on Bevis Marks.

In 1830 the authorities renamed the market's central artery Middlesex Street. Few traders or customers took any notice. Street atlases and council documents use the new name, but everyone else still calls the road and its market Petticoat Lane.

By the 1850s, huge clothes auctions were being held every week on Goulston and Wentworth Streets. Henry Mayhew tells of 2–3 miles of old clothes up for sale, calling it 'a vista of multi-coloured dinginess'. As with many of London's markets at this time, Petticoat Lane was unlicensed. As late as the 1900s, hucksters used to fight each other for the best pitches, resulting in mayhem first thing in the morning. The opponents of Sunday trading tried to abolish the market but eventually, in 1928, Stepney Borough Council stepped in and licensed the traders.

In 1936, Mary Benedetta remarked that '80% of [Petticoat Lane's] wares are said to be genuine.' In those days there were nearly 200 pitches, and Cobb Street, Leyden Street and Strype Street had stalls full of kosher chickens. The place was a haven for eccentrics. Benedetta tells of 'Old Heyday, with his silver hair, rosy cheeks and gentle, courtly manners', who sold rubber stamps and spectacles, and who spent harvest time selling his wares around Norfolk villages; and the foot clinic where customers sat on a table in front of the crowds 'having their corns cured for a few pence'. William Addison, writing in 1953, describes the patter of Mike Stern, president of the Stepney Street Traders' Association. Dressed in Lord Mayor's garb, Stern would declaim in Shakespearean tones: 'Oh, when I am dead and forgotten as I shall be, and sleep in dull, cold marble with...[waiting for the crowd to take notice] these lovely utility towels, ten bob a pair, ten bob a pair.'

Though there are more stalls now, most of the characters have gone; their oddball descendants are more likely to grace Brick Lane, half a mile to the north. But Petticoat Lane still has a great deal of life. Best come early, while the streets are passable. At 8.30am the stallholders are still cranking up for the day's business. They clear their throats and practise calling across the street to each other: 'Oh – only £7.99, come on!'

Interestingly, Mary Benedetta's book contains a photo of Indian traders selling clothes on the Lane 65 years ago. But it wasn't until the 1970s that large numbers of Bangladeshis moved into the area. Young Asian men, probably London-born and certainly well-cockneyfied, now run several of the garment stalls. Jewish clothes traders are still in evidence, but

Food and Drink

Bagel lovers are well fed round here. Try the **Kossoff Bakery** at 91 Middlesex Street. A pleasant sit-down Sunday lunch can be had at the **Woodin's Shades** pub opposite.

most now live in comfortable suburbs and only visit the East End on Sundays. The closure in 1996 of London's most famous Jewish restaurant, Blooms, on Whitechapel High Street, is further evidence of the diaspora away from the East End.

Nearly all the clothes are new. Petticoat Lane attracts businesses that buy stock from huge discount wholesalers to sell on a stall. Underwear, socks, shirts (£5), coats, towels, duvets, blouses, jeans, dresses and shoes: dozens of stalls duplicate these wares on both Middlesex Street and Goulston Street. There are also scores of traders selling leather luggage, handbags, purses and jackets. Many of these will have been made locally by low-paid Bangladeshi workers. Prices are much less than in West End shops, but higher than in the Brick Lane leather emporia.

If you're after a leather jacket, the best place to look is in the covered section of the market in a concrete car park off Goulston Street below a sign bearing the legend 'This is the famous Petticoat Lane'. Here dozens of traders compete with each other. The choice is large, with jackets hanging up to the ceiling. Most stalls in the covered section have a similar stock, but if you're lucky you might spot a trader who sells a unique collection of sequin-strewn tops and dresses.

Among the clothes on Middlesex, Wentworth and Goulston streets are occasional stalls selling tourist rubbish – Union Jack hats and busby-wearing dolls as well as football shirts. You'll also come across the odd cockney shyster trying to flog the latest wonder product.

It's always worth joining the small knot of people around these 'demmers' just to listen to the outrageous spiel as they eulogize their vegetable peelers, glass cutters and window cleaners. The undisputed champions of this kind of salesmanship, however, are the 'mike-men' of the clearance sales; there are usually at least a couple on duty every Sunday and you can easily waste half an hour or more listening to them drumming up custom for their weekly once-a-year never-to-be-repeated spectaculars.

'You're all looking at me like I'm some sort of raving lunatic. You're thinking "How can he do this? How can he sell a Sony Walkman that retails in the shops for £42 for just £3? What's the catch?" you're asking, "what's the angle?" Well, I'll tell you now. There is no catch, there is no angle. These are shop window goods. You see that the packaging is a little damaged. Shops, by law, cannot sell goods with damaged packaging. That's where we come in. We don't mind if the box is a little tatty coz the contents is perfect. I'll say again, the contents is perfect and that's why we can sell this Sony Walkman for just £3. So you've got everything to gain and...[big pause] nothing to lose. So, who's first?'

Practically everyone, to judge by the tumult resulting from this soliloquy. If the crowd seems a little tentative, however, the mike-man will do his best to entice customers forward: 'Don't be shy, come to the front. If you put one foot in front of the other, you'll find your body follows – it's called walking.'

Of course, once the punters are in, he wants to make sure they stay in. 'If you want four video games for £10 then stay here and don't let dynamite move you.' Remember, these men do not indulge in idle bragging but are willing to offer hard proof of their goods' saleability. 'If I don't sell these here and now then I'll eat them in front of you, and I tell you, ladies and gentlemen, it's not fit food for a mad dog.'

Cheap CDs, low-quality hi-fis, trashy jewellery, lights, film prints, electronic watches, hairbrushes, holograms, toys, crockery, tablemats and poor-quality pottery can also be found on these busy streets, and cheap perfume is sold by **Perfume Mad House**. Connoisseurs of kitsch could have a field day; others might find themselves examining the wares for longer than they'd like, as the crowds make the going slow.

Most of the traders are on Middlesex Street, Wentworth Street and Goulston Street, although you may find secondhand clothes being sold on Leyden Street and there are some traders around the junctions of Middlesex Street and Wentworth Street, including a stall at the end of Toynbee Street selling furry mock-leopardskin fabric. There are no food stalls – apart from **Tubby Isaacs**, which sells jellied eels at the end of Goulston Street, and some hot food stalls: Thai noodles, fried shellfish and the odd burger van.

There's a change on New Goulston Street. Here, the remnants of the Cutler Street gold and coin market congregate. In the early 1980s, about 40 stalls were packed into Cutler Street, about a 4-minute walk from Petticoat Lane, until redevelopment forced them to move here. Only a handful of dealers are left, selling old silver and gold jewellery. As you inspect their stock, try to get them to talk about the old days. There's a rich fund of stories to be told about Petticoat Lane.

QUEEN'S MARKET

Off the junction of Green Street and Queen's Road, E13, **t** *(020) 8430 5760.*
Transport: ⊖ *Upton Park; buses 58, 104, 238, 330, 376.*
Open: *Tues and Thurs–Sat 9am–5pm.*
Best time to go: *Saturday.*
Parking: *Try the side streets off Plashet Grove or Green Street.*
Main wares: *Clothing, fruit and veg, household goods.*
Specifics: *Asian and Caribbean foodstuffs.*

The parish of West Ham dates back to the Middle Ages, when a weekly mart was held there. Today's Queen's Market, however, goes back little more than a century, to the time when traders set up stalls on Green Street to cater for the inhabitants of the newly built terraced houses. In the 1900s, the market was turfed off the main street to ease the flow of traffic, and transferred to Queen's Road. At the end of the 1960s, Newham Council built a market square off the road; 10 years later the council decided to put a roof on top.

The result is rather like an underground car park. But the market is thriving, providing multiracial Upton Park with a fine blend of foodstuffs, household goods, fabrics, electrical equipment and clothing. Over 100 stalls set up regularly in the square; more businesses occupy permanent shops around the perimeter.

The local Afro-Caribbean and Asian communities shop here, so the market has an exciting variety of fruit, veg, spices, meat and fish. As well as radishes, cabbages, boiled beetroot and oranges, you'll find mangoes, peppers, pomegranates, soursop, guavas and green coconuts. One fish stall might have cod, whiting and hake, while its neighbour sells jackfish, snappers and cuttlefish. African food and spices are available from **Africana Spot**, a tropical delicatessen, while a sheep's head takes pride of place at the nearby halal meat store.

A couple of stalls sell beautifully embroidered clothes as worn by Asian children; smart *kurtas* and flowing saris are also on display. A few yards away, an Afro-Caribbean store stocks a bewildering array of hair accessories, including long black wigs. Other stalls sell greetings cards, bed linen, net curtains, watches, shoes and jewellery. Walk to one side of the square and you'll hear lovers' rock thumping out of the reggae shop; across the way it's bhangra that blares from the Asian food emporium; in the middle is cacophony. Queen's is cooking. For a while, the future of Queen's Market looked uncertain, but happily the council has got behind the market and its future is safe.

Food and Drink

There are a couple of caffs and a sandwich bar around the market's perimeter. Alternatively, head to **Mobeen**, 222–6 Green Street, for cheap, authentic Pakistani food (no alcohol).

RIDLEY ROAD

Ridley Road, off Kingsland High Street, E8.

Transport: ⇌ *Dalston Kingsland; buses 30, 38, 56, 67, 76, 149, 236, 242, 243, 277.*

Open: *Mon–Wed 9am–3pm, Thurs 9am–12pm, Fri and Sat 9am–5pm.*

Best time to go: *Saturday morning, before the crowds; Friday morning for stalls run by Jewish traders.*

Parking: *Try St Jude Street or other residential side streets to the west of Kingsland High Street.*

Main wares: *Fresh food, clothing, household goods, records, tapes and CDs, fabrics, haberdashery, electrical goods.*

Specifics: *Fish, Afro-Caribbean foodstuffs, Turkish foods, fresh herbs, eggs, fruit and vegetables, reggae and calypso records.*

It's faster if you dance along Ridley Road on a Friday or Saturday, propelled by the bone-resonating thuds of the record stalls that give this market its rhythm. Turks, Jews, Asians, cockneys, Africans and Afro-Caribbeans – East Londoners all – join the throng pushing past shanty-town shacks, lock-up shops and old wooden barrows.

The food is similarly diverse: pigs' tails and sheep's heads are displayed with aplomb by the butchers shops. A long-pronged fork is on hand to help customers

Food and Drink

Sadly, Dalston's Edwardian pie-and-mash shop has closed down, becoming **Shanghai** (41 Kingsland High Street), a Chinese restaurant with good dim sum snacks. If you don't fancy a meal, just pop your head in to admire the magnificent tiled and mirrored interior.

On Ridley Road itself you could try the greasy spoon café in the Ridley Road Shopping Village.

One of London's largest shops for Turkish food, the **Turkish Food Centre**, can be found at 89 Ridley Road. **Istanbul Işkembecisi**, at 9 Stoke Newington Road, is among the best of the many Turkish restaurants in the area.

rifle through the goats' tripe. Chicken and geese are hung with plastic bags tied around their necks to catch the still-dripping blood. In one meat emporium, staff have given names to the Christmas turkeys; one enormous bird used to answer to 'Humphrey', apparently.

At **Milly's** tiny salmon stall (closed on the sabbath), old friendships are renewed, petty grumbles are warmly exchanged, and condolences offered with slivers of fish. **Mr Bagel 2000** will provide further ingredients for a snack.

Despite the building of Dalston Cross Shopping Centre in the early 1990s, the market is thriving. It began in the 1880s, and during the early years of the 20th century was started each morning by a policeman with a whistle. The market expanded to its present size (about 180 stalls) in the 1920s. As with Brixton, Ridley Road has benefited enormously from the influx of immigrants. Paradoxically, they have helped to retain the feel of a

traditional East End market – full of zip and bustle. There's nothing like a trip here to buck you up.

Such is the cosmopolitan mix of the place, you might find Turks selling African food, Asians selling West Indian food and cockneys selling Asian produce. Fill up on mangoes (eight for £2) or papayas that are twice the size of those you will find in the supermarket. The market is excellent for fresh fish (from tilapia and jackfish to scallops and lobster), and has strong lines in fruit, vegetables, fabrics and lace, with traders earnestly vying with each other for custom. 'Who's gotta bit o' money for Rodney?' roars one seasoned coster-monger with a laugh that makes Sid James sound like Charles Hawtrey.

Halfway down Ridley Road on the left is an indoor market, **Harmer's Ridley Road Shopping Village**, with about 40 stalls selling Afro-Caribbean fashions: puffa jackets, trainers, hair and nail extensions, plus an assortment of jewellery, toys, CDs, food and household goods. There's also a pet shop and a café.

At the other end of the market from Kingsland High Street, the atmosphere becomes more Caribbean, helped along by joss-sticks from the 'freedom fragrance' stall. Hot red-pepper sauce, black-eye beans, yams and plantains are all up for grabs. An African stall sells Nigerian-brewed Guinness. At the wig stall, a couple of spirited black women try on hair extensions. Nearby, Harry at his record shack takes note of this and plays some thundering calypso. Hips start swaying, hands start clapping... Who needs Notting Hill Carnival?

The market extends on to a piece of land off St Mark's Rise with several more stalls, one of the most interesting selling Nigerian food.

ROMAN ROAD

Globe Town, west of Usk Street off Roman Road, E2; Roman Road, from St Stephen's Road to Parnell Road, E2; t (020) 7377 8963.
Transport: *⊖ Bethnal Green, then bus 8; buses 8, 277, 309, 339, 903, D6, S2.*

Open: *Globe Town – Mon–Sat 8.30–4pm; Roman Road – Tues 8am–2pm, Thurs and Sat 8am–6pm.*

Best time to go: *Thursday and Saturday.*

Parking: *Try the backstreets to the south of Roman Road (turn off along Grove Road: it is pedestrianized after St Stephen's Road), or there is a pay and display off St Stephen's Road, just before the market.*

Main wares: *Clothing, household goods, fruit and veg.*

Specifics: *Cheap clothing (underwear, socks, woollens, women's and men's wear, shirts, jackets, babies' and children's wear, large sizes), fabrics, jewellery, bathroom-ware, cosmetics, CDs.*

Roman Road is the East End of pie and mash, boxing clubs and street barrows. There are really two markets here.

Globe Town has occupied an austere, purpose-built square off the road since 1961. Only a dozen or so stalls trade at this six-days-a-week market, which provides the local housing estate with essentials such as household goods (from crockery to light bulbs), fruit and vegetables. There's also a good fish stall, **G. T. Downey & Sons**.

Roman Road market proper couldn't be more different. The street is lined with modest Victorian buildings rather than municipal blocks, and the 150-year-old market is one of the East End's largest weekday knees-ups. Even on a Tuesday there are over 150 stalls along the quarter mile of pedestrianized street.

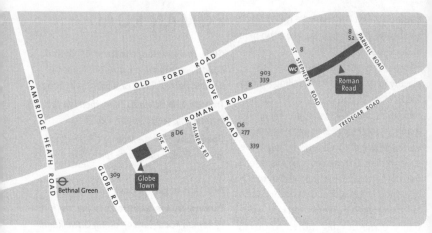

As you stroll between the stalls you'll begin to notice something. This is a women's market. Most of the goods for sale are aimed strictly at one half of the population and the crowd is accordingly overwhelmingly female. Everywhere you will hear the cries – 'Jumpers and cardies a fiver, girls', 'come and have a look, ladies', 'come on girls, don't be shy' – of traders who know their audience.

Food and Drink

Eels and mash at **G. Kelly** (526 and 600 Roman Road) is the costermongers' choice for lunch. The No.526 branch also does smashing plum pies. Alternatively, walk 5 minutes up the Roman Road towards Bethnal Green and try the area's third great pie and mash shop, **J. Kelly** at No.150. Excellent seafood can be had at **Winkles**, at No.238, a modern and bright seafood restaurant and oyster bar, with reasonable prices, near the Regent's Canal.

A complete alternative can be found at 241–5 Globe Road, where **Wild Cherry**, a vegetarian café, resides.

Back on Roman Road, a few minutes towards Bethnal Green, you can visit **Friends Organic** at No.83 to stock up on organic foodstuffs.

Fabrics, haberdashery and shoes are plentiful, and prices are keen – the seasons' favourite high-heeled gold strappy sandals for a tenner, sheepskin coats for £5, a 'Mulberry' handbag for £15, shirts for £3, macs for £3 and jeans for £10. Some stalls sell designer clothes, for instance coats that were samples; others feature high street names such as Wallis, Oasis, French Connection and River Island. Larger sizes are also available; one stall sells Evans clothes, sizes 16–26. You might pass a throng crowded around a furtive man pulling new clothes out of a box and selling them for a pittance as fast as he can. Ask no questions as to their origins. Secondhand clothes and 'cabbages' (new clothes made from off-cuts) are piled on barrows and rifled by industrious, sturdy women used to getting elbow room. There are plenty of underwear stalls too, for both sensible and glitzy lingerie, with racks of 'M&S' matching knickers and bras on sale for £8.

Food is of secondary importance, but you'll find a large egg stall and a few fruit and veg traders with wooden barrows full of root crops, including freshly boiled beetroot in season. One stall has West Indian produce (there are a few traders from the Asian or black communities); while Mickey's Sweets ('Established 25 Years!') has brightly coloured, old-fashioned sweets. There are also toys and CDs (check out the stall selling great mixes of R&B and dance music), and a few curtain and bed linen stalls, also peddling towels, duvets and tea towels.

SPITALFIELDS MARKET

Commercial Street (between Lamb Street and Brushfield Street), E1, t (020) 7247 8556, www.visitspitalfields.com.

Transport: ⊖/⇌ *Liverpool Street; buses 8, 26, 35, 47, 48, 67, 78, 149, 242, 344, 388.*

Open: *Mon–Fri and Sun 10am–5pm.*

Best time to go: *Sunday.*

Parking: *There are car parks in Lamb Street and Steward Street.*

Main wares: *Organic foods, crafts, bric-a-brac.*

Specifics: *Organic fruit, veg and bread.*

Spitalfields takes its name from the hospital fields that once belonged to the priory and hospice of St Mary. Trading began in 1682, when a local silk-thrower, John Balch, was granted a charter to hold a market in Spital Square. It grew into one of London's main wholesale fruit and veg markets. The present warehouse-like buildings were completed in 1893, five years after Spitalfields gained notoriety for the Jack the Ripper murders. The premises were extended in the 1930s to include a flower market; development work has more than halved the size of the site.

In 1991, the wholesale market moved to more spacious premises in Hackney Wick. Its old buildings now contain several permanent shops and cafés and a new retail market built around Spital Square which has been redeveloped and covered under acres of concrete overseen by steel and glass edifices.

In the week, only a few traders turn up and the site seems empty and cavernous. On Sundays, however, the space is full of stalls, surrounded by a Camden-like crush. Within walking distance of Petticoat Lane and Brick Lane, Spitalfields is these days significantly more well-to-do than either, more like Camden or Portobello than its neighbours. The sound environmentalism of many stallholders reveals their middle-class credentials.

There are usually around 15 organic food sellers occupying the space near the Commercial Street entrance, and there is an excellent wholefood shop. Regulars include **Long Wood Farm**, selling organic meat and cheese; an organic fruit juice bar; a couple of bread and cake stalls with up to 20 varieties of bread, including olive focaccia; and a stall selling delicate shades of alpaca wool and knitting needles. You can also find organic wines, a tofu stall selling smoked and spiced tofu, home-made fudge, organic chocolate truffles in exotic flavours (try orange and cardamom), fairtrade coffee and a huge dried fruit and nuts stall. There are up to four fruit and veg pitches. The largest of

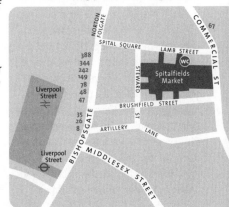

Food and Drink

Around the perimeter of the market there are various wooden stalls and restaurants selling food from around the world: Thai noodles, pasta, satay, nachos and falafel. Stock up on burritos and tacos at **Mesón Los Barriles**, an excellent traditional Spanish tapas bar, or meat lovers could try **Arkansas Café**, at the Commercial Street end of Spitalfields. **The Spitz**, near gate 5, is popular for its brunch, while **Mediterraneo** provides some good pasta.

these is **Global Organics**, with its impressive variety of produce: alfalfa, grapes, kiwi fruit, salsify and mooli, as well as the more mundane root vegetables.

Around this area there's also a range of food stalls selling everything from falafels to Indian curries and specialities from the Pacific. Long rows of trestle tables give buyers a chance to sit and eat their food and the atmosphere here is very family-friendly, with young children happily accompanying chirpy parents.

In the crafts market you might find silk-screen prints, sinewy glass ornaments, silk clothes, rugs, harlequin hats, wrought-iron candlesticks, chunky knitwear, handmade jewellery, and hand-painted plant pots. If you're lucky, the trader selling customized male underwear will make an appearance – gape in wonder at the size of the posing pouches. Among the regulars is a large stall selling cards and T-shirts emblazoned with feminist and left-wing slogans. Stalls selling twee rubbish are thankfully in a minority – most of the goods here are very individual and high-quality. Several stalls sell wares that are actually useful – well-made wooden toys, underwear of unbleached cotton, handloom bedspreads woven by the Bengal Women's Union,

buttons made from coconuts and seashells – and even some of the purely ornamental wares have an aesthetic appeal.

Elsewhere you can find stalls selling musical instruments, chess sets, magic-eye pictures that no one bought the first time round and some secondhand goods such as old typewriters, golf clubs and lamps on the Lamb Street side. There are several stalls featuring sheepskin goods from multi-coloured throws to boots and slippers to keep you cosy in winter. A trader has an interior design operation that is publicized here by the cushions and throws he displays – and be sure to check out Grace with her range of home-made organic creams and beauty potions, cooked up in her kitchen in Dorset and called The Graceline Body. There's a stall selling guitars and guitar accessories with posters of Jimi Hendrix, and a sweet shop selling handmade chocolate and jelly beans. Other stalls stock LPs, old stamps and postcards, and secondhand books, including Penguin Classics and volumes of poetry. **Bookworm** sells both new and secondhand titles, including marvellous magazines from the 1940s and 1950s such as *Practical Wireless*, with its pictures of pipe-smoking men and smiling housewives gazing lovingly at Bakelite.

There is a lot of art for sale here too, from the sublime to the ridiculous. Here, practicality gives way to conceptuality: abstract paintings, wire sculptures, angry collages and broken-glass mosaics are the order of the day. The individual artists are usually on hand to talk you through their 'visions'. For those preferring something safer, there's a variety of stalls selling mounted-up colour photographs of both abstract and floral themes.

After a slow start, Spitalfields became an attraction in its own right and is a great

Nearby Attractions

William Morris Gallery, *Lloyd Park, Forest Road, E17,* **t** *(020) 8527 3782, www.walthamforest.gov.uk/wmg;* ⊖ *Walthamstow Central.* **Open** *Tues–Sat 10am–1pm and 2–5pm, plus first Sun in the month 10am–1pm and 2–5pm.* William Morris's childhood home, with a fascinating exhibition about his life and work.

venue for a Sunday outing. In particular, it is heartening to see small-scale food producers thriving, despite the challenge of the ubiquitous supermarket chains. The redevelopment may have made Spitalfields smaller and more expensive (Sunday rents for its stalls have rocketed and this is reflected in the prices charged) but it has done nothing to dampen the creative and fun atmosphere of this wonderful market.

WALTHAMSTOW

Walthamstow High Street, E17.

Transport: ⊖ *Walthamstow Central;* ⇌ *Walthamstow Central, St James Street Walthamstow, Walthamstow Queens Road; buses 20, 34, 48, 58, 69, 97, 212, 215, 230, 257, 275, 357, 505, 905, W11, W12, W15.*

Open: *Mon–Sat 9am–5pm.*

Best time to go: *Thursday or Saturday before 4pm.*

Parking: *Try the residential side streets to the north of the High Street.*

Main wares: *Clothing (mostly new), fruit and veg, food, household goods, fabrics, pet food, toys, kitchenware, cosmetics, lace, electrical goods, cheap jewellery, handbags, bedclothes, cassettes and CDs,* dried flowers, cushions, lace doilies, leather gloves, Hoover spares, leather belts, tablecloths, fresh flowers, secondhand pulp fiction, tools, hats.

Specifics: *Haberdashery, pet food, cheese, sausages, outsized men's trousers, football strips.*

Fanatical supporters of Spurs and Chas 'n' Dave, yet living in E17 and fond of pie and mash, the people of Walthamstow are uncertain about their geographic identity. Are they north or east Londoners? What is certain is the esteem they hold for their market, claimed to be England's longest (at half a mile), and one that is busy all week.

The High Street is really a series of well-rounded local markets serving this highly populated region. Fruit and veg, household goods and cheap clothes are liberally scattered among over 450 pitches, but several more fascinating stalls are worth seeking out.

Say Cheese, a caravan about halfway down the market, has a good stock of British cheeses; **Joshua Hills'** sausage stall nearby displays about 20 varieties of

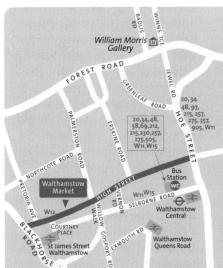

Food and Drink

L. Manze's pie and mash shop at No.76 has been serving Walthamstow's market-goers since 1929. On the menu are meat pie, mash and eels, with fruit pies for pud. At No.151 is the self-styled 'cockney diner' **Market Café**, a more modern pie and mash shop, which also sells jacket potatoes and salads.

For alcoholic refreshment, or just for a sit down halfway along the market, try the **Chequers** pub, favoured by the stallholders.

banger. Gaze in awe at the voluminous grey flannel garments at the **Trousers for Big and Small Men** stall (waist sizes from 30in to 54in), near the junction with Vernon Road. Competition has led to low prices among the fruit and veg sellers. You might snap up 2lbs of mushrooms for as little as £1, 10 large navel oranges for £1 or a box of mangoes for £2. Take a look at **Billy Grubb's** stall towards the western end of the market; pineapples and nuts are laid out pretty as a picture.

Although there's a dearth of Asian and black traders, there's a stall full of South Asian vegetables, plus a couple of Afro-Caribbean food stalls where, along with yams and plantains, you might find more unusual produce such as sorrel (not the green-leafed plant, but a type of hibiscus whose pink flowerheads are used to flavour a traditional Caribbean Christmas drink). There's also a takeaway stall selling tasty Caribbean fast food: spicy dumplings, Jamaican patties and Guinness punch.

But, even if you don't intend buying, it's worth strolling along Walthamstow market for the spectacle. See the more conscientious traders near the Chequers pub taking surreptitious sips from their pints behind their stalls while, nearby, one stallholder's 10-year-old son takes control of business as his dad 'recharges his batteries'; the lad's patter and salesman's manner are every bit as sharp and polished as a man five times his age.

Drool at the shellfish on **H. Clare's** old whelk barrow (est. 1890), also near the Chequers; hear news of Tottenham Hotspur's latest game by the football-kit stall; join the knees-up by the large music stall playing Chas 'n' Dave's singalong favourites; and call at the indoor mini-market at No.146–8 to peruse pot-pipes at the Rastafarian stall.

Victorian terraces line much of the street, but there's a jumble of other styles, from 1930s flat-tops to the new shopping centre. The market started in the 1880s, when the High Street was known as Marsh Street. In his autobiography *A Hoxton Childhood*, A. S. Jasper describes the market in the early 1920s, when his mother sold home-made frocks and trousers to get enough money for Christmas presents. And today, though the market prospers, the same cannot be said for all its customers: knots of pensioners and hard-up mothers delve for bargains at a stall full of dented tins of food; more rummage through a pile of secondhand clothes dumped on a barrow.

Waltham Forest Council, eager for its share of tourism, has worked laudably hard at promoting the market, even making the extravagant claim that it is now Europe's longest (note longest, not biggest – and Portobello Road could dispute Walthamstow's claim even to be London's longest), and there are street performers dotted through the market during summer weekends.

WHITECHAPEL

Whitechapel Road, between Vallance Road and Cambridge Heath Road, E1, **t** *(020) 7377 8963.*

Transport: ⊖ *Whitechapel; buses 25, 106, 205, 254, D3.*

Open: *Mon–Sat 8am–6pm.*

Best time to go: *Saturday.*

Parking: *Difficult; try parking meters to the north of Whitechapel Road.*

Main wares: *Clothing, fruit and veg, electrical goods, cheap jewellery, shoes.*

Specifics: *Asian fruit and veg, curtain material.*

Whitechapel Road is so wide that you could have a chariot race down the middle of it. This isn't so far from what used to happen: until the mid-19th century, drovers used to steer their livestock along this stretch of road on the way to Smithfield, and one of London's main hay markets was held here until 1920.

The road is now busy and grey, yet there are some fascinating historical nuggets to be found. At the **Whitechapel Bell Foundry** (Nos.32–4), churches have been kitted out with their sound equipment since the 15th century. The **Trinity House**

Food, Drink and Shopping

The **Blind Beggar** pub has been dolled up, and has a veranda where you can order pub food of the lasagne and chips variety. On the pavement, at the western edge of the market, is **Taja**, an Indian restaurant housed in a building which looks like an enormous Portaloo, where you can get an all-day buffet for £4.95. Otherwise the curry houses of Brick Lane are only a short walk away (*see p.101*).

Hidden down an alley to the west of the market is the **Freedom Press Bookshop** (Angel Alley, 84b Whitechapel High Street), a tiny place well stocked with political pamphlets and treatises, and run by bookish folk awaiting the revolution.

almshouses (at Trinity Green, about 100 yards from the eastern end of the market) were built in 1695 for old seafarers and their widows. More recent history was made at the **Blind Beggar** pub in 1966, when Ronnie Kray, of the notorious Kray gang, walked in and gunned down George Cornell from the rival Richardson gang.

The market takes place on Whitechapel Road's wide northern pavement, next to a large branch of Sainsbury's built in the early 1990s. As yet, the supermarket has had little effect on the street trading. This is probably because the market has accommodated traders from the local Bangladeshi population better than most in the district, so produce sold here is geared more directly towards the needs of the local community – the market feels almost completely Asian. A few stalls stock good-quality Asian fruit and veg: okra, herbs, beans and several varieties of mangoes. A handful of stalls sell long-distance phone cards, and mobile phones – I caught a loud fracas between a dissatisfied customer claiming he had

Nearby Attractions

Whitechapel Art Gallery, *Whitechapel High Street, t (020) 7522 7888, www. whitechapel.org; ⊖ Aldgate East; buses 5, 15, 15A, 25, 40, 67, 78, 254. Open Tues–Sun 11am–6pm, Thurs 11am–9pm; closed Mon.* An innovative contemporary gallery in an impressive Art Nouveau building.

been sold a broken phone and a disgruntled stallholder who was having none of it. Other traders sell the colourful, smart tunics and frilly dresses favoured by Bangladeshi parents for their young children. Elsewhere, teenagers can pick up puffa jackets and cheap trainers, while many of the stalls display embroidered tunics and spangly saris as well as fabrics for making your own. There are cheap pashminas (£1.25, no joke), in every colour of the rainbow, and beautifully embroidered shawls. Sequinned Indian slippers complete the look while there are a couple of stalls selling fashionable high-street clobber from the likes of Top Shop. There are 'M&S' bras and a stall selling Indian and African bold-print kaftans, as well as flannel pyjamas.

Most other traders sell new, everyday items – socks, underwear, cheap jewellery, watches, shoes, cut flowers, fruit and veg, fish, baby clothes, kitchenware, biscuits and sweets – and there are enough stalls and variety to make a healthy number of East Enders shop here, making it an atmospheric local market.

Southwest London

BRIXTON

Electric Avenue, Pope's Road, Brixton Station Road, Electric Lane, SW9, t (020) 7926 2530.

Transport: ⊖ *Brixton;* ⇌ *Brixton; buses 2, 3, 35, 37, 45, 59, 109, 118, 133, 159, 201, 250, 322, 333, 345, 355, 432, P4, P5.*

Open: *Mon, Tues and Thurs–Sat 8am–5.30pm; Wed 8am–3pm.*

Best time to go: *Good on any day, but busiest on Friday and Saturday.*

Parking: *The side streets off Railton Road, a 10-minute walk to the south of the market, have free parking, but it can be hard to get a space; there's a multi-storey car park in Wiltshire Road.*

Main wares: *African and Caribbean foodstuffs, fruit and vegetables, fabrics, clothing, records, tapes and CDs, secondhand clothing, bric-a-brac, haberdashery, electrical goods.*

Specifics: *Fish, Afro-Caribbean fruit and vegetables, meat, African fabrics and clothing, black music.*

Brixton market is dynamic, tense and vital. People gather simply to watch the entertainment. And by doing so they become part of that entertainment, the parading, cosmopolitan crowd that's as essential to the spirit of the market as the 300 or more stalls and lock-ups that open for business six days a week.

Street trading began in the 1870s along Atlantic Road, and quickly expanded down Electric Avenue to cater for the massive increase in the area's population. The market soon drew customers from all over south London, and became known for its eccentric characters. By 1936, Mary Benedetta, in her own survey of London's street markets, complained that customers at Brixton were a joyless lot,

mainly 'serious-minded housewives'. But the stallholders more than made up for it, and she went on to describe folk such as 'Long Dick', who sold a game called hookum for 3d, 'Bertie Bacon', whose streaky never cost more than 8d a pound, and 'Fatty', who sold bargain tinned foods.

Afro-Caribbeans were invited to work in Britain to help solve the post-war labour shortage. They began to settle in Brixton in 1948, drawn by the availability of lodging houses within easy reach of central London. There have been problems in the community's assimilation. High unemployment and aggressive policing helped fuel tensions. These reached explosive levels in 1981 and 1985, when riots broke out in the area, and there have been further disturbances since. However, it would be wrong to think of Brixton as a ghetto, as blacks and Asians together represent only about 30 per cent of the local population. Though economic problems remain, the local community has worked together in the past decade to ease the tension. Since the latter half of the 1990s, the area has become one of London's funkiest, with new bars, trendy restaurants and equally modish clubs opening up.

You might think the market has changed out of all recognition since the days of Bertie Bacon. Not a bit of it. Though Brixton is now reputed to have the largest selection of African and Caribbean food in Europe, the traders from these communities not only operate in the same arcades and streets as their 1930s predecessors, they have also kept the jolly, noisy atmosphere and the unashamedly carnivorous feel of the place.

Electric Avenue

Built towards the end of the 1880s, Electric Avenue was one of the first shopping streets to be lit by electricity. The road curves round elegantly, giving a fine view of the late-Victorian housing. But, while the market is on, architecture takes second place. Stalls are on the right-hand side as you walk up from Brixton Road, competing for attention with a varied collection of lock-up shops. A crowded pavement separates the two sets of traders. Standard fruit and veg is sold at the first stall. Then come women's clothes, a cheap electrical goods pitch ('any watch £10') and a trader in haberdashery. It's not long before you come across the first stall of African and Caribbean goods; excitingly exotic, it carries contorted black segments of dried fish, dried pulses, bitter leaf and something named 'nzu edible chalk'. Further along, a stall has a mix of colourful materials and fabrics; next to it, gospel music is blaring out from the CDs pitch.

Many of the barrows on Electric Avenue are stocked with fruit and veg. There's a good mix of Afro-Caribbean and traditional British stalls. One trader might have plantains, yams, guavas and red-hot chillies; the next could be selling spuds, apples, cabbages and beetroot. Several of the lock-up shops also sell Afro-Caribbean fruit and vegetables, along with spices and tinned foods. Despite the variety and number of stalls, prices aren't rock-bottom, though, given the quality, value is good.

A small crowd is gathered round the fishmonger's, viewing the milk fish, butter fish, blue runners, snappers, yellow croakers and talapias. Just one such shop with half this variety is more than most British towns can muster; Brixton has over half a dozen of them. The remaining barrows along Electric Avenue sell the type of goods found at a thriving local market: underwear, socks, shoes, haberdashery, household goods and toiletries, greetings cards, bedlinen and towels, inexpensive suits for women, curtain fabrics, and hats with fur trim. But there are twists to show that Brixton is more than simply a local market: the barrow full of traditional sweets sells slices of dried mango and bags of Bombay mix alongside the humbugs; and one electrical goods stall is packed with expensive stuff such as new car radios.

Along with Brixton's indoor arcades, Electric Avenue is the best place to buy offal and halal meat. At a couple of lock-ups along the south side of the street there's an awesome display of carnage. In one, a gang of butchers is chopping joints, their heads knocking into a dangling row of pallid, plucked chickens. Vegetarians who've survived thus far would surely blench. It is a mark of how divorced many British meat-eaters are from the food production process that they would do likewise.

Pope's Road

There's a brief hiatus in the proceedings as Electric Avenue hits Atlantic Road. It was here that the market started in the 1870s, but stalls were banned from Atlantic Road some 80 years ago because of the obstruction to traffic. However, the beat soon picks up again as you cross over Atlantic Road to Pope's Road and hear the thud of reggae coming along the street. The road curves round a Victorian railway viaduct as trains thunder overhead, providing counter-beats to the music. The claustrophobic atmosphere at street level is intensified by stalls packing both sides of the narrow thoroughfare. No car could get through here during the market, even if allowed.

There are three or four traditional fruit, vegetable and salad stalls along the road, but otherwise little fresh produce on this stretch of the market. Near one of the railway bridges, a couple of chaps deal in dried foods from Africa: big kola nuts, black desiccated uda beans, and 'akawu', which looks like chunks of white stone. Another food stall sells sarsaparilla, spices, pulses and creamed coconut. You might also find sorrel syrup being sold in winter. This traditional Christmas drink from the West Indies is made from the pink flowerheads of the roselle plant, mixed with ginger and sugar.

New clothes account for many of the stalls. Here you can restock your wardrobe with trainers, silky nightshirts, jeans, tracksuits and half-price out-of-season garments (woollies in summer, skimpy tops in winter). If you're after a secondhand bargain, wait for Brixton Station Road. Further along is a barrow completely overwhelmed by the mass of net curtains piled on it and over it. Look carefully and you can just make out the head of the stallholder peering from within. At a nearby brassware pitch, there's an assortment of candlesticks, plus delicate little weighing machines – useful for measuring out small chunks of valuable material. Other stalls worth making for sell bags and suitcases, telephones and good-value watches.

Brixton Station Road

The market spread into Brixton Station Road in the 1920s, when stallholders were removed from Atlantic Road. In market terms, it is a road of two halves. The stretch running east from Pope's Road to Valentia Place is full of secondhand goods, both on stalls and in lock-ups under the railway arches.

A score of temporary stalls are crammed with good-quality, cheap secondhand clothes and shoes. The garments – dresses, jeans, army-surplus clothing, suits, denim jackets, leather jackets, shirts, overcoats – are hung on rails rather than dumped on tables. Clothes aren't called 'vintage', 'retro' or 'antique' here; they're just secondhand and inexpensive. Lee jeans in reasonable condition cost under £10 and most suits go for little more than £20.

On tables beneath the clothes rails you'll find a disparate collection of goods. Some of them could pass as antiques – the odd pair of old opera glasses, say – while others are just secondhand: videos of old films; computer games and Playstations. Root about and you might find a bargain, for few antiques dealers venture here.

The lock-ups on Brixton Station Road inhabit cavern-like dens under the railway bridge and keep varying hours. Come on Saturday to find most open. Stock varies widely and wildly: secondhand clothes, cutlery, crockery, washing machines. One enterprise that trades on most days concentrates on records; there's a welter of vinyl, with the entire space full of LPs and 45s. The soul selection attracts many young locals, though the gamut of popular music is covered, from Mantovani to garage thrash. Cool music from a cheap hi-fi accompanies your browsing.

Turning west onto Brixton Station Road from Pope's Road, you'll find mostly new goods. The premises under the arches this side of the junction have been converted into shops. This stretch of road is best populated by stalls on a Saturday, when tinned food, clothing, shoes, and household and electrical goods are sold. But on most days you'll find traders in jeans, fresh flowers and CDs. Two lads at one stall are swaying to hefty bass rhythms from their own selection of 'jam mixes'; the sound blends with calypso music coming from a nearby CD, DVD and video stall.

Market Row

Entrances on Atlantic Road, Coldharbour Lane and Electric Lane.

Brixton's indoor arcades are inseparable from the market. In both Market Row and the Granville Arcade, the music, crowds, aromas and tumult of the street continue indoors. Both halls date from the 1930s and contain permanent kiosks and lock-up shops arranged in avenues. Astonishingly little has changed in the structure of the arcades since they were built. Several lock-ups still have shelving reaching the ceiling, thwarting any attempts at self-service. But on the shelves the bully beef and tinned carrots of 60 years ago have been replaced by jars of palm oil or tinned callaloo (the green-leafed tops of yams).

Market Row holds a fine array of household essentials together with fresh and preserved foods. A pig's head squints

out at Atlantic Road from **Philips Butchers**, while at the **Twin Peaks Fish Co** a fishmonger is cheerfully de-scaling a croaker. **Capelstone Ltd** displays lurid pink and peach bedspreads from its premises, but also specializes in mosquito nets. Several businesses sell African fruit and vegetables, and there's also a black haircare and wig salon, a trader in fancy satin dresses for little girls, and a store full of bright material and African costumes.

Other businesses worth looking for include **Yen**, which sells women's coats, suits, slinky halterneck tops and sequinned dresses in sizes 16–26. **Blacker Dread**, a record store, graces the Coldharbour Lane entrance to the market. It's good for US and Jamaican imports, and has its windows plastered with album covers. Nearby is a store devoted to religion; the smell of incense that seeps from it is almost overpowering. Within you'll find figures of saints for sale, along with model heads of Native American chiefs, prayer books, bottles of holy water and tapes of Dolly Parton singing *Give Me that Ole Time Religion*.

Reliance Arcade

Entrances on Brixton Road and Electric Lane.

The smallest of the arcades, the Reliance is simply a narrow, walk-through thoroughfare with lock-ups on either side. Highlights within include African crafts (wooden masks and jewellery), a wig stall, the **CD Bar** with its stock of black records, Hoover spares, leather jackets, and a takeaway caff specializing in home-made Jamaican patties. I order a pattie and am given a boost as the café owner raises his hand and sends me on my way with a cheerful 'Respect!'

Brixton Village Market

Entrances on Atlantic Road, Pope's Road and Coldharbour Lane.

This was formerly Granville Arcade but has been refreshed and turned into Brixton Village. Upbeat reggae blasts out of **LonDisc Records** at the Atlantic Road entrance, setting the rhythm to the hubbub within. It holds a similar variety of goods to Market Row, but it's bigger. Built in 1937, it is divided into half a dozen avenues, with lock-ups on either side. There has been a lot of collaboration with local artists, and their work adorns the Coldharbour Lane entrance; look out for the vivid artworks.

There's a big queue at **Trinder's**, which is divided into a butcher's and a fishmonger's section. The fish are the attraction: customers can hardly keep their eyes off the display of salted mackerel, glisteningly fresh butter fish, salmon heads, crabs and raw king prawns. A couple of lads weave through the queue, full of vim and singing 'Hoo, wheeee!'

It's worth inspecting all the fish stalls at the Village – they're among London's best, full of a bi-cultural mix of North Sea and Caribbean species. Atlantic blue crab, silver fish, jackfish, pollock, butterfish, exotic-coloured parrot fish, doctor fish, talapia, mackerel, cod (both fresh and salted) and yellow snapper are just some of the varieties on the slabs. The arcade is also a good place for meat, especially offal, sold by Asian Muslims to mostly Afro-Caribbean customers. Several lock-ups sell tinned provisions and spices along with the fresh produce, and there are also a couple of Caribbean bakeries.

Several more of the Village's businesses cater for the cultural and sartorial tastes of Brixton's African and Caribbean locals.

Food and Drink
Cafés and Fast Food

Max Snack Bar & Café (under a railway arch at 18 Brixton Station Road) has Portuguese *petiscos* (like tapas) such as green soup, boiled salt cod and fried squid. **Take Two**, at 1 Brixton Station Road, is a takeaway place selling Afro-Caribbean food, including cow's foot soup, Jamaican patties and jerk chicken. **Garden Jacaranda** (11–13 Brixton Station Road) is probably the most amenable café in Brixton. Open all day, there's a constant bustle of young Brixtonians; the food goes from jollof rice with chicken and hot pepper sauce to salads and sandwiches.

At the Coldharbour Lane end of Market Row, **Café Pushkar** sells vegetarian snacks and coffee.

Restaurants

Bah Humbug, in St Matthew's Peace Garden off Brixton Hill, is an inventive vegetarian restaurant, while **Brixtonian Havana Club**, 11 Beehive Place, serves excellent Caribbean and 'Black British' cuisine.

Pubs

The Dogstar, at 389 Coldharbour Lane, is a large, lively pub selling bar food, juices and flavoured vodkas. It becomes a club at night.

A store on 4th Avenue has vibrant African tunics hanging outside; a video shop specializes in Nigerian films and music cassettes; wigs can be bought from **The Wig Bazaar** (which has a sign in the window reading 'Sale. Human hair from £10'); **African Spot** sells African-style clothing and jewellery. A couple of the best groceries are run by Africans and can be found on 3rd Avenue. **Kumasi Market** must have more than 10 types of salted and dried fish, some looking as though they've been washed up on a beach. It also sells chewing sticks (resembling the stalks of ice lollies), bambara beans, powdered okra, tins of mentholated dusting powder, and beautiful wooden eating bowls. Opposite are the premises of the **Sierra Leone Groceries**, where a jolly bunch of lads sell a fascinating variety of exotic produce (frozen cassava leaves, potato leaves, sawa sawa, crain, greens and fufu). Other businesses include **The Bible Bookstore** on 3rd Avenue, selling gospel music, pictures, videos and greetings cards. You can buy Slim Tea and have IBS (Irritable Bowel Syndrome) cured at **The Green Healer**, which sells Chinese Herbal Medicines, and purchase cheap designer clothes at **The New Galaxy**.

It is sometimes easy to forget that the West Indies aren't far from the coast of South America. However, there are several food vendors selling *chorizos* and *arepas*. **El Pilón Quindiano**, a Colombian café and restaurant, sells snacks such as *arepas* (cornmeal buns) and *empanadas* (pasties stuffed with chopped meat, eggs and olives), and a nearby butcher's, **Carniceria Los Andes**, has a Spanish price list and sells uncooked *chorizo* sausage.

I stare incredulously at **Witchdoktor Studios**, a body-piercing and tattooing salon, which has close-up photos of its practitioners' work displayed in the windows. Without warning, I find myself in the middle of one of Brixton's periodic bouts of tension. A gang of police, perhaps ten of them, have entered the arcade. A staring match ensues between policemen and local shoppers. And then someone in **All Tone Records** ('specialists in Studio 1, Rock Steady, R&B, Ska, Roots, Motown and Dub') flips on a disc, and the irresistible rhythms of early ska come echoing down the arcade's old avenues. The effect is

palpable: everyone loosens up and this astonishing market resumes its rhythm.

HILDRETH STREET

Hildreth Street, between Balham High Road and Bedford Hill, SW12.

Transport: ⊖ *Balham;* ≥ *Balham; buses 155, 249, 315, 355.*

Open: *Mon–Wed, Fri and Sat 9.30am–5pm; Thurs 9.30am–1pm.*

Best time to go: *Saturday.*

Parking: *There's roadside parking on the streets east of Bedford Hill.*

Main wares: *Fruit and veg, flowers, eggs.*

Specifics: *Caribbean fruit and veg.*

Barely 50 yards long, Hildreth Street has been the home to Balham's market since 1903, when traders were swept off Bedford Hill, where they had been operating since about 1900, to make way for trams. Now pedestrianized, it's an odd prong of a road, lined by four-storey gabled red terraces that might seem elegant were it not for the jumble of activity taking place at ground level.

About half a dozen stalls are constructed on both sides of the road on a Saturday,

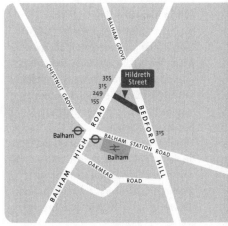

Food and Drink

M&M Bakery (11 Hildreth Street) sells various takeaway snacks, including ackee and saltfish, and Guinness punch. The dumplings – heavy, doughy grenades of fried bread – will fill you up for a pittance. If you're in need of something a little more refined, there is a popular French café-pâtisserie, Ann Marie, opposite the market at the corner of Ramsden Rd, selling a delicious cakes and coffees.

The **Bedford** (77 Bedford Hill) is a traditional local pub that does a good Sunday lunch. **Balham Kitchen & Bar** (15–19 Bedford Hill) is a trendy brasserie that's very popular with the locals, especially for brunch.

fewer in the week. They complement Hildreth Street's collection of useful small shops – a well-stocked fishmonger's, a halal butcher's, an Afro-Caribbean baker's, a Caribbean food shop and a caff. Fresh fruit and vegetables are the main commodities. Prices, though they knock spots off those at local supermarkets, are generally higher than at Brixton or Tooting. Several stalls specialize in the usual potatoes, cabbages, apples and oranges, perhaps with some Brazil nuts and walnuts in winter. Because of Balham's sizeable Afro-Caribbean community, however, you might also find the odd mango or even some prickly pears. Two black stallholders concentrate on West Indian produce: yams, plantain, salted mackerel, dried pulses, bottles of sarsaparilla, tins of gunga peas and packets of saltfish.

The cut-flower stall makes a grand display on Balham High Road with its abundant red and white carnations. A greetings-card seller is a regular through the week here, though it's best to come on Saturdays to catch the household goods stall. Gloves for a cold winter's day were also up for grabs in December.

The High Road, once part of the Roman Stane Street which ran from London to Chichester, is now Balham's main shopping street. A few independent shops find space among the chains – a halal butcher's here, a discount jeweller's there.

Balham Continental Market, a small indoor concourse occupying a dilapidated building opposite Hildreth Street on Bedford Hill, finally closed in 1995 after more than a decade of decline. It has long seemed that the outside market is also on the wane with the local council demonstrating its allegiances by allowing a huge supermarket to be built on Bedford Hill. However, plans are under way to make the street more attractive, with £150,000 earmarked to regenerate the street. New paving is being laid down and businesses are being encouraged to spruce up their merchandising. The council is hoping to make Hildreth Street more of a meeting place for locals, encouraging cafés to spill tables out onto the street and the market stalls to move to the middle of the street with better lighting and a wider entrance to help bring people in. Once all this has taken place, the hope is that the market will bring in new stallholders as well as perhaps a farmers' and a French market.

KING'S ROAD ANTIQUES

Antiquarius, 131–41 King's Road, SW3,
t (020) 7351 5353.
Transport: ⊖ *Sloane Square; buses 11, 19,*
22, 49, 211, 239, 319, 345.

Open: *Mon–Sat 10am–6pm.*

Best time to go: *Tuesday–Thursday, Friday afternoon, Saturday.*

Parking: *Difficult nearby; try the parking meters around Paultons Square. South of the river Surrey Lane, off Battersea Bridge Road, usually has spaces and is a 20-minute walk away.*

Main wares: *Antiques.*

Specifics: *Jewellery, silverware, ceramics, vintage clothing, cinema memorabilia, watches and clocks, Art Nouveau and Art Deco artefacts.*

Chelsea's high street, the King's Road, dates back to the 17th century at least. Despite this, it has no long history of street trading. Until 1830 it was literally the king's road, a private thoroughfare of the monarch. Charles II travelled along it to Hampton Court, and it was George III's favourite road to Kew. Private citizens could only use it with a copper pass stamped 'The King's Private Roads'. Although costermongers did try to set up stalls on the road towards the end of the 19th century, they were forced off their pitches by local shopkeepers and went instead to North End Road (*see* p.139). In the 1960s the King's Road gained

---

Food, Drink and Shopping

The Chelsea Kitchen (98 King's Road) is a decent budget diner. Part of the Stockpot chain of restaurants, it remains a favourite with students, serving popular international dishes. **Chutney Mary** (No.535) is an upmarket Indian with an excellent menu and wine list. The **Coopers Arms** (87 Flood Street, south of the King's Road) is a bar-style pub selling food and Young's beers.

There is, of course, a plethora of antiques shops and boutiques along the King's Road, but, if you want an expensive treat after parading along its length, visit **Rococo**, one of London's best chocolate shops, at No.321.

---

international fame as the epicentre of swinging London. Dozens of boutiques were set up, mostly along the middle third of the road's 2-mile stretch. The Rolling Stones and the Beatles came to be kitted out with psychedelic clobber, and there was a free fashion show as groovy young things paraded up and down the street. The King's Road maintained its position as the headquarters of hipness in the 1970s, when punk gurus Vivienne Westwood and Malcolm McLaren opened a clothes shop called Sex. The latest manifestation of Ms Westwood's shop, **Vivienne Westwood**, is still at No.430 with the clock with its hands spinning backwards outside.

There used to be three antiques markets along the King's Road. Two have closed, yet the sole survivor, **Antiquarius**, is well worth a visit, containing dozens of stalls packed with high-quality stock. However, since Chelsea is one of London's most expensive districts, don't come here expecting bargains.

Most stallholders accept credit cards and operate the export scheme whereby

Nearby Attractions

Carlyle's House, *24 Cheyne Row, **t** (020) 7352 7087;* ⊖ *Sloane Square, then bus 11, 19, 22, or 15-minute walk;* **buses** *11, 19, 22, 49, 239.* **Open** *25 March–Oct Wed, Thurs, Fri 2pm–5pm, Sat–Sun 11am–5pm;* **adm** *adults £4.20, children £2.10.* Attractive Queen Anne building that was home to the historian Thomas Carlyle and has been kept just as he and his wife left it.

Chelsea Old Church, *Old Church Street (off Cheyne Walk),* **t** *(020) 7795 1019;* ⊖ *Sloane Square, then bus 11, 19, 22, or 15-minute walk;* **buses** *11, 19, 22, 49, 239.* **Open** *daily 9.30am–1pm and 2–4.30pm.* This church is a memorial to Sir Thomas More, the author of *Utopia*, who lost his head standing up to Henry VIII. He built the South Chapel and there is a monument to him in the sanctuary.

Chelsea Physic Garden, *Swan Walk (off Royal Hospital Road),* **t** *(020) 7352 5646, www.chelseaphysicgarden.co.uk;* ⊖ *Sloane Square;* **buses** *11, 14, 19, 22, 49, 137, 211, 239, 349.* **Open** *April–Oct Sun 12–6pm, Wed 12–5pm, Tues and Thurs 18 July–7 Sept 12–5pm;* **adm** *adults £6.50, children £3.50.* A wonderfully unusual garden containing many examples of rare trees, plants, herbs and seeds, dating back to 1676.

Cheyne Walk, ⊖ *Sloane Square, then bus 11, 19, 22, or 15-minute walk;* **buses** *11, 19, 22, 49, 239.* Beautiful 18th-century buildings line this street, where former residents include George Eliot (No.4) and Henry James (Carlyle Mansions), and more recently Mick Jagger (No.48) and Keith Richards (No.3).

The Royal Hospital, *Royal Hospital Road,* **t** *(020) 7881 5204;* ⊖ *Sloane Square;* **buses** *11, 14, 19, 22, 49, 137, 211, 239, 349.* **Open (museum)** *Mon–Sat 10am–12pm and 2–4pm, Sun 2–4pm (closed Sun in winter).* Wren's answer to the Invalides in Paris (1682), housing 400 Chelsea Pensioners, war veterans famous for their distinctive scarlet frock coats and three-cornered hats. Every May the gardens host the famed, week-long Chelsea Flower Show.

National Army Museum, *Royal Hospital Road,* **t** *(020) 7730 0717, www.national-army-museum.ac.uk;* ⊖ *Sloane Square;* **buses** *11, 19, 22, 137, 239.* **Open** *daily 10am–5.30pm.* Telling the fascinating history of the British army, from Agincourt to the SAS, from the perspective of the soldiers themselves.

visitors from outside the EU can claim back VAT on goods. Ask for a form at the time of purchase. The site has a bureau de change.

Some shops open onto the King's Road, including **At the Movies**, a business specializing in vintage film posters. As you approach the entrance to the market you might see a display of Rolex watch straps and Art Deco jewellery in the window: indication of the luxury goods within. The first stalls you'll encounter inside are the most expensive and intimidating. Goods are kept under polished glass counters,

like museum exhibits. Even the floor is of polished stone tiles. Muzak plays as you glance at the bronze statuettes of Victorian worthies, or the collection of leather purses and riding crops. Antique Persian rugs are displayed in one window; silverware from R. E. Stone, Gilbert Marks and Liberty & Co adorns another. Art Deco ceramics, sparkling silverware, Islamic art and oriental pots also await the opulent collector.

If you're a seasoned market buff and find vast prices scary, you should quickly descend the five steps into the main market hall where things are more relaxed and prices lower. Over a hundred traders sit at their stalls, chat with a nearby dealer, or take a break at the café (breakfast fry-ups and pasta are specialities). One long-established trader deals in old polished leather, redolent of public school and Empire: bowls sets, shooting sticks, suitcases, boxing gloves, rugby balls and well-seasoned cricket bats. A nearby stall is hidden under a plethora of old photo frames, made of materials varying from gold to bronze to wood.

Wander along the narrow walkways, with neatly partitioned stalls on either side, and you might discover battalions of model soldiers, or an array of elaborately adorned snuff boxes. Wedgwood ceramics on one stall are followed by silver table-ware at the next. One dealer has a stock of 19th-century prints, kept under headings such as Sporting, Architecture, Hunting Scenes and Maritime.

For a fancy vintage party frock, look for the stall packed with 1920s evening wear. Not far away is a trader specializing in antique handbags. Children's clocks from the 1960s (featuring Noddy and Big Ears, among others), old kitchenware, and a large collection of military medals, swords, globes and buttons are among the more quirky selection of goods. And, even if you're not buying, it's worth visiting the antique timepieces stall with its fascinating collection of clocks. Come on the hour for a festival of chiming.

There is a Gents WC in the main hall and a Ladies just inside the Flood Street entrance. As is the case with many of London's antiques markets, if you're planning to visit Antiquarius on Friday, better go after lunch, as many traders pay an early morning visit to Bermondsey market (*see* p.150) to replenish their stock.

MERTON ABBEY MILLS

Watermill Way (opposite Savacentre), off Merantun Way, SW19, **t** *(020) 8543 9608.*

Transport: ⊖ *Colliers Wood; buses 57, 152, 155, 200, 219.*

Open: *Sat and Sun 10am–5pm; it starts winding down around 3.30pm.*

Best time to go: *Sunday.*

Parking: *There's a free car park right by the market; the entrance is via Watermill Way.*

Main wares: *Crafts, clothing, toys, books, records, sheet music, flowers, jewellery, paintings, fast food.*

Specifics: *Designer and ethnic clothes and jewellery, secondhand books, wooden toys.*

> *'Have nothing in your houses that you do not know to be useful, or believe to be beautiful.'*

Perhaps William Morris's words should be writ large over the entrance to Merton Abbey Mills, to prod the consciences of all who trade there. Several craftsworkers would be able to walk underneath with

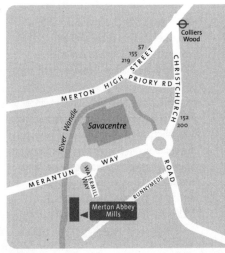

head held high; there are some beautiful, practical and worthwhile goods sold here, many of them skilfully made by hand. But, as with all crafts markets, there's also codswallop: twee twaddle and hideous knick-knacks sold at ludicrous prices.

William Morris, the 19th-century socialist, poet, designer and multi-talented craftsworker, expanded his arts and crafts business to Merton Abbey in the 1870s. In this southwest London suburb he revived the art of tapestry weaving, experimented in the use of vegetable dyes and continued his wallpaper-designing work. Young workers were recruited to be trained in techniques that had all but died out. All were encouraged to use their creativity.

Although Morris was the major inspiration behind the Arts and Crafts movement, it was Arthur Liberty who provided more substantial assistance for today's Merton Abbey market. Liberty, a follower of Morris and founder of the famous Regent Street department store, bought this site by the River Wandle in 1904. He used existing buildings and constructed more to house his fabric-printing works. The half-dozen or so structures were restored in 1989 and are now occupied by a restaurant, a café, a pub, several crafts shops and, at weekends, an indoor crafts market.

Though the market is held on both days of the weekend, Saturday trading is a relatively small affair. On Sundays, dozens more traders arrive and most pitches are taken, both indoors and outdoors around the buildings. In the car park there is often a bouncy castle and swing carousel, and just inside the entrance there is go-karting for children.

It's 9.25am on a Sunday morning and many of the outside stalls are still being constructed. Craftsworkers are later risers than costermongers. A man with a wicker basket full of plant pots staggers by, followed by a woman wheeling a trolley on which a stripped-pine chest of drawers is precariously balanced. Nearby, a couple of lads are hanging their agate wind chimes around a stall. The tinkling sounds like thousands of jostling wine glasses. 'It's the wrong time of day for this,' remarks a trader at the vintage jeans stall, nursing a hangover.

There's more than a passing resemblance to Camden Lock, but everything is a little more manicured. Families from the sedate sitting rooms of Wimbledon account for many of the customers. Quite a crowd arrives on fine Sundays, but you won't get the irksome throngs that bedevil central London crafts markets.

The **1929 Shop**, a former print shop raised slightly above the other buildings, houses several businesses. There's a pizza and pasta restaurant, **Mamarosa Ristorante**; **Carina Prints**, with art reproductions, limited editions (including autographed prints of sports stars in action), engravings and posters; a rather twee lace shop, **Abbey Lace**, which also sells porcelain dolls, mobiles, picture frames and pillowcases; **Dragon's Hoard**, which sells sci-fi and film/TV-related items such as prints and dolls; and **Charlie's Rock Shop**, with polished fossils, necklaces, shiny pebbles and the aforementioned wind chimes. Shortly before 10am, a knot of casual traders gathers round the entrance to the main market hall. The market supervisor then reads out numbers, as if calling a raffle. This is how pitch positions are decided. By now, most of the regular traders are putting the finishing touches to their displays. A man surrounded by stripped-pine furniture adjusts a mirror; clothes sellers organize their piles of Andean jumpers, or vibrant-coloured skirts, or T-shirts with African designs. One trader specializes in waistcoats, with styles ranging from suede, through bucolic-looking wefts, to vivid prints for children; another has a big collection of cheap CDs.

By 10.30am the stalls are all up and the punters are beginning to arrive. There's plenty for them to peruse at the outside stalls: chunky pottery cups and plates, flat caps and women's headgear (all looking homespun and utterly worthy), candlesticks, thick jumpers and rugged checked shirts. New Age sun and moon symbols are everywhere, on mobiles, ornaments, brooches and earrings. The market also attracts a few young clothes designers who bring their velvet and silk tops, their mini-skirts made from blanket material, and their floppy hats.

Alongside the market hall are a batch of shops that are open through the week. At weekends some place stalls outside. Haberdashery, ceramics, pot plants, garden gnomes and ornaments in wood, pottery, stained glass and metal are among their wares. One stocks a wide array of records, tapes and CDs: outside, albums are sold for £1, singles for 50p; inside, you'll find framed autographed photos of rock stars.

A stall near these shops sells door stops in the shape of pigs, metallic money boxes in the shape of General Pershing, and unnervingly lifelike dolls. The stallholder approaches, concerned. 'You're not nicking our ideas are you? People do, you know.'

Skip past more garden gnomes and you might encounter brightly and wildly painted wooden furniture, smartly upholstered stools (made to order),

children's clothes (mostly in tartan) and a large stall full of beautiful but expensive wooden toys, from colourful little rocking chairs to penguins that totter down a slope. There are also a few more designer clothes stalls as well as a couple of clairvoyants: 'Janet and Avis invite you to come to the caravan'.

Near the eastern limits of the market is another Victorian structure, the **Coles Shop**. At the front of the building, near the market's main entrance, is **The Tradehouse**, a soft furnishings shop specializing in gaily coloured rugs and throws. Picture framers **Abbey Framing** work next door to the WC. The Coles Shop also contains the **Commonwealth Café** (see Food and Drink, p.136).

The open-air stalls tend to vary from week to week, but there's always plenty of jewellery (both ethnic and locally designed) and clothing. Jumpers might come from the Himalayas, Ecuador, Peru or Wandsworth. Highlights might include home-made cakes, wooden chess and backgammon sets, embroidered waistcoats from Thailand, home-made salad oils (containing mixtures such as rosemary, garlic and lemon, or chilli, cinnamon and ginger), legitts (small wooden stilts for children), handmade lingerie, Kate Bramwell-Cole's gorgeous ceramic bowls, and Peruvian moccasins, ponchos and mirrors. Apart from the cakes and salad oils, there's a wealth of food stalls from around the world, including a wholefood stall or Indian pickle-maker's, as well as an aromatic coffee-bean and leaf-tea stall. There are also stalls selling farm produce – not quite a farmers' market but obviously cashing in on their popularity. You can find free-range eggs, home-made honey, and farm-produced bacon, sausages and cheese.

There are four other buildings in this odd little commune near the river. **The Apprentice Shop** now contains a large secondhand bookshop which puts much of its stock outside on fine days. There's a huge number of paperbacks, with authors ranging from Aristophanes to Barbara Taylor Bradford. Most cost around £1.50. It also has an impressive history section. Another bookshop specializes in old sheet music, with thousands of popular and classical scores (a hardback book of Gilbert and Sullivan songs costs £7). **Greencades** sells herbs, aromatherapy oils, oil burners, candles, soap and food. **The Colourhouse**, one of London's oldest industrial buildings (dating from 1730), now houses the Colourhouse Theatre, where children's and family shows are staged at 2pm and 4pm on weekends as well as drama workshops for children; call **t** (020) 8542 6644 for details. **The Wheelhouse** contains a watermill and information about the history of the site. There's usually a group of children watching the wheel spin, and then looking at the dials indicating the electricity generated. Occasional demonstrations – of traditional hand-spinning, for example – are also held in the Wheelhouse. The Wheelhouse Pottery, a stall just outside the building's entrance, sells sturdy-looking ceramic plates, bowls and jugs.

The remaining building holds the **indoor market**, where the smell of flavoured coffee beans is overwhelming. It has space for scores of traders, with stalls neatly arranged in lines. Several sell similar goods to those you might find at Covent Garden or Greenwich, with plenty of jewellery, handmade greetings cards, candlesticks, oil lamps and cutesy pottery. Some natty handmade dungarees for children might catch your eye, or you might prefer a

Food and Drink

Fast food stalls are grouped in a semi-circle at the western end of the market. Lentil burgers, Mexican tacos, Belgian waffles, hot doughnuts, Filipino or Thai noodles, Indonesian satays and British roasts are at the various pitches, but before midday it is only the egg, bacon and sausage stall that does good business. I usually plump for British food and receive a bending plateful of faggots, mushy peas, creamy mashed potatoes with onions, stuffing and lashings of gravy – smashing. Pity, then, that there seems to be nowhere to consume the feast apart from perching on a disused railway sleeper in the car park.

The **Commonwealth Café** serves sandwiches and greasy spoon fare, with tables inside and out.

Behind the 1929 Shop (*see* p.134) is the **William Morris** pub, with its patio overlooking the canal-like banks of the little River Wandle – a view only partially marred by the enormous electricity pylon opposite. The pub (open from midday on Sundays) has a choice of real ales, pub grub (steak and Guinness pie, vegetable Kiev), a Thai menu, and chicken nuggets and other stuff deemed fit for kids.

limited-edition print of photographer Mike Furber's British landscapes.

'Smoker, mate? Like a puff?' murmurs a bloke rather at odds with this genteel setting. He sells various mixtures of herbal tobacco. 'Just like the real thing – but legal.' Some of the more interesting stalls of ethnic goods are also inside the hall. One has Native American artefacts, including peace pipes and beads; another displays chunky Kenyan jewellery; a third has handmade recycled Nubian glassware from southern Egypt.

Here you can also have your future told by a tarot-card reader, have your name written in Chinese at the Chinese calligraphy stall, buy a pottery pendant imprinted with runes or a piece of toast turned into a clock, procure a leather punch-bag and boxing gloves, or order a wedding cake. There are a couple of antiques stalls full of old glassware and crockery, but most goods are new. Sadly, a stall of crockery in bright, original designs attracts less interest than a nearby pitch filled with dreary Victoriana.

Yes, it's all rather dignified at Merton Abbey Mills, without Camden's rough edges or Brick Lane's spontaneity. But mass-produced goods are, for once, in a minority here, so there are plenty of diverting wares to look at, even if you don't buy. What's more, the market makes a fine place for a family outing, sited away from busy roads and with plenty for children to enjoy, be it the toy stalls, the theatre, the watermill, or the faggots and mushy peas (*see* Food and Drink, p.136).

NINE ELMS SUNDAY MARKET

New Covent Garden Market, Nine Elms Lane, SW8, **t** *(01895) 639912.*

Transport: ⊖ *Vauxhall;* ⇌ *Battersea Park, Vauxhall; then buses 44, 344.*

Open: *Sun 8am–2pm.*

Best time to go: *Early for the secondhand bargains.*

Parking: *There's free parking on site, but space is limited.*

Main wares: *Clothing, tools, meat, fruit and vegetables, secondhand books, bric-a-brac and junk.*

Specifics: *Look for bargains among the secondhand stalls.*

Since fruit, vegetable and flower trading moved out of Covent Garden to Nine Elms in 1974, over a million tons of produce have passed through the drearily functional buildings of Britain's largest horticultural market every year. But Sunday is the wholesalers' day of rest (at least until 11pm), so once a week the wide open spaces where juggernauts are loaded become the site of a retail market. Or rather two markets. For, as well as the dealers selling new goods, there's a car boot sale tacked on each week. Altogether, more than 150 traders turn up.

The approach to the market can seem off-putting. Railway sidings, the famous disused Battersea Power Station and Battersea Dogs Home are near neighbours, and the 68-acre site has been designed to ease the access of immense cabbage-laden lorries, rather than with any aesthetic consideration. Cars are ushered along concrete ramps and thoroughfares to be parked by the main market buildings.

Food plays only a minor role and, despite the location, there's only one fruit and vegetable stall. Here the stallholders tempt customers into buying at least 2lbs of produce at a time, bellowing 'Any scoop you like for £1.' The selection is fairly unadventurous. A big meat lorry turns up each week, and the butcher also sells in bulk, asking £5 for 4lbs of pork chops, for instance. Otherwise, you might find eggs, a stall full of bread and pastries, and the ubiquitous burger van.

Though most of the stalls in the new goods section are typical of Sunday markets – sweatshirts, jumpers, sportswear, cushions, leather jackets, greetings cards, dresses, underwear, bedsheets and duvets, cheap CDs, car-cleaning stuff, pyjamas,

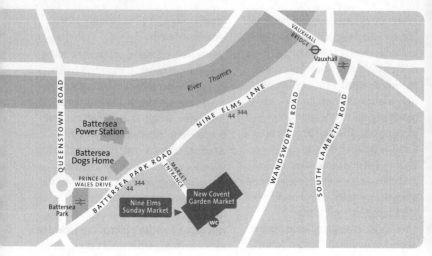

training shoes and electrical goods – there is the occasional oddity. One stallholder has a bewildering variety of goods, stocked higgledy-piggledy: royal jelly and cod liver oil, tools, nails and screws, cassettes and video tapes, cheap oil paints for artists, and plastic dinosaurs. A few stalls display children's wear, and you'll also find pet food, leather bags, jewellery, toys, watches, cameras, boots and shoes, wooden fruit, dried flowers, tools, lace, candles and aromatherapy goods. There are several household-goods pitches, including a particularly well-stocked stall full of unglamorous but useful bits and bobs, such as packs of indigestion tablets, umbrellas and plastic food bags. Another stall sells smoking paraphernalia: pipes, bongs and papers.

It is the 30 or 40 stalls selling second-hand clobber that hold most interest for the market connoisseur, however. The scope is wide: old clothing, scuffed suitcases, curled-up shoes and golf balls, as well as a variety of elderly electrical goods – TVs, videos, stereos, laptops. The stallholders seem scrupulously honest when it comes to pricing. One trader, when asked the cost of an ancient-looking video, replied: 'Well, this morning it was £20, but then I found out it doesn't work, so it's a fiver.'

Occasionally you might be tempted to make a beautifully pointless purchase, perhaps a pocket diary that got wet in a flood and now has a nasty stain across half the pages – it only costs 10p, and so what if all the days are marked in Portuguese?

There's a mix of genuine part-time car booters and professional traders. One of the former has some fantastic bargains among his boxes of old books: eight Penguin Classic paperbacks in good condition (by Nabokov, Sartre and Somerset Maugham, among others) go for 50p. Of course, stock changes every week, so get ready to encounter anything:

Food and Drink

Apart from the burger vans and stalls selling spit-roasted chicken (a whole bird for £5) at the market, the only chance of food nearby is at the **Market Café**, inside the market buildings. All the usual breakfast fry-ups are served.

The **George II**, at 339 Battersea Park Road, is an upmarket pub incorporating a restaurant area.

a collection of old toilets, army-surplus clothes, vast numbers of records, books, and even a stall full of press photos.

A couple of the shadier professional operators arrive in battered lorries and sell old televisions or vacuum cleaners from them. Fortunately they also carry generators, so you can test the stock before purchasing it. One trader has the nerve to offer six-month guarantees. Another likely lad is selling arson-proof letter boxes and some new books. His stock includes a pamphlet entitled *How I Cured My Duodenal Ulcer*. He displays it with his cookery books... Perhaps it *is* a cookery book.

As you trudge back towards the car park, loaded with bargains or baloney, just occasionally you'll spot an enormous carrot or a squashed onion lying on the tarmac, to remind you of the other market that takes place here the rest of the week.

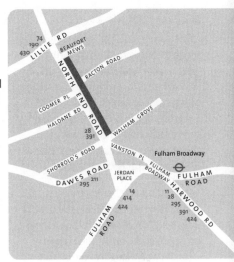

NORTH END ROAD

North End Road, SW6.

Transport: ☉ *Fulham Broadway; buses 11, 14, 28, 74, 190, 211, 295, 391, 414, 424, 430.*
Open: *Mon, Tues and Thurs–Sat 9am–5pm; Wed 9am–12.30pm.*
Best time to go: *Saturday, early afternoon.*
Parking: *There is pay-and-display parking off North End Road on Racton Road, Coomer Place or Sedlescombe Road.*
Main wares: *Fruit and veg, household goods, clothes.*
Specifics: *Cheap fruit and veg, fish.*

Unlike Chelsea, which has always been associated with the nobs, Fulham was once a working-class area. And – despite gentrification during the 1970s and 80s – parts of it still are. This helps to explain why North End Road has the only traditional street market north of the river in southwest London. It is probably one of the city's older markets; street trading took place at Walham Green (now the area around Fulham Broadway) in the Middle Ages. The traders moved on to North End Road in the 1880s, spreading northwards almost as far as Hammersmith until 1927, when the council limited them to the area south of Lillie Road.

Well into the 19th century, Fulham was noted for its market gardens, and no doubt these once provided the traders with much of their produce. Today North End Road is still an excellent source of cheap fruit and vegetables, with traders in fresh food taking the lion's share of the 60 or so pitches from Walham Grove to Beaufort Mews on the east side of North End Road. Old Crowther Market, the antiques market, has been replaced by a housing development.

The costermongers take great pride in their stalls, and much of the produce is beautifully displayed. Traders tend to specialize, selling fruit ('Geoff's the name

Food and Drink

There are a couple of fish and chip shops along the market stretch of North End Road. Try **The Café Fish Bar** at No.348, which is clean, has somewhere to sit and also serves kebabs and Jamaican patties.

Another option is the **Fox & Pheasant**, an old-fashioned little pub that's a 10-minute walk away, past Chelsea Football Club's ground at No.1 Billing Road.

– fruit's the game'), vegetables or salad goods. There are two cheese stalls with a large selection of different cheeses, and an egg stall which sells ducks' eggs.

For the whole length of the market, pitches are cut into the pavement so that trading doesn't hinder the busy traffic on the road. The space also gives stallholders enough room between the pavement and the road. There are always plenty of shoppers, as local stores complement the market well. One of the best butchers is **Dickenson's** at No.365, which has wall-to-wall meat inside, and up to a dozen lads getting down to it with cleavers.

There are other traders who don't sell food. You can buy posters (£1 each), football hats and scarves, net curtains (£10) and jewellery. Several traders deal in new clothes – however, there's little out of the ordinary. In winter, one does a good line in woolly hats, scarves and gloves. Further along, women's coats and jackets go on show.

A brace of stalls specialize in cut flowers, while mobile-phone holders, calculators, handbags, duvet covers, rugs and greetings cards can also be had along the street. But North End Road is principally a food market, and, in addition to the wealth of fruit and vegetable stalls, you'll also find sweets, cakes and biscuits, and a splendid wet-fish stall where grass carp, crabs and talapia might be exhibited alongside the cod and mussels.

NORTHCOTE ROAD

Northcote Road, SW11, **t** *(020) 8871 6384.*

Transport: ⇌ *Clapham Junction; buses 35, 39, 77, 219, 319, 344, C3, G1.*

Open: *See individual markets.*

Best time to go: *Saturday.*

Parking: *There are pay-and-display machines on the west side of Northcote Road and most side streets.*

Main wares: *Fruit and vegetables, fish, clothes, antiques.*

Specifics: *Flowers, foliage, crafts, antique jewellery.*

The semi-gentrified districts of London are a joy. In the 1980s, houses in several areas that had traditionally been home to the families of office clerks or factory foremen were snapped up by young professionals. By the time of the collapse in property prices of the early 1990s, these districts had a noticeable but not overwhelming cluster of new arrivals. Northcote Road typifies the colourful clash of class cultures that ensued.

Though the gentrification process has marched on into 2006, Northcote Road remains a cosmopolitan, stimulating area and its markets reflect this diversity. The general market provides most daily essentials, while the antiques market stocks mantelpiece fillers prized by couples restoring their late-Victorian abodes. The new arrivals support a scattering of alluring luxury food shops, while local people with modest incomes keep the fry-up cafés and cheap hardware stores in business.

General Market

Northcote Road (west side), between Bennerley Road and Battersea Rise, SW11.
Open Mon–Sat 9am–5pm.

Northcote Road and its market have a similar ancestry to several other shopping streets in London's suburbs. First came the railway station, in this case Clapham Junction, built in 1863 and now one of the busiest train stations in the world. Then followed the housing: grey-brick Victorian terraces were built all around the Northcote Road area during the 1870s and 1880s. Soon after came the market.

At first traders gathered on Lavender Hill, Falcon Road and St John's Road, as well as Northcote Road. But in 1910 they were evicted from St John's Road (where most of the dull high-street chains can now be found) and Northcote Road became the prime site. In recent years the success of the market has been helped by the proximity of New Covent Garden wholesale market, which moved to Nine Elms in the 1970s. Northcote Road is now a healthy local market, with about 30 traders setting up stall on a Saturday and over half that number in the week.

Most of the traders here deal in fresh produce. A flower seller takes one of the first pitches at the northern end of the market. As well as the usual blooms, she stocks the dried and fresh foliage used to decorate fashionable Clapham homes; there's also a good choice of perennials. A nearby salad stall also has some upmarket touches, displaying *lollo rosso* and *frisée* as well as the traditional bunches of watercress. Vegetable stalls might have fresh thyme, butternut squash and artichokes, as well as the more usual British crops; fruit stalls could have papaya, figs and coconuts alongside their grapes, apples and oranges. There's a well-stocked bread and cake stall offering a wide range of speciality breads, home-baked carrot cakes and French chocolate eclairs. There are also two French deli stalls that sell cheese, olives, olive oil and soap, in addition to the French market that Northcote Road regularly plays host to. Another stall has silk clothing and handbags, while yet others sell shirts, socks, jumpers and rugs.

Antiques Markets

155a Northcote Road, SW11, t (020) 7228 6850, and 70 Chatham Road, SW11. Open Mon–Sat 10am–6pm, Sun 12–5pm.

Ten minutes' walk south of the fruit and veg stalls is the main site of the indoor antiques market. It opened in 1986, occupying the ground and first floor of a Victorian terraced shop. In 1994 another

Food, Drink and Shopping

Eating places vary from basic caffs to fashionable Italian venues. **Crumpet** (No.66), fantastic, child-friendly 'tea room' with good selection of cakes and sandwiches; baby menu, too. **Osteria Antica Bologna** (No.23) is a cosy Italian restaurant with a modish regional menu. It's open all day on Saturdays. The most popular place to hang out at lunchtime is **Buona Sera** (No.22), a crowded but usually enjoyable pizzeria with tables outside so you can eye up the market crowds.

There are several enticing food shops along Northcote Road. **A. Dove and Son**, the butcher's at No.71 (established in 1889), has a fine stock of game in season and organic meat all year round. **Hamish Johnston's** cheese shop, at No.48, has a range of British and Continental cheeses, plus extra-virgin olive oils. **Kelly's Organic Foods** at No.46 is popular with the new locals, while near the antiques market, at No.135, is the **Grape Shop**, with cases of vintage wines.

annexe was opened further up the street, at the corner with Chatham Road.

A big advantage here is that you can be fairly sure that all the stalls will be open, as traders co-operate in running the venture and look after each other's businesses on a rota basis. There's space to cram 40 dealers into the small building. To make more room, some pieces are kept outside in fine weather. Within are traders specializing in jewellery, glassware and Art Deco ceramics. Most, however, have a selection of goods, perhaps some silver cutlery, a few murky old paintings, the odd necklace or set of cut-glass drinking vessels, and various pieces of Wedgwood-like crockery.

A silver cigarette case from 1936 is displayed on one stall; on another there's a section devoted to cricket prints, but more interesting is the picture of a hot-air balloon ascent at Vauxhall Gardens. Some 19th-century corkscrews are also diverting, widely varying in their designs. Silverware, jewellery and ceramics account for the wares on most of the remaining stalls.

Upstairs there's more of the same. The display of Clarice Cliff ceramics from the 1930s is particularly impressive, but equally alluring (and a great deal cheaper at £2) is a kitsch My Little Pony snow jar. Such is the range of goods that at the next stall you might find a Napoleon III *encrier* (inkpot) or an early TV in Bakelite. **Wally's Lunch Box**, an inexpensive café, takes up the remaining space, serving all-day breakfasts, lunches such as chicken and mushroom casserole or *salade niçoise*, and sandwiches to dealers and their customers.

The annexe to the market is even smaller. Old chairs, bedside cabinets and the like are put out for display, and the furniture theme continues on the ground floor, with pine dressers and tables. A selection of glassware and cutlery is also on show. In the basement is a greater variety of goods in a slightly bigger space. A chipped enamel soup ladle costs a pricey £12 at the antique kitchenware stall, while nearby a 1940s Anglepoise lamp has a £85 price tag. You'll also find a fine collection of vintage fountain pens (a Swan Blackbird from the 1920s costs £40), some glassware and ceramics, and a little cubby hole full of old prints and paintings.

Though a notch above most bric-a-brac, the goods sold at both these sites tend to fall into the category of 'collectibles' rather than that of expensive antiques. The polished presentation and hefty prices of Chelsea and parts of Portobello or Camden Passage are absent here, making browsing all the more pleasurable.

TOOTING

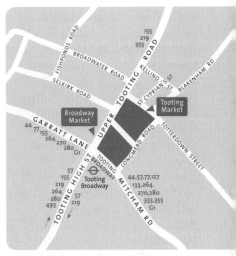

Upper Tooting Road, SW17.

Transport: ⊖ *Tooting Broadway; buses 44, 57, 77, 127, 133, 155, 219, 264, 270, 280, 333, 355, 493, G1.*

Open: *Mon, Tues and Thurs–Sat 9am–5pm; Wed 9am–1pm.*

Best time to go: *Friday and Saturday.*

Parking: *Try the side streets to the north of the markets.*

Main wares: *Fruit and vegetables, meat, fish, clothes, household goods, records and tapes, fabrics, furniture.*

Specifics: *Afro-Caribbean foodstuffs, fish, pet foods, babywear.*

Tooting remained a small settlement until late in the 19th century. But soon after the London County Council was formed in 1889 it decided to turn the Totterdown area of Tooting into a housing estate. The district was covered in the suburban terraced houses that still provide homes to the customers of Tooting's two markets. These occupy almost adjacent indoor halls, both built in the 1930s off one of the borough's main roads. They look similar to the indoor arcades found at Brixton (*see* p.124), with fixed lock-up stalls on either side of a corridor, but here trading is on a more modest level.

Tooting is an appealing place, a typical London suburb but none the worse for that. You'll rarely find excesses of wealth or poverty, and there's a pleasing mix of communities – Afro-Caribbean, Irish,

South Asian and English. Both markets reflect this, and provide a useful range of goods that undercut the chainstores on Tooting Broadway and Mitcham Road and complement the collection of takeaways, Indian food shops and discount stores on Tooting High Street and the Upper Tooting Road.

Tooting Market

Entrance also on Totterdown Street, SW17.

I like starting an exploration of Tooting's markets from this building, the furthest from the tube station, though only a 5-minute walk away. And I always begin the adventure from Totterdown Street, partly because of the splendid name, but also to approach the market from a residential street. This makes it seem all the more part of the neighbouring community – a local treat.

Though the structure of the 1930s building is somewhat spare, all corrugated roofing and metal girders, the lock-ups within are colourful and brightly lit. Two of the best food stalls greet you at the Totterdown Street end. **Steve's** green-grocers has a large stock of traditional root vegetables, oranges and lemons, but also exotic fruits such as prickly pears and pomegranates. Next, the large butcher's shop usually has some goat's meat (often used in Caribbean cookery) among its stewing steak and loins of pork. But, unlike the halal meat merchants of Brixton and Ridley Road, these butchers – a cheery gang of lads who heave great trolley-loads of carcasses in from the street first thing in the morning – steer clear of offal specialization.

The 30-odd businesses at Tooting Market provide a well-balanced mix of goods. **Mac's** children's wear stall ('the best for less') has baby clothes, rattles and bottles. There's a large cut-flowers stall and another selling oriental foodstuffs (packets of noodles, fresh beansprouts and the like), and a women's wear trader with a yen for polyester and sequins and jeans for £10. Close to the corner of the L-shaped trading floor is the **Tropicana Café** where you can wolf down a fried breakfast, 'dripping toast' or two eggs and bubble and squeak, while gazing at the wood-veneer walls.

Khan's Music Centre specializes in Indian and Arabic CDs and DVDs with a good stock of Bollywood movies. Near the High Street entrance there's a **Chinese Medicine Clinic** to treat all ailments.

Meat is mundane by comparison, but **Stannards of Tooting** stocks great mounds of it at low prices (5lbs of oxtail for £4.99). Nearby, **Caribs International Foods** sells a fine array of packaged and fresh Afro-Caribbean foods including fresh 'garden eggs' (small yellow Ghanaian aubergines) and pigs' tails. Hot snacks, drinks and breakfast are available from **Nandino's Diner Delight**. Further along, a greetings card stall also has boardgames, jigsaws and stationery. A sizeable haberdashery

stall comes next, while another Tooting lock-up will supply much of what you might need to equip a kitchen, including glasses, crockery, cutlery and swing bins. **Tiêm Vàng** sells and repairs jewellery.

The remainder of the market is taken up by **Swan's** bookshop, dealing mostly in secondhand pulp fiction; **Gary's Galleries**, with Gary's collection of shiny, cheap ornamental brassware; and **AJ's Allsorts**, which resembles a corner shop in its range of packet foods and household goods. At the Upper Tooting Road end is an old-fashioned tobacconist (selling clay pipes, pipe cleaners and 'Medicated No.99 Snuff'), and a bright and bustling fruit and veg pitch, where the traders flog their surplus off cheap at 5pm on Saturdays.

As you leave Tooting Market and emerge onto the main road, take a look at the building's Art Deco façade, which makes it seem almost like a cinema. But there's scarcely time to muse, as bellowing fruit and veg traders from both here and the Broadway Market spill out onto the pavement, nearly colliding in the middle.

Broadway Market

Entrance also on Longmead Road, SW17.

The Broadway Market, built in 1936, is a little larger and a mite gloomier than its neighbour. It also duplicates several of the stalls of Tooting Market: there are a couple of large fruit and vegetable pitches (one does a good line in fresh herbs), a butcher's (selling pheasants, in season), a florist's, a fishmonger's, a haberdashery stall and a key cutter.

You'll find a better choice of Afro-Caribbean produce at the Broadway, with two well-stocked stalls. I saw some enormous shellfish-type beasts, which turned out to be African land snails, and there were some of the small, dried

Food and Drink

Harrington's pie and mash shop, just across Upper Tooting Road on Selkirk Road, is a peach among pie shops, open since 1916 and with prices among London's lowest. Tooting is also a great area for Indian food; three of the best restaurants, all low-priced, are: **Shree Krishna** (192–4 Upper Tooting Road), a south Indian specialist; **Jaffna House** (90 Tooting High Street), a Tamil Sri Lankan café; and **Lahore Karahi** (1 Tooting High Street, at the corner of Totterdown Street), with superb Pakistani tandoori food.

The **Castle** (38 Tooting High Street) is a large, friendly pub where Young's ales are quaffed in earnest.

variety, along with soursop nectar, tinned ackee, a contorted mass of dried fish, yam flour, four species of hot pepper and eight types of yam. One of the stalls, **Tropical Fresh**, lists: 'grace mackerel, Yeoman's Indian Head, saltfish, pigtails, egg nog and oblayo' among its stock. If you're hungry and wary about taking a nibble at Yeoman's Indian Head, try the Caribbean takeaway stall which is close at hand. I've tried *kenkey* (a glutinous cornmeal paste with a sour lime flavour) before, and didn't relish the experience, but the rice and peas with chicken, and fried fish seem alluring. Other snacks are provided by a hot doughnut stall, **Carlo's** coffee bar, which does all-day breakfasts, a fried fish and *kenkey* stand, and **Poppashaw**, which supplies copious quantities of fresh popcorn.

A few of the clothes stalls also veer from the norm. Keep an eye out for the Indian women's wear stall **Saree Hut** and its striking *salwar khamese* robes, saris and pashminas for £1.99. **Kim Thanh Nails and Fashions** sells Thai clothing for women,

and nail accessories. There are two boutiques run by Afro-Caribbean women and both have a good line in snazzy party clothes; one sells wedding dresses, too. Several other stalls are also aimed at the black women's fashion market. The beautiful, exuberantly coloured fabrics favoured by African women are stocked by one; another deals in wigs and hair accessories. There are also cosmetics and perfumery stands and several nail bars with an array of false nails, sporting incredible designs, on offer.

Close by is a specialist in reggae, ska, soul, swing, soca, gospel, African and dub-imports; perturbingly, these CDs also share shelf space with a Des O'Connor album and *Mrs Mills' All Time Party Dances*. Similarly odd mixes of wares are sold at a stall where fresh eggs are stocked next to artificial flowers and foliage.

Also worthy of mention at Broadway Market is the large and well-stocked discount stationery stall, a watch and clock vendor's, a wool stall, a hairdresser's, a dealer in leather jackets, and Tooting's best pet store – to find it, just follow the chirping of birds that fills this section of the market. The latter is divided into two. Part one contains livestock, including tropical fish and goldfish, hamsters, several finches and budgerigars. Next door is an abundance of pet foods and accessories, from 'pussy pyramids' (for cats to scratch) and dog baskets, to books.

Whereas Tooting Market is L-shaped, the Broadway more resembles a Y. The remainder of its space is taken up with a shoe-repairer's, a discount warehouse (with all manner of household goods stacked up under its 'everything for £1' sign) and traders selling leather belts, nighties, duvets, curtains, pillows, bags and party goods.

Both markets at Tooting have a fine, community feel to them. At 'knocking out' time on a Saturday, it's almost a local custom for a crowd to gather by the fresh produce stands, waiting to pounce on a bargain.

WIMBLEDON STADIUM

Wimbledon Stadium car park, Plough Lane, SW17, t (07956) 961640.

Transport: ⊖ *Wimbledon Park;*
≳ *Haydons Road; buses 44, 77, 156, 200, 270, 919.*

Open: *Sun 9am–2pm.*

Parking: *Plenty of free parking in the stadium car park. Arrive early.*

Main wares: *Clothing, tools, electrical goods, food, toys, toiletries, pet food, car and phone accessories, greetings cards, tapes, videos and CDs.*

Specifics: *Football strips, women's outsized clothing.*

Greyhounds bound around Wimbledon Stadium on weekday evenings, stockcars smash themselves to scrap on Sunday nights, but on Sunday mornings the stadium car park is given over to equally entertaining – and only slightly less frenetic – activity as over 80 stalls are set up for trading. As is the case with many of the newer breed of Sunday markets, cheap mass-produced clothing makes up a large slice of the wares sold here each week. Dozens of traders deal in jumpers and women's tops, and you'll have no trouble finding socks, underwear, shirts, women's jackets, skirts, new shoes and children's clothes. A few stalls have leather jackets, but not as many as you'll find at Petticoat Lane (*see* p.109) or Wembley (*see* p.91).

Wimbledon does a better line in football strips, with most of the Premiership teams represented; several stalls also sell mugs, scarves and hats emblazoned with team names.

A couple of traders specialize in large clothing for women. One, sadly, has stock that wouldn't look out of place at a Richard Clayderman concert, but the other has some more modish prints and frocks ranging from size 12 to size 30. Most jeans sold at the market don't have famous labels, but the going rate is under £20. There's also a good lingerie and bed-clothes stall, and two traders who sell waxed jackets for under £30.

The clothes stall with the most earnest group of customers sizing up its garments deals in imitation designer menswear – the ink barely dry on the labels. Calvin Klein, Ralph Lauren and Armani (long-sleeved grandad shirts for £15) all have their names displayed on the shirts. 'Guaranteed fakes', a scrawled notice proudly proclaims. Another stall, which must be equally unpopular with large fashion houses, sells fake perfumes. 'I smell like Opium' is one of a dozen or so signs written above the bottles. Each perfume costs about £5 – a snip, if you can stand the whiff.

Food forms only a minor part of the market's business. There's a small collection of fast food vendors, with baked potatoes, ice cream, doughnuts, Thai noodles, hamburgers and salt beef among the attractions, and a burger van advertising 'traditional home-cooked food'. Away from the rest of the stalls is a shellfish stand with the usual crab sticks, winkles, whelks and cockles. If you're shopping for your Sunday lunch, look out for bargains at either of the two meat lorries; one butcher is trying to sell three large joints of Scotch beef for £15. There's a big stall of sweets and two bakery stalls, one with soda bread and bread pudding as well as more mundane loaves, the other full of doughnuts and cakes. Close by, a trader is selling nuts, biscuits, cheese and gruesome-looking sealed plastic packs of cooked meat. At the three large fruit and veg stalls, all the traders try to sell in bulk, tying up plastic bags full of produce and flogging them for £1.

The social gap between punters that come to Wimbledon and those at Merton Abbey Mills (see p.133), little over a mile away, is almost as wide as the chasm between local dog-race enthusiasts and the select clique that occupies the Centre Court during Wimbledon fortnight.

Food and Drink

The **White Lion** and the **Plough** public houses are both opposite the entrance to Wimbledon Stadium on Plough Lane, and there are cafés on Summerstown Road. Alternatively, if you've a car and it's a fine day, take the 10-minute drive westwards for a picnic on Wimbledon Common (see Nearby Attractions).

Nearby Attractions

If you've come by car there are a couple of places a short drive away:

Wimbledon Common, ⊖ *Wimbledon*; ⇌ *Wimbledon*. Large common (over 1,100 acres) about a 10-minute drive from the market. There's a windmill with a museum and tea room attached, nature trail and golf course. If you're feeling active, there are tennis courts, playing fields and horse riding areas.

Wimbledon Lawn Tennis Museum, *Church Road, Wimbledon, SW19, t (020) 8946 6131, www.wimbledon.org/museum*; ⊖ *Wimbledon*; ⇌ *Wimbledon*. **Open** daily 10.30am–5pm; **adm** adults £6.50, children £5.50. Learn all about the famous international tennis tournament, including the quantity of strawberries consumed by spectators each year, at the reconstructed museum, reopened Easter 2006.

You won't find any secondhand or antique goods at Wimbledon. Rather like Wembley market, on a smaller scale, it provides high-street goods at less than high-street prices.

Pot plants and flowers, new books (mostly romances, thrillers and children's books), greetings cards, wrapping paper, towels and duvets, garden ornaments, pet food and curtain fabrics are all up for grabs. Two large stalls sell tools to Sunday DIYers: saws, clamps, chisels, wire brushes, paint sprays. One is full of electrical goods for the kitchen: irons, vacuum cleaners, kettles and saucepans.

As well as the usual cosmetics, blank video and cassette tapes, cheap jewellery, hair accessories, pot-pourri and handbag stalls, there's also stuff only seen at larger markets: video games, car accessories (seats, tow ropes, mats and the like), and two stalls selling mobile-phone carriers and batteries. One trader will even cut kitchen blinds to order. More mundane household goods range from light bulbs and soap to bin bags and bubble bath.

The large video stall sells new feature films for under a tenner, while children's films and 'pre-viewed' videos go for as little as £5. There are two traders in tapes and CDs. One is geared to dance music and has two large speakers belting out chart hits. He also sells empty CD cases and cardboard slips for 45rpm records. The other has plenty of Irish music, but also soul and reggae.

A few traders sell toys: one gigantic stall occupies a juggernaut at the northern end of the market. A crowd gathers as the seller goes through his spiel, with his helpers carrying large robots, Action Men and Tonka trucks out to the buyers. Towards 2pm the action reaches a climax as the toy seller drops his prices and his (amplified) voice competes with the lusty roar of a costermonger flogging the last of his produce off cheap. A mad cacophony ensues as 'Who'll give me £5 for a dinosaur? Come next week and it'll be twice the price,' coalesces with 'A pound a bag of peppers.'

Five times a year there is a record/CD fair (9am–3.30pm) held inside the stadium, specializing in nostalgia, but also offering pop music.

As you leave, you might catch a glimpse through the stadium fencing of a sign urging owners to extract as much urine as possible from their greyhounds for chromatography testing. On Sunday mornings, the fun is in watching traders trying to perform the same task on the punters.

Southeast London

07

BERMONDSEY (NEW CALEDONIAN)

Bermondsey Square, SE1, t (020) 7525 5000.
Transport: ⊖ *Borough, London Bridge;*
⇌ *London Bridge; buses 1, 17, 21, 35, 40, 42, 43, 47, 48, 78, 133, 141, 149, 188, 343, 381, 521, night buses N1, N21.*
Open: *Fri 4am–2pm; traders start packing up around 11am.*
Best time to go: *As early as possible.*
Parking: *There's usually space in the side streets away from the square, but don't leave valuables in your car.*
Main wares: *Antiques.*
Specifics: *Paintings, ornaments, jewellery – anything collectible; expect low prices, but no 'finds'.*

Dawn on Long Lane. A paltry procession of grey-faced commuters, in cars and on foot, heads for the City and the early shift. No sign of life there. A gale is blowing, and it's raining. Then you notice a few figures darting in and out of a Victorian warehouse. As you approach, more people emerge. These are no commuters: they look wide awake. Many have been here for hours, buying and selling at London's biggest wholesale antiques market.

This weekly event has one of the longest and most fascinating histories of all London markets. Its lineage can be traced back to the Middle Ages, when a Friday market was held near Smithfield on the site of the annual Bartholomew Fair (immortalized by Ben Jonson in the play of the same name). Traders used to vie for the custom of farmers who had brought their livestock to market at Smithfield. When the livestock market was moved to Copenhagen Fields near Caledonian Road in 1855, the pitchers, who by then dealt mainly in old clothes, followed. The Friday market grew tremendously in the first decades of the 20th century, fuelled by the new fashion for collecting antiques, which the traders had begun to stock. In the 1920s and 30s the 'Cally', as it became known, reached its zenith, filling the square-mile site and attracting more than 2,500 stalls and crowds of up to 100,000.

The Second World War closed down this magnificent spectacle. When the conflict was over, the traders were refused permission to return. In 1949, 13,500 people signed a petition demanding the market's reopening. The Court of Common Council rejected the petition, and in the following year the present site in war-damaged, working-class Bermondsey was found. All that remains of the old Cally are three huge pubs, the central clocktower, and a few street names such as Pedlars Walk and Market Road. Although the New Caledonian attracts over 250 stalls each week, including dealers from all over southern England plus a fair few from the Continent, the huge crowds and cockney 'silver kings' of the 1930s have gone.

The traders of Bermondsey market proper occupy two patches of land by Bermondsey Square, where their treasures are exposed to the weather. Most articles up for sale date from 1850 to 1950; the majority are English. Several paintings go on display each week, most by obscure artists in styles varying from pastoral to Cubism. Other traders specialize in farmyard animals, writing cases, carriage clocks, silverware, workmen's tools, binoculars, model vintage cars or trains, golfing equipment, perfume bottles, or old walking sticks. Some stalls are well ordered, others not, but there is little that seems worthless. You won't find the piles of junk you get at Brick Lane or Westmoreland Road, but nor will you uncover giveaway bargains; the prices here are on the high side, but it's worth haggling.

This said, there's plenty to engross even the most eccentric of enthusiasts. Why not start a collection with a croquet mallet, a Victorian urine-testing kit, a boxed set of dumbbells from the 1950s, an edition of *Playboy* magazine from 1954, an Empire State Building ashtray, a stuffed boar's head, some ancient luggage (apparently made out of solid oak) and a cumbrous 19th-century diver's helmet straight out of a Jules Verne novel? One stall has old rifles, guns, swords, scabbards and various African curios including a crudely carved wooden figure from which nails protruded; it turned out to be a nail fetish from Zaire. Another's stock consists entirely of old spirit levels and wooden bowls. Some of the traders seem equally bizarre, wearing battered top hats or ancient fur coats while pouring a cup of tea from their Thermos.

There are stalls specializing in old ship equipment (an 1895 single bridge telescope for £325) and late 19th-century ceramic pots – these formerly contained such tasty delights as anchovy paste, tooth powder and the wonderfully named Darby's Fluid Meat, as well as various concoctions from the halcyon period of patent remedies. Pity the poor soul whose affliction forced the use of D. Nelson's Improved Inhaler for Hot Water Infusions. Tucked away among the antiques a man has organic runner beans and rosemary for sale, and there are a couple of burger vans selling hot food. You can also find a good deal of Charles and Di wedding crockery for sale – much of it suspiciously well preserved.

The warehouse at the junction of Long Lane and Bermondsey Street contains the first of several privately run indoor sales that surround the main market. This one, confusingly, is named **Bermondsey**

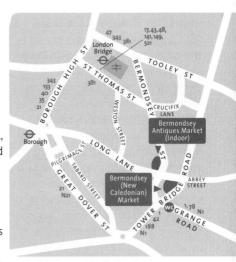

Antiques Market. The half-dozen or so stalls outside are just a prelude to the scores that fill every cranny of the ramshackle building. Antiquarian books (mostly Victorian), wooden carpenters' tools (beautifully worn), silverware, jewellery, pocket watches, prints, ornaments – the variety is stupefying. Some stalls are well ordered, others higgledy-piggledy, but most stock is in good repair, and everything seems to have a price tag: this is no junk market. One stall has a fascinating collection of Victorian mechanical devices, including several symphonions – Swiss-made musical machines from the turn of the 20th century, which briefly rivalled the phonograph in popularity. Best described as a cross between a gramophone and a music box, they play record-sized discs in which are cut small holes to allow rows of tuned metal teeth to pick out a merry tune (invariably a waltz). A small gramophone-sized model will set you back at least £1,000, while the Wurlitzer-sized version can cost 20 times as much. The basement contains an antique furniture shop, while upstairs there are more stalls, including a bookshop accessible via the coffee shop.

Just off the market, on Tower Bridge Road, is another indoor market bearing the words, 'Shipping Goods, Clocks, China and Brass' over the door. Inside you'll discover a variety of knick-knacks, pieces of furniture and silverware.

It's worth exploring the area around Bermondsey Square, as much of it is given over to the antiques trade. You're likely to encounter dealers, hunched over the back of a Volvo estate, haggling over the price of an *objet d'art*; or you might see a van drawing up and being emptied of Victorian armchairs. Bermondsey Street, a rather dingy old road to the north of the square, has warehouses full of antiques, especially furniture. A stone's throw along Tower Bridge Road, southwest of the antiques trading, is a smaller general market. Up to a dozen stalls are set up on the wide pavement outside the oldest pie and mash shop in London (**M. Manze** at 87 Tower Bridge Road). Fruit, vegetables, household goods, sweets and eggs can be bought here.

Over the years, more and more tourists have discovered Bermondsey market, but before 9am few of them are simply sightseers. Knowledgeable American, German, Japanese and French collectors come to scrutinize the goods, perhaps realizing that many of the articles bought and sold here will reappear at Portobello Road or Camden Passage at a higher price. Some stallholders proffer joke quotes in euros, no doubt a foretaste of things to come. A bureau de change on the ground floor of the Bermondsey Antiques Market does some brisk early morning trading.

On Bermondsey Street, there are a few more antiques shops and indoor salerooms mostly selling furniture; they include **Penny Farthing Antiques** at No.177.

As 9am approaches, the pace at the antiques market gets less frenetic as late risers come to browse along the stalls.

Food and Drink

For liquid refreshment, try **The Hand and Marigold** pub, at the corner of Cluny Place and Bermondsey Street, which opens at 7am on Fridays. Early-morning fried breakfasts, including black pudding and bubble and squeak, can be had at the **Rose Dining Room** (210 Bermondsey Street). Otherwise, there are vans in the square dispensing mugs of tea and filling the market with the smell of fried bacon.

Some visitors wander around the square – not an ugly place, with some Victorian buildings as well as a few grim modern flats. In the Middle Ages Bermondsey Abbey stood just off the present square on Bermondsey Street, next to St Mary Magdalen church. Behind its late-Georgian 'Gothick' façade, the present church is mostly 17th century. On the Tower Bridge Road, commuters in their cars seem oblivious to what they are missing.

BOROUGH

Off Borough High Street, London SE1, t (020) 7407 1002, www.boroughmarket. org.uk.

Transport: ⊖ *London Bridge;* ⇌ *London Bridge; buses 17, 21, 35, 40, 43, 47, 48, 133, 141, 149, 343, 381, 501, 521, RV1.*

Open: *Fri 12pm–6pm, Sat 9am–4pm.*

Best time to go: *Lunchtime.*

Parking: *Try Jubilee Market off Winchester Street, or Southwark Street on a Saturday; within the congestion charge zone.*

Main wares: *Organic food, farm produce, delicatessen food.*

Specifics: *Swedish delicatessen, ostrich meat and blown ostrich eggs.*

Borough Market is a busy, bustling food market located just off Borough High

Street opposite London Bridge station, with entrances from Stoney Street, Bedale Street or Borough High Street. Borough market differs from farmers' markets because it attracts traders from other countries, whereas farmers' markets only allow food produced locally. Occasionally, events and festivals are held here; see the website for details. A wide variety of produce is available at the market, from locally produced organic meat, dairy and veg to more exotic delicatessen food from round the world. The place has a lively atmosphere and can get very busy, but it is much more fun shopping here than in a supermarket and there's plenty of choice, although prices aren't low. There are also eight permanent food shops dotted in streets around the market, such as the **Monmouth Coffee Company** and **Neal's Yard Dairy**, both on Stoney Street.

As you go in the Stoney Street entrance, a bunch of traders sell seasonal veg such as kale and squashes in autumn and bright green and purple cauliflowers. They also stock cheese, dried mushrooms and fresh herbs. Next is the Wild Mushroom Company, which sells every variety of mushroom you can imagine. Opposite is

Elsey and Bent, with its collection of plants, herbs, bamboo and window boxes made to measure. There are lots more fruit and veg stalls inside the main hall. Two to look for are: **Turnips Distribution**, where if you're lucky you may experience opera singing as you're being served; and **Total Organics**, with 'vegetables that won't bite back', hot takeaway organic food, and soya products such as soya yoghurt.

Meat-eaters are catered for as well. You can buy ostrich meat and blown ostrich eggs (£8.50) from **Gamston Wood Farm**; **Mrs Elizabeth King's Pork Pies** from Melton Mowbray; venison from the west country; pork, ham, bacon and sausages from **The Ginger Pig**; and **Sillfield Farm**'s wild boar from Cumbria, sold by workers dressed in aprons and bowler hats.

A host of stalls stock goods from further afield. The Scandinavian delicatessen sells herrings, smoked eel, gravlax and meat-

---

Food and Drink

Hobbs Pie & Mash, on Bedale Street, under the bridge by Green Market, has takeaway pie and mash for £3.50. There's also a café in Southwark Cathedral. **Roast**, on the first floor of Floral Hall, Stoney Street (**t** (020) 7940 1300), is a stunning and smart new restaurant overlooking the market and specializing in British food with the emphasis on the quality of the produce – there are even unusual foraged vegetables on offer. You have to book ahead. On Stoney Street you'll also find **Konditor and Cook**, a bakery and café, at No.10, and for Japanese food go to **Feng Sushi**, at No.13. The pan-Asian deli and takeaway **Fuse Box**, at No.12, has delicious takeaway food boxes. **Cantina Vinopolis**, a wine bar and brasserie, is located at 1 Bank End. Wine buffs should head for **Vinopolis Wine Wharf**, on Stoney Street.

Nearby Attractions

Tate Modern, *Bankside Power Station,* **t** *(020) 7887 8000, www.tate.org.uk;* ✆ *Southwark;* **buses** *45, 63, 100, 344, 381, RV1.* **Open** *Sun–Thurs 10am–6pm, Fri and Sat 10am–10pm; charges for some special exhibitions.* London's most exciting museum of modern art, housing the national collection of international 20th-century and new art.

Millennium Bridge, ✆ *Southwark, Blackfriars;* **buses** *45, 63, 100, 344, 381, RV1.* The problem of the 'wobbles' has been solved and in early 2002 the first bridge across the Thames in more than a century reopened to pedestrians after being closed for almost two years.

Shakespeare's Globe, *21 New Globe Walk, box office* **t** *(020) 7401 9919, www.shakespeares-globe.org;* ✆ *Southwark, London Bridge;* **buses** *45, 63, 100, 344, 381, RV1.* **Performances** *May–Sept; tickets from £5. Shakespeare's Globe Exhibition* **open** *Oct–May daily 10am–5pm, May–Oct 9am–12pm and 12.30–5pm;* **adm** *adults £9, children £6.50.* A reconstruction of the original Globe theatre, where many of Shakespeare's plays were performed for the first time. See a performance of Elizabethan theatre, or take a tour.

HMS Belfast, Morgan's Lane, *off Tooley Street,* **t** *(020) 7940 6300, www.iwm.org.uk;* ✆ *London Bridge;* **buses** *17, 21, 43, 47, 48, 149, 381, 521, RV1.* **Open** *March–Oct daily 10am–6pm, Nov–Feb daily 10am–5pm;* **adm** *adults £8.50, under 16s free.* A survivor from the Second World War; its seven floors are open for you to wander round.

---

balls. The Spanish stall, **Brindisa**, now in a permanent spot by Floral Hall, sells olive oil, vinegar and *chorizos*. You can also buy Viennese jam or sausages and mustard from the German delicatessen and there are numerous chances to sample and buy olives and olive oil from Italy, feta cheese from Greece, chillis from Mexico – not to mention the dried fruit and roasted nuts from as far afield as Iran.

Other stalls in the main section include: one selling New Forest fruit wines, cider, perry and apple juice, and hot spiced cider – very warming on a cold day; **East Tea**, selling teas from Japan, Korea and Taiwan; coffee beans from **Monmouth Coffee Company**; pasta stalls with own-made pasta and sauces; several honey stalls selling many different varieties of honey, such as lavender; and a fish stall with Morecambe Bay potted shrimps, squid, swordfish and salmon.

There are lots of cheese stalls; one stocks goat's cheese, another specializes in cheese from Cheshire, there are pungent cheeses from France, and another sells delicious Welsh Caerphilly. Most traders put samples out to taste – it's quite possible to fill up completely on the little samples as you go round the market. You will also find vegan bread, fresh shellfish, cut flowers and chocolates, and in one corner of the market there is a man juggling fruit. Nearby there are fresh fruit smoothies on offer and the queue by the barbecued burger stall is always long.

Many more stalls can be found in the smaller section of the market. A trader selling garlic and tomatoes from the Isle of Wight has 'vampire relishes' and Transylvanian pickled garlic. Other stalls in this section include the **Dorset Blueberry Company**, **Mrs Bassa's Indian Kitchen**, selling sauces and pickles, and another Mexican food stall.

Food is not all you will find at Borough; there are also a handful of arts and crafts retailers, such as **Richard Bramble**'s hand-made porcelain plates and kitchenware, as well as organic beauty products such as

Wild Wood Grove's argan oil which is wild harvested in Morocco. Wine and beer lovers can visit a handful of vintners and, at **Utobeer**, find a range of organic beers impossible to find elsewhere.

This fine-food retail market is a new development, dating back to a Food Lovers' Fair organized here in 1998. However, the wholesale fruit and veg market that still trades on the site in the early hours of the morning can trace its history back to the Middle Ages (see p.8). Both markets are run by the Borough Market Trustees, with profits helping to fund local community projects.

The glass-and-iron structure that accommodates traders was constructed in 1851, though needed altering in 1862 after the building of the South Eastern Railway viaduct, which passes right over the top (clanking trains provide the market's muzak). It has been redeveloped sensitively, losing none of its original atmosphere, and now houses a huge range of stalls, many with painted signage above and dispensing a cornucopia of fresh and gourmet food to the hordes of people that flock to Borough. The market incorporates Covent Garden's Victorian cast-iron Floral Hall Portico into the Stoney Street frontage of the market, and a new two-storey building houses a stunning new restaurant on the first floor (see p.153) and food retailers and whole-sale businesses on the ground, such as **The Ginger Pig**, **Sillfield Farm** and **Brindisa**. Borough market's fine food reputation is now such that it was recently voted *Time Out* magazine's most popular market, and similar accolades have been heaped on the market by other London publications and visitor organizations. It is very rare in London in being able to accommodate visitors – from other parts of London, the UK and abroad – without losing its appeal

to locals. On Fridays and Saturdays, the place fairly fizzes with life and there is nothing else quite like it in London.

DEPTFORD

Deptford High Street, from Deptford Broadway to the railway bridge, SE8; Douglas Way, from Deptford High Street to Idonia Street, SE8; Douglas Square, off Douglas Way, SE8; **t** *(020) 8314 7111.*

Transport: ⇌/*DLR Deptford Bridge; buses 47, 53, 177, 188, 199, 225.*

Open: *Wed and Fri 8.30am–5pm, Sat 8.30am–6pm.*

Best time to go: *Saturday.*

Parking: *The side streets south of Deptford Broadway often have spaces.*

Main wares: *Deptford High Street – fresh food, household goods, clothing, bathroom goods, eggs, greetings cards, perfumes, cosmetics, lingerie, jeans, gold jewellery, books, stockings, socks, shoes, watches, hair accessories, net curtains, cut flowers; Douglas Way – secondhand clothing and records, bric-a-brac.*

Specifics: *Fabrics, children's clothes, haberdashery; look out for secondhand bargains.*

'You'd better watch it mate, they'll have your guts for garters down there.' This welcome to Deptford market, by a cheery trader who spotted my notebook and took me for a spy from the authorities, shows how the district is perceived from both within and without. To many north Londoners, Deptford symbolizes the untamed south: wild and forbidding. Even locals would term it rough and ready, with the emphasis on the rough. Although parts have been spruced up in recent years, you'll find nothing of Greenwich's gentility here. But Deptford flourishes on Saturdays,

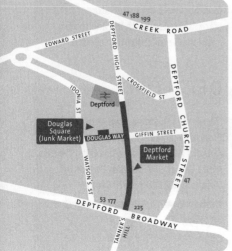

as well as the usual country and western, and 'hits of the 1960s' compilations for £3.99. It also has a small collection of video games. There are different sounds blasting from every few stalls, giving the market a varied soundtrack.

Although most of the stallholders are white, the Afro-Caribbean presence at the market has increased in recent times and now better reflects the ethnic make-up of the area. Stalls such as **African Ties** and **Cards of Colour** at **Trading Places**, a small arcade near the anchor, cater specifically for this section of the community. The **Kosan Café** here serves West Indian dishes such as jerk chicken and salt fish. Even the old costermongers whose families have run a stall for decades now sell okra and fresh ginger, and even a few yams, alongside their cabbages. It's the same story with the High Street's butchers; though many are long-established, they now sell cows' feet and goats' meat.

The market is particularly well supplied with fish; sea bass, conger eels, red snapper and catfish can all be picked up relatively cheaply. For electrical goods try **Electric**

when it is home to one corker of a market. The area is set for regeneration, meaning that the usual struggle with property developers for the future of the market is in the offing: go while you still can.

Starting at the Deptford Broadway end of the High Street, the first thing you'll notice is a huge anchor, a reminder of the district's maritime connections. The market crowds surround it, gathered in front of a trader selling knives for all he's worth: 'You know, they retail for £14.95 at a certain shop, but I'm not allowed to tell you the name of the shop...Asda [uttered in the largest stage whisper in Deptford]. Eeyaa, I'll tell you what I'll do, while the guvnor's on holiday. (We always have a sale when he goes missing. Don't tell him when you see him next week.) I'm not going to charge you £8 or £6. Not even going to charge you £5. *Three pounds to clear*.'

Prices are low throughout the market's 250 or so stalls. Along the High Street are dozens of clothes pitches, going from piles of garments on a barrow, all for £1.50, to women's glitzy nightclub wear. A CD and tape stall has some chart albums selling for about half the price you'd pay in a shop,

Food, Drink and Shopping

W. H. Wellbeloved Butchers, just across Deptford Broadway from the High Street on Tanner's Hill, is a great old-fashioned butcher's shop, established in 1829, that specializes in hot baked pies. Deptford has two pie and mash shops on the High Street north of the market. **Manze's**, at No.204, is the most attractive. The **Hales Gallery** (70 Deptford High Street) is decidedly upmarket for the area, with Tuscan bean soup and vegetarian pizzas.

Just past the northern end of the market, **Eunice's Tropical Food Shop** stocks a wider range of African provisions than you'll find on the stalls.

Avenue, a shop named after the Brixton market street and Eddie Grant song.

Some stalls have spread onto Giffin Street, where there are some handy public toilets. Opposite Giffin Street is the market's other main thoroughfare, **Douglas Way**. Lewisham Council maintains that this is a completely separate market, but it keeps the same hours as Deptford High Street. Douglas Way traders sell fruit and veg, new clothes, household goods, fabrics, plants, leather bags, pet food and electrical goods, but the most interesting section is on Douglas Square, a small patch of land on your right as you walk from the High Street. Here, about 40 stalls display a wild variety of junk, from old records to lengths of electric flex and piles of old clothing. You may even come across secondhand spotlights or bathroom scales. One trader's wares consist solely of old cameras and mobile-phone batteries.

Deptford High Street market has existed for over a century, but has often had to battle with the street's shopkeepers for its existence. One such battle to save the market from being cleared off the road was won in the 1950s by Bill Gallagher, chairman of the Deptford Street Traders' Association. Mr Gallagher ran his stall for 70 years, dying in November 1994 at the age of 84.

The market has been at the forefront of Deptford's resurgence, attracting crowds to the area. On a Saturday afternoon, it's an exciting place to be.

EAST STREET

East Street, from Walworth Road to Dawes Street, SE17.

Transport: ⊖ *Elephant and Castle;*

⇌ *Elephant and Castle; buses 1, 12, 35, 40, 42, 45, 53, 63, 68, 100, 133, 155, 168, 171, 172, 176, 188, 343, 468, P5.*

Open: *Tues–Sat 8am–5pm, Sun 8am–2pm.*

Best time to go: *Sunday.*

Parking: *Try the side streets west of the Walworth Road.*

Main wares: *Clothing, household goods, fruit and vegetables, flowers and plants (Sunday only).*

Specifics: *Net curtains, haberdashery, shellfish, cheap jewellery, cut flowers, electrical goods, suitcases, foam rubber, shoes and trainers, cosmetics, women's hats, pet food, spectacles, carpets, crockery, cheap dried herbs, martial arts videos, mobile phone accessories.*

Busy through the week and heaving on Sundays, East Street – known to locals as 'the Lanes' – is where southeast Londoners like to come for a knees-up. Like its neighbour Westmoreland Road (*see* p.170), the street is in the heart of a huge working-class district built in the mid-19th century. Until 1880, traders set up their stalls on the main Walworth Road, but traffic and the laying of tram-rails forced them off. Nine years after the market moved to its present site, Charlie Chaplin was born at a house on East Street. Right up until 1939, one of the market's busiest times was Saturday

night, when women poured in after collecting their husbands' wages and trading went on to 11pm.

East Street traders guard their licences jealously, and several stalls have been passed down the generations. Only on Wednesdays can casuals get a look in. As a result, there are few black stallholders, despite the fact that many market customers are Afro-Caribbean. Even the stall selling West Indian fruit, veg and breads is run by a white costermonger.

There's a good spread of merchandise among the 250 or more stalls. The fish stalls sell mainly seafood, such as prawns and crab. Fruit and veg traders tend to occupy the Walworth Road end. However, though there are enough of them to keep prices low, food is only a sideline at East Street. As with most London markets that have been long-established on a Sunday, several stalls are run by Jewish traders; many of them deal in fabrics, mostly for curtains or upholstery, but there's also one who sells suit material.

There are plenty of cheap new clothes available: jeans for £10, skimpy tops for £4.99, trainers (Reeboks for under £40), two T-shirts for £5, football shirts for £15 – you can kit yourself out from head to toe in the red and blue of south London's premier football team (Crystal Palace, in case you were wondering) for under £50. Cheap socks are the stock in trade of 'The Sock King'.

At the Walworth Road end of East Street is a stall selling Moroccan crafts: tagines (the dishes with a conical shaped lid used for cooking stews); lamps with hand-painted leather lamp shades; pouffes; wooden furniture and sequinned slippers for a fraction of the price you pay in smart Notting Hill shops.

There are mobile phone stalls which sell sim cards, phone cases and other

Food and Drink

Marie's Snack Bar and Café (84 East Street) has salads, sandwiches, fry-ups and beans on toast. There are also burger vans, and one selling Chinese food.

There are several pubs along East Street, but try **The Bell**.

See also Westmoreland Road, p.171.

accessories. One trader resets security codes and unlocks mobile phones. Another sells 'magnets for health' which 'fight arthritis, rheumatics, migraine and many more illnesses'. Aloe leaves, the juice of which is good for the skin, can be found on one of the fruit and veg stalls. There are CD stalls selling Latin American, flamenco, soca and reggae. Other traders deal in perfume, books, net curtains, bedcovers, crockery, saucepans, spectacles and DIY tools – one has a box of drill bits, screwdrivers and other useful bits and bobs for £1 each.

Few shops would turn down the chance to cash in on crowds like these, so most of the small businesses that line East Street are open on Sunday. Some of them have their wares displayed outside. There are several discount stores stocked with the type of goods more often sold in markets, but also a good helping of butchers, including Mitchells of East Street, which supplies Arment's pie and mash shop on Westmoreland Road with its pies.

On Sundays, Blackwood Street, halfway along East Street, becomes south London's answer to Columbia Road flower market. About a dozen big stalls sell cut flowers, bulbs and shrubs, while Gypsy women proffer their sprigs of heather at the junction with East Street.

At Portland Street there's a minor hiatus, as this is the only thoroughfare where cars are allowed to cross East Street on Sundays. As you shuffle along with the crowd, look out for the beach stall full of bikinis and rubber rings (even in winter), another selling those Ronco labour-saving devices from the 1970s (the type that cut as they peel as they cook as they cut your hair), and yet another which sells nothing but doorknobs and masking tape. You'll also find stalls stacked with cheap Hollywood videos, the legal status of which is best indicated by the fact that you're not allowed to open the boxes until you've handed over your money. One of them specializes in the latest martial arts films. Nearby, a couple of lads are discussing last night's boxing match down the Old Kent Road. On Sundays the market ends at Dawes Street, which has about half a dozen stalls on it, including one selling 'cabbages': cheap clothes made from off-cut material.

The only thing missing from East Street is a secondhand and junk section, but Westmoreland Road is only a 10-minute walk away (see p.170). Taken together, these two markets make for an exhilarating Sunday treat.

GREENWICH

Off College Approach, Stockwell Street, Greenwich Church Street, Thames Street and Greenwich High Road, SE10, t (020) 8293 3110, www.greenwich-market.co.uk; see individual markets for details.

Transport: *≥/DLR Greenwich; buses 170, 177, 180, 188, 199, 286, 386, night bus N1.*

Open: *See individual markets for details.*

Best time to go: *Sunday.*

Parking: *Very difficult – most of the roadside parking is for residents only; try the area off Thames Street, or the meters on streets off Greenwich High Road.*

Main wares: *Secondhand goods, crafts, clothes, books, antiques.*

Specifics: *Prints, books, old jackets, dresses, military uniforms and collectibles; organic food (Sat only); look for secondhand bargains at the flea market (Sun only).*

Only Camden Lock can compare with the astounding success of the markets of Greenwich over recent years. And in many respects Greenwich is similar to its illustrious north London counterpart. Before the 1980s, Camden only had its costermongers on Inverness Street, and Greenwich had a dying wholesale fruit and veg market plus a clutch of stalls off Trafalgar Road. Today the two boroughs have London's most dynamic markets, attracting thousands of visitors from around the world.

The major difference is that, while flocks of tourists are attracted to Camden simply by the market, Greenwich has some of London's most famous sights. England's greatest architects of the 17th and 18th centuries – Inigo Jones, Christopher Wren, John Vanbrugh and Nicholas Hawksmoor – all contributed to the banquet of classical and Baroque buildings to be found here. The *Cutty Sark*, the sleek 1869 tea clipper, also draws crowds to the riverside and the opening of the Jubilee Line extension and DLR have made the area more accessible.

Though many of Greenwich's markets are held on Saturday – the small organic food market is only held on that day – the area truly comes to life on Sunday. None of the main markets listed below is geared to providing locals with shopping basics; for these you'd best travel to the markets at Woolwich (see p.171) or Deptford (see p.155) or, failing that, to the few stalls that trade on Colomb, Earlswood and Tyler Streets, off Trafalgar Road, from Monday to Saturday.

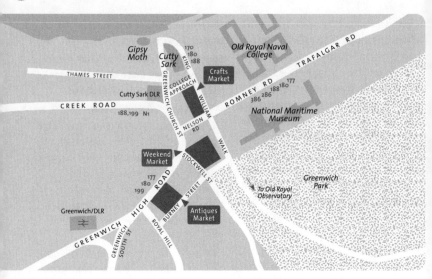

Weekend Market

*Stockwell Street, opposite the Hotel Ibis, SE10. **Weekend Market open** Sat and Sun 9am–5pm (organic food market Sat only); **Village Market open** Fri and Sat 10am–5pm, Sun 10am–6pm.*

Of all Greenwich's markets, this most resembles Camden's shindig, both in the goods sold and its setting. Sited on a largish patch of land off Stockwell Street are scores of outside stalls, a dozen or so lock-ups and a couple of old buildings filled with yet more stalls. Far more activity takes place on Sunday than Saturday.

A few of the traders with stalls facing Stockwell Street deal in books (new hardbacks at half-price; tatty old hardbacks for £1; new travel guides; Penguin Classics in good condition for £2). They are in front of the **South London Book Centre**, a two-storey literary emporium. At the Book Gallery, the illustrated books section on the first floor, you can reclaim all your old *Beano*, *Dandy* and *Monsterfun* annuals from the 1970s or flick through a couple of thousand *Marvel* comics featuring the Silver Surfer,

Fantastic Four, Spiderman et al. You can even find ancient editions of *Playboy* and *Screamqueens* (with useful advice on 'How to find a naked woman').

The remaining stalls in this section are strewn with old jewellery, crockery, footstools, copper saucepans and glassware; a few of the pretensions to be found at the Crafts Market are stripped away here (where stalls cost less to rent), and you might find some genuine craftsworkers selling their wares at fair prices: mirrors with distressed pine frames painted in Mediterranean greens, for instance. Behind the Book Gallery, other street traders might tip out a pile of clothes and sell 'anything for £1', or gather together a collection of old tools and traffic warning lights.

To the left of the South London Book Centre (looking down from the Stockwell Road) is the **Village Market**, housed in a large two-storey building. It has about 40 partitions for stalls downstairs; upstairs are about 10 more, and a crêperie/café. There's a toilet halfway up the stairs. Books were once the main commodity sold here, but now the ground floor is given over to mawkish framed pictures of teddy bears, new mirrors with pine frames, lacquer cabinets and spice chests. Upstairs (on Sundays) are books (hardbacks all £1), film posters and stalls such as **Lame Duck**, specializing in 1950s and 60s collectibles: a fantastic white, red and chrome Coca-Cola vending machine for £2,000, four bubblegum machines for £375, a mini Wurlitzer for £225. A fortune teller does tarot card readings, palmistry and crystal ball readings. The most fascinating item of all, however, is without doubt a bright orange, helmet-shaped eight-track tape player. Standing next to it is a basket of tapes featuring such legendary titles as *50 Guitars for Midnight Lovers*, *The Sound of Chris Montez*, and, of course, *Vicki Carr Live* – no wonder they became obsolete. If pop memorabilia is your thing, it's hard to see how you could be without a Shakin' Stevens cloth carrier bag, complete with concert scarf, cap and badges, for sale at another stall for just £16.

Grouped behind the Village Market are lock-ups and open-air pitches where traders sell secondhand goods. There are usually a couple of stalls packed with old and new stocks of records and CDs, with all types of music. Rails of old leather, suede, denim and sheepskin jackets are lined up nearby. Prices are high if, to you, 'secondhand' means 'worn and fraying'. If, however, it means 'vintage cool', you'll be queuing to pay £30 for a Levi's denim jacket, or £30 for a decrepit leather coat in an original 1960s design.

Furniture and other booty from house clearances accounts for much of the stock in the lock-ups; the more expensive stuff – ornaments, clocks, dressing tables, candlesticks, paintings and the like – is kept under cover, while inky school desks and an elderly standard lamp soak up the showers outside. A few traders sit

themselves down round a dilapidated table and open a Thermos of tea. On Sundays a large shed at the rear of the site is unlocked, and traders in furniture and collectibles (including old musical instruments) set up stall. To its right, one of the lock-ups has been taken over by some Thai noodle sellers.

There's a second storey above a couple of the lock-ups where you can find the **Military Shop** and **Bottle Shop**. If you're planning a fancy-dress party, try the former, where you can pick up a Royal Marine dress uniform or British Seaman's white uniform for £45, a Wren's outfit for £30 or camouflage helmets for £30. Alternatively, relive your childhood among the shelves of Airfix models. The Bottle Shop is packed to the rafters with bottles of every size, shape and colour. In many ways, this place seems more like a museum than a centre of commerce. It's pleasant to browse through the racks of brown glass 19th-century beer bottles, 1950s Bovril jars and assorted chemist 'poison' bottles, but only collectors are likely to make a purchase. Beer mats (10p each) and bar towels are also sold. In the building next door you can buy organic coffee, bread and olives. The building also contains furniture and **Third Eye**, where you can buy crystals or get a massage (£20 for 15 minutes).

There are fewer than half Sunday's number of stalls on Saturday, but one reason for coming to the Weekend on Saturday is to visit the small **organic food market**. This is held to the left of the Village Market (looking from Stockwell Street). Only about half a dozen traders turn up each Saturday, including the butcher from **Longwood Farm**, who also visits Borough (*see* p.152) with his range of organic meats, cheeses, butter and sheep's yoghurts. Next to him, a bread stall has an enticing collection of organic loaves, including *bara brith* (Welsh tea bread), olive and onion focaccia, and buttermilk and honey soda bread. An organic fruit and veg stall sells most of the usual produce, from watercress, carrots and celery, to avocado, kiwi fruit and lemons. It also has dried organic herbs and spices, vegetable juices and olive oils. A run-of-the-mill fish van (oysters, mussels, trout, cod, bloaters) and a less-than-organic burger van and jacket potato stand complete the picture.

If you return to Stockwell Street and cross the railway line, you'll find a small patch of land (almost opposite St Alphege's church) that contains a batch of fast food stalls known as the **Fountain Food Court**. Here you can stoke up on curry, burgers, Thai noodles, crêpes, chicken kebabs, falafels, caramelized peanuts, fresh fruit juice or cappuccino. Chairs are placed outside on the unattractive concrete courtyard.

Crafts Market

*College Approach, with entrances on Turpin Lane (off Greenwich Church Street) and Durnford Street, SE10, **t** (020) 8293 3110. **Open** Sat and Sun 9.30am–5.30pm.*

If the Weekend Market is Camden, this is Covent Garden. Slap in the centre of Greenwich, the Crafts Market occupies the site of a former fruit and veg mart that fizzled out in the 1980s. The cobbled paving has been retained, but a translucent corrugated roof keeps the rain off traders. The little alleyways surrounding the market were once the home of greengrocers; now they are crammed with gift shops.

Around the perimeter of the trading area are more shops of the same ilk, plus a café and a pub.

Food and Drink

Cafés, Restaurants and Fast Food

One place in Greenwich that has avoided much touristification is **Goddards Old Pie House**, at 45 Greenwich Church Street. Along with minced beef pie and mash, this caff has a range of other pies and pasties. For breakfast, you can pick up a croissant or *pain au chocolat* at a huge branch of **Café Rouge**, on the corner of Stockwell Street next to the Ibis Hotel. There are a couple of places on Nelson Road: **Bar du Musée** (No.17), which is a French-style bar, and **Saigon** (No.16), a long-standing reliable Vietnamese. **Time Bar and Restaurant**, at 7a College Approach, serves excellent global cuisine. Main courses are £8–10. **Noodle Time**, at 10–11 Nelson Road, is a popular stop for cheap, filling noodle dishes.

Pubs

The **Trafalgar Tavern**, part of the Royal Naval College, overlooks the river and serves reasonable bar food and a good pint. The **Auctioneers** pub on Greenwich High Road is a good final pit-stop before the station and the train journey home.

Up to 120 stalls are jammed into the small central space; more pitches are taken on Sundays than Saturdays. Here you can buy mounted butterflies and spiders (a tarantula, mounted and framed, costs £23, a sleeker-looking Malaysian scorpion £26; keyrings cost £3–4); designer jewellery, mobiles made of spoons, model boats, boomerangs, porcelain dolls; artefacts from Asia, the Middle East and Africa; wacky candlesticks; a variety of wooden goods, some useful (an egg-timer, a bowl), some not. Framed cartoons and sporting prints from *Punch* are sold for upwards of three times the price charged

Nearby Attractions

The Cutty Sark and the Gipsy Moth, *by Greenwich Pier, t (020) 8858 2698, www.cuttysark.org.uk;* ⊖ *North Greenwich, then bus;* **DLR** *Greenwich Cutty Sark.* **Cutty Sark open** *daily 10am–5pm, last admission 4.30pm;* **adm** *£5. Gipsy Moth closed to the public.* The *Cutty Sark* is a memento of Empire days, the last great tea clipper from England to the Far East and one of the fastest sailing boats of its day. Next door is the *Gipsy Moth*, in which Sir Francis Chichester sailed solo round the world in 1966–7.

Greenwich Park, ⇌ *Greenwich;* **DLR** *Greenwich Cutty Sark;* **buses** *53, 188.* Elegant park which was once a royal hunting ground.

Old Royal Naval College, *King William Walk, recorded information* **t** *0800 389 3341, www.greenwichfoundation.org.uk;* ⇌ *Greenwich;* **DLR** *Greenwich Cutty Sark;* **buses** *53, 188.* **Open** *daily 10am–5pm, last adm daily at 3.30pm.* Originally a naval

hospital designed by Christopher Wren, these grand buildings are now leased by the University of Greenwich. The Chapel and Painted Hall are open to the public.

Old Royal Observatory, *Greenwich Park,* **t** *(020) 8858 4422, recorded information* **t** *8312 6565;* ⇌ *Greenwich;* **DLR** *Greenwich Cutty Sark;* **buses** *53, 188.* **Open** *daily 10am–5pm.* The Observatory is where Greenwich Mean Time is measured and contains a museum on the history of navigation and time and how the problem of measuring longitude was solved.

The Queen's House and the National Maritime Museum, *Trafalgar Road,* **t** *(020) 8858 4422, www.nmm.ac.uk;* ⇌ *Greenwich;* **DLR** *Greenwich Cutty Sark;* **buses** *53, 188.* **Open** *daily 10am–5pm.* A thoroughly engaging museum dedicated to all sorts of boats, naval weapons, paintings and lots of interactive exhibitions. The Queen's House is a grand private villa, commissioned by Anne of Denmark, James I's wife.

---

at the Weekend Market. You can compare markets past and present at a stall selling old photographs. One of the albums is full of market pictures from the early part of the 20th century (£3 each; a large, 10x20-inch framed shot of the Crystal Palace taken just a couple of years before it burnt down will cost £60), and football club prints from the late 19th century onwards.

There's a food court area near the College Approach entrance where you can buy olives, cheese, honey, jams, juices, sauces, sausages, different kinds of bread and fresh herbs, all very hard to resist. There's also a small organic food stall, and on the way into the market you can smell the different flavoured coffees available from the tea and coffee trader.

There are plenty of clothes stalls, mainly selling alternative clothing: Indian, punk,

designer. Gothic clothing is available from **Circa** in one corner of the market, which is a good place to look for something out of the ordinary. In addition, you can get a tarot card reading, psychometry, pewter hip flasks, Russian dolls (one painted as Santa Claus), astrological readings and Etruscan money pots. At one stall you can have your name handpainted with illustrations, and at another you can have your name written in Chinese characters.

Tourists and locals mingle among the stalls, but the place has a rather contrived air. Over the exit of the old market buildings, built in 1831, is the inscription 'A false balance is an abomination to the Lord, but a just weight is his delight.' Outside, a new sign bears the disingenuous inscription 'Greenwich Market, since 1737'.

Antiques Market

Off Greenwich High Road, between junctions with Stockwell Street and Royal Hill, SE10. **Open** *Thurs and Fri 6.30am–5pm.*

Trading takes place on a patch of tarmac off the busy Greenwich High Road. Some of the old jewellery or 19th-century prints (sold at lower prices than you'd find in the Crafts Market) might be described as antique. More of the goods would be in the 'collectible' category: Oxo tins, door-knockers, comics, annuals, old wood-carving tools, Tonka models of the 1986 French World Cup squad, or a variety of smoking paraphernalia, including cigarette cards and old match boxes. Others still fall into the secondhand or junk genre: rolling pins, oil cans, furniture, books, fishing nets, secondhand blow football kits (who buys secondhand blow football kits?).

There are also secondhand clothes stalls: leather jackets, hats, mock-fur coats. Some look as though they've come straight from a jumble sale or charity shop, but a price tag of £25 for a jacket isn't uncommon. The Antiques Market's future is under threat, as the site is due to be replaced by luxury flats, so enjoy it while you can.

LEWISHAM

Lewisham High Street, SE13,
t (020) 8314 7111.

Transport: *≷/DLR Lewisham; buses 21, 47, 54, 75, 89, 108, 122, 136, 178, 180, 181, 185, 199, 208, 225, 261, 273, 278, 284, 321, 380, 484, P4.*

Open: *Mon–Thurs 10am–4pm, Sat 9am–6.00pm, Sun 10am–4pm.*

Best time to go: *Saturday.*

Parking: *There are parking meters along Albion Way, to the east of the High Street.*

Main wares: *Fruit and veg, flowers, fish, haberdashery, clothing.*

Specifics: *Cheap fruit and veg, fish.*

The part of Lewisham High Street which holds the local market has been pedestrianized and at the weekends there is often a bouncy castle and merry-go-round, so there is a real family atmosphere. Lewisham, more than most markets, deserves its new-found serenity. In 1944, a V1 rocket fell directly onto the market, killing 56 people and wounding 99 others.

There are only about 50 stalls, but these are, in the main, enormous (or at least noticeably bigger than the average market

Food and Drink

Something Fishy, on the High Street by the market, is the enticingly named caff that attracts many locals. As well as fish and chips, and eels, pie and mash, it has a choice of fried breakfasts and ice creams. Similar English-style fare can be found upstairs at **Blighty's**, where you can get a superb full fried breakfast for £4.50. A short walk south of the market along Lewisham High Street will take you to the **Welcome Noodle House** at 47–9 Lee High Road.

stall). Many shoppers are drawn away from Lewisham Shopping Centre's stultifying chainstores by the market's low prices. This is one of the best places in the area for fruit and vegetables. Some traders go for high-quality produce, making beautiful displays out of their wares; others prefer the 'pile 'em high, sell 'em cheap' approach, flogging 2lbs of 'nanas for 40p, a dozen Coxes for £1, seedless grapes at 2lbs for £1, or five coconuts for £1. A few sell more unusual produce: artichokes, Chinese leaves, chicory and *frisée* lettuce. One stall sells eggs, crisps, drinks and other cheap packaged food.

As with many markets that attract Afro-Caribbean shoppers, there's a very good fish stall. **R. J. Davis & Son**, which has traded here for years, sells a wide variety of swimming creatures: crab, salmon, snappers, yellow croaker, octopus, Dover sole, bream, trout, mussels, red mullet, kippers and cooked roe. The remainder of the stalls supply locals with everyday merchandise: clothes, pet accessories, cut flowers, haberdashery and greetings cards, plus the occasional oddity: porcelain dolls and the like. On Sundays the emphasis is on fashion with bags and all sorts of accessories attracting the locals, while towels, bed linen and toys bring in housewives. There is a burger and Thai food stall too for when hunger calls.

LOWER MARSH

Lower Marsh, from Westminster Bridge Road to Baylis Road, SE1.

Transport: ⊖ *Lambeth North, Waterloo;* ⇌ *Waterloo; buses 1, 12, 53, 59, 68, 76, 148, 159, 168, 171, 172, 176, 188, 341, 453, X68.*

Open: *Mon–Sat 9am–5pm.*

Best time to go: *Friday lunchtime.*

Parking: *Difficult; there are some meters in the area, or an (expensive) car park a 10-minute walk away on Library Street; within the congestion charge zone.*

Main wares: *Fruit and vegetables, household goods, clothes, electrical goods, haberdashery, bric-a-brac.*

Specifics: *Classical CDs.*

Two old women once took me around this part of south London showing me cheap places to eat. Almost as an aside, they started talking of the New Cut market of their youth. I was enthralled. The market they described was not only a meeting place and shopping centre; it was free entertainment that lasted until midnight on Saturdays. Henry Mayhew, in the 1850s, gives a vivid portrayal of the mid-Victorian atmosphere of the place:

> *There are hundreds of stalls, and every stall has its one or two lights... One man shows off his yellow haddock with a candle stuck in a bundle of firewood; his neighbour makes a candlestick of a huge turnip, and the tallow gutters over its sides... Then the tumult of the thousand different cries of the eager dealers...is almost bewildering... 'Come and look at 'em! here's toasters!' bellows one with a*

Food and Drink

Masters Super Fish, a 5-minute walk away at 191 Waterloo Road, has some of the best fish and chips in London. **The Fire Station** (No.150) is a laid-back pub-style eatery in a converted fire station, while the **Waterloo Bar and Kitchen** (No.131) serves good modern European food with set menu prices for lunch and dinner.

On Lower Marsh, **Barbarellas** (No.141) is a café serving sandwiches and jacket potatoes, and **Coopers** (No.17) is a wholefood shop with a vegetarian café selling organic coffee and vegetarian food. There's also **Sine Thai** restaurant which serves a special buffet at lunchtime (£4 per person). **Cubana** (No.48) is a cheap and cheerful café, which serves large jugs of cocktails in a rowdy, party atmosphere.

Yarmouth bloater stuck on a toasting fork... A little further on stands the clean family, begging; the father with his head down as if in shame, and a box of lucifers held forth in his hand... Then is heard the sharp snap of the percussion-cap from the crowd of lads firing at the target for nuts; and the moment afterwards, you see a black man half-clad in white, and shivering in the cold with tracts in his hand, or else you hear the sounds of music from 'Frazier's Circus', on the other side of the road, and the man outside the door of the penny concert, beseeching you to 'Be in time – be in time!' as Mr Somebody is just about to sing his favourite song of the Knife Grinder. Such, indeed, is the riot, the struggle, and the scramble for a living, that the confusion and uproar of the New-Cut on Saturday night have a bewildering and saddening effect upon the thoughtful mind.

Sadly, the market today is a husk of its former self. It has become a lunchtime affair catering mainly to local office workers, and is now based only on Lower Marsh, but you can get everything from quality veg to cheap potatoes to cutting-edge fashion here. Midweek, there can be as few as 30 stalls trading at lunchtime, though more come on Fridays.

A couple of stalls sell secondhand bric-a-brac (including brassware, old tapes and pulp fiction), but otherwise most goods are new. Office workers come to peruse the audio and computer equipment, stock up on underwear, buy a good luck card and flowers for colleagues moving jobs, or browse through the excellent collection of classical CDs at the stall linked to **Gramex**, which has a shop on the street (No.25). But the area also contains much council housing, and the market provides locals with cheap tins of food, fruit and veg, inexpensive clothing, pirate videos and (piled haphazardly in a tangled litter of cardboard boxes) a variety of household goods – from umbrellas and can openers to bed linen and alarm clocks. One of the first stalls at the Baylis Road end of Lower Marsh seems to sell everything for £1: a bottle of oregano-flavoured olive oil, two packets of out-of date ground coffee, a few packets of cashew nuts. There is also a good deal of booze-cruise booty on sale: cheap batteries (three large Duracell for £5, down to 16 for £5 by 1pm), Belgian chocolates, beer, even French red table wine at £2 a bottle – all sold in super-quick fashion auction-style, with many a sidelong glance up the road. Meanwhile, a section of the crowd has turned its attention to the miracle cleaner man: 'I'll tell you what I'll do today. I don't do this Monday or Tuesday but I've had a quiet day today so I'm going to offer you not one, not two, but three bottles for a fiver. Three bottles, and remember one bottle is equal to 32 bottles of normal cleaner...you all know me, don't you? You've seen me

Nearby Attractions

British Airways London Eye, *Jubilee Gardens, bookings* **t** *0870 5000 600, www.londoneye.com;* ✛ *Waterloo, Westminster, Embankment;* **buses** *11, 24, 211.* **Open** *daily 10am–8pm, summer until 9pm;* **adm** *adults £13, 5–16s £6.50.* You'll probably get the best view of the city from this giant ferris wheel.

Dalí Universe, *basement of County Hall,* **t** *0870 744 7485, www.daliuniverse.com.* **Open** *daily 10am–6.30pm;* **adm** *adults £9.75, 5–16s £6.25.* Poorly laid out but interesting exhibition of Dalí's work.

IMAX 3-D Cinema, *1 Charlie Chaplin Walk, SE1,* **t** *0870 787 2525, www.bfi. org.uk/imax,* ✛ *Waterloo;* ⇌ *Waterloo;* **buses** *1, 4, 26, 59, 68, 76, 77, 168, 171, 176, 188, 211, 243, 341, 381, 501, 505, 507, 521, RV1.* **Open** *Mon–Thu 12.30–8pm, Fri 12.30–9.15pm, Sat 10.45am–9.15pm, Sun 11–9.30pm;* **adm** *adult £7.90, 5–16s £4.95.* Britain's largest cinema screen (the height of five double-decker buses), in a seven-storey glass cylinder in the middle of a roundabout, showing films in 3-D format.

London Aquarium, *basement of County Hall,* **t** *(020) 7967 8000, www.london aquarium.co.uk.* **Open** *daily 10am–6pm, last adm 5pm;* **adm** *adults £11.75, 3–14s £8.25.* The three-storey tanks let you get close up to a large selection of sealife.

See also Riverside Walk, p.170.

before, haven't you love? Exactly, so what you do is you take the bottles away over the weekend and, if you're not happy, bring 'em back and I'll give you your money back.' Of course he will.

PECKHAM

Choumert Road, between Rye Lane and Choumert Grove, SE15; Rye Lane indoor market, 48 Rye Lane, SE15; Agora indoor market, Rye Lane (opposite No.98), SE15.

Transport: ⇌ *Peckham Rye; buses 12, 37, 63, 78, 197, 343, 363, P12.*

Open: *Mon–Sat 9am–5pm.*

Best time to go: *Saturday.*

Parking: *There are spaces along Bournemouth Road (to the east of Rye Lane).*

Main wares: *Afro-Caribbean foodstuffs, clothing, household goods, pet food.*

Specifics: *Afro-Caribbean fruit and veg, meat, fish, Afro hair accessories.*

Although Peckham has become the butt of many jokes and been mythologized by the TV show *Only Fools and Horses*, it is not really a stark urban wasteland seething with shysters, wide boys and Robin Reliants. Although there's plenty of urban deprivation if you look for it, Rye Lane on Saturdays is a cheerful, buzzing place, with two indoor markets, an outdoor market on Choumert Road, and side streets dotted with stalls. Moncrieff Street, Atwell Road and Park Stone Road have half a dozen stalls each, selling cheap clothes and fruit and veg. Rye Lane itself is not overwhelmed by chainstores, but has a fine variety of shops (although, strangely, no newsagents'), including butchers, Afro haircare stores, and fishmongers' stocked with a wide variety of seafood.

Peckham is a multiracial area with large Afro-Caribbean and Asian communities. The markets reflect the district's cosmopolitan population. **Choumert Road**, with about 30 stalls, is geared towards Caribbean foodstuffs. There are jackfish and snappers (three for £7) on the two well-stocked fish stalls, with a good supply of salmon heads and fish bones for making fish soup; papayas, yams, mangoes, coriander and plantain on the fruit and vegetable stalls; and reggae on

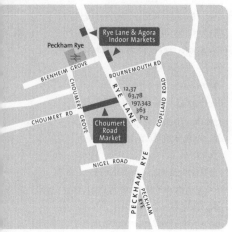

engraver, jewellery, reggae and soul records, videos and CDs of African artists, dried flowers, wool, a printing and photocopying service, a mobile phone stockist and a health food stall. One stall sells teddy bears and porcelain dolls. There are two travel agencies, a garden centre also dealing in aquatic supplies, and an employment agency. There's also African craftwork, such as large wooden giraffes.

The main **Rye Lane indoor market**, sometimes called the Bargain Centre, is across the road to the north. Traders moved here from the old Rye Lane street market in 1931. It was bombed in the war but soon rebuilt, and now has an old-fashioned, murky feel, like the arcades of Brixton or the great indoor market halls of northern England. It is currently being refurbished and with luck will continue as a market.

The butchers at **Terry's Meat Market** 'knock out' at the end of the day on Saturday. A crowd of people wait eagerly for cheap chops and joints. The neighbouring businesses are a unisex hair salon, a haberdashery stall and a trader selling bedding. In one corner of the building, an old-established pet stall sells birds, small furry animals and all manner of pet food – 'day old chicks are a speciality' it claims, in language perhaps more suited to a restaurant. Nearby is **Tropical**, a stall selling dub reggae vinyl, and an Afro-Caribbean café, **Aunty's**.

There's a complete change at the far end of this avenue, where **Steptoe & Sons** has its premises. Piles of old books, records and tapes vie for space with disparate pieces of furniture and non-specific junk with plenty of people having a rummage.

Video games, greetings cards and perfumes can also be bought in the

the record stalls. There are also Afro haircare stalls and a trader selling the sort of felt hats much loved by Afro-Caribbean women of a certain age. The lock-up shops along the street are really part of the market, with many of their goods displayed outside. Several of the businesses, including the butcher's shop (where you can get boiler chickens for £2.50 each and a whole goat for £25), are run by Asians, but more often than not their customers are Afro-Caribbean.

Back along Rye Lane, the **Agora indoor market** is held in a long, narrow building. Inside it is bright and quite modern, with about 50 traders cramped between partitions off the central walkways. There's a wide variety of goods and services: Afro hair accessories, clothes (mostly women's and children's), toys, secondhand TVs, a key-cutter and

Food and Drink

At the back of the Agora indoor market is the **Agora Café**, with a menu of hot food, meatballs, chickpeas and spinach. **The White Horse**, at 20 Peckham Rye, the southern continuation of Rye Lane, has a pleasant atmosphere, friendly staff and fabulous Sunday roasts.

indoor market. Before you go, don't miss a look at **Brenda's** toiletries stall, with its row of wigs and hair extensions hanging like scalps from the ceiling.

RIVERSIDE WALK

Riverside Walk, in front of the National Film Theatre, SE1.

Transport: ⊖ *Waterloo;* ≋ *Waterloo; buses 1, 4, 26, 45, 59, 63, 68, 76, 77, 100, 139, 168, 171, 172, 176, 188, 243, 341, 381, 521, RV1, X68.*

Open: *Sat, Sun and weekdays 12–7pm (earlier in winter).*

Parking: *At weekends there might be spaces on the side streets south of Stamford Street; there's a big NCP car park on Stamford Street; within the congestion charge zone during the week.*

Main wares: *Books, prints.*

Specifics: *Secondhand play texts, old editions of guide books, prints of English architecture, maps.*

The Riverside Walk book market is a hardy animal. Even in the depths of winter its long trestle tables are set up under Waterloo Bridge. The concrete surrounds of the South Bank and the wind off the river are mellowed by the quiet

bookishness of the customers. You may even find yourself serenaded by virtuoso buskers, fiddling for their passage through music college.

Hardbacks and paperbacks, both fiction and non-fiction, are displayed on eight rows of tables. Quality is high, both in content and condition – there's precious little pulp fiction, and even the oldest books are generally in fine fettle. Second-hand paperback novels cost upwards of £1.50. Virago and Women's Press are well represented, and most of the classics of English literature can usually be found. You might also discover boxloads of science fiction or detective stories, or the final G. A. Henty (the Blackie edition, of course) to complete your collection.

Both new and secondhand non-fiction is stocked; most new books are remainders, covering subjects from natural history to embroidery, and from politics to pets. Classification is sometimes rudimentary: *The History of the Second World War* might be next to *Understanding Your Dog*. But film, art, food and books for children usually have their own sections. As the National Theatre is only a stone's throw away, it's no surprise to see a good collection of secondhand play texts: Beckett, Ayckbourn, T. S. Eliot, Pinter, Brecht and, of course, Shakespeare – all at slightly more than half-price. There's also a wide choice of travel guide books that are a

Nearby Attractions

Oxo Tower, ⊖ *Waterloo;* **buses** *45, 63, 100, 381, RV1.* Art Deco tower that houses several designer and jewellery workshops, restaurants and bars. A great view of London is offered from the free public viewing gallery at the top of the tower.

South Bank Centre, ⊖ *Waterloo, Embankment;* **buses** *1, 4, 26, 59, 68, 76, 139, 168, 171, 172, 176, 188, 243, 341, 521, X68.* Arts centre composed of the Royal Festival Hall, National Film Theatre, Hayward Gallery, Queen Elizabeth Hall, Purcell Room, Royal National Theatre and the Museum of the Moving Image.

See also Lower Marsh, p.166.

year or so out of date; many are sold for less than half-price.

The market has a good line in old prints and maps, culled from 19th- or early 20th-century books and magazines, including some great old colonial views such as *Sunset in the Tropics* and *Elegant Elephant Hunting*. Engravings of historic buildings and landscapes of England are ordered by county. A series of 1950s adverts features vacuous housewives gazing yearningly at the latest labour-saving devices.

It is often hard to divine who is running stalls here; as often as not, the owners are poring over books alongside their customers. This adds to the charm of the market, and the pleasure of browsing is enhanced if you're lucky enough to uncover gems such as *Scouting Thrills* by Captain G. B. McKern VC, published in 1925.

WESTMORELAND ROAD

Westmoreland Road, from Camberwell Road to Queen's Row, SE17.

Transport: ⊖ *Elephant and Castle;* ⇌ *Elephant and Castle; buses 12, 35, 40, 42, 45, 68, 171, 176, 343, 468, X68.*

Open: *Tues, Wed, Fri and Sat 9am–4pm; Thurs 9am–2pm; Sun 8.30am–1pm.*

Best time to go: *Sunday.*

Parking: *Try the side streets west of the Walworth Road.*

Main wares: *Secondhand junk, old books, tapes and CDs, clothes (Sun); fruit and veg (rest of week).*

Specifics: *Secondhand clothes, possible antiques bargains.*

In an era where junk is described as 'heritage' and sold at inflated prices, Westmoreland Road's Sunday market is a joy. It benefits from the crowds visiting nearby East Street (*see* p.157), yet keeps its own neighbourhood atmosphere.

This is still a close-knit working-class area. Away from the noise of the Walworth Road, you'll find stallholders who live in the nearby council flats chatting with their friends about the day's takings, and whether it'll be worth paying for a pitch next week. Many are casual traders who have a weekday job, or are unemployed, and have raided their attics for merchandise. Hardly any professional dealers bother to scour the stalls.

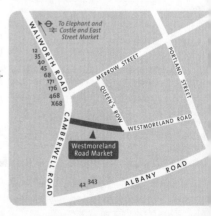

Few traders turn up during the week; a single fruit and veg seller and a household goods stall at most. Over the years the weekday market has dwindled, unable to compete with East Street. A couple of fruit and veg dealers and an egg seller also turn up on Sunday, when trade is brisker. They are joined by a shellfish stall, which dispenses cockles to the punters. Otherwise, virtually all the 50-odd Sunday traders sell secondhand goods – tapes, records and CDs, old crockery, a box of toy cars, boots and shoes, books – and oddities such as garlic-flavoured chewing gum. One stall is full of DIY bits and pieces: nails, screws, washers and the like. There's also a good line in secondhand kitchenware: pots and pans and old cutlery.

Some traders seem to be selling the contents of their granny's flat; disparate pieces of furniture line the pavements. Other stock has been put in order by eccentric stallholders with a yen for pen nibs, pocket watches, old sewing machines or coins and medals. Some pitches display a glorious madness of junk: a pair of patent leather shoes resting next to tubes of oil paints and a watering can. Others specialize in the exquisitely sordid: a half-used bottle of roll-on deodorant, semi-fresh from an elderly relative's armpit; an old, clearly used, plastic potty; or bunches of withered flowers pilfered from a neighbour's garden.

The Sunday market is particularly good for cheap secondhand clothes, untainted by the high prices that go with trendiness:

a rail of shirts for a pound each; workaday suits for £10; fake fur coats for £1.50. Many of the clothes are wrapped in plastic bags and hung on rails to give the appearance of having been dry-cleaned. Other traders make no such effort, tipping bags of musty garments directly onto the street.

Unlike East Street, most shops on Westmoreland Road are closed on Sundays, though a halal butcher's continues trading. No matter: you'll be fully occupied by the market, for if you're prepared to root through the rubbish you might snap up a bargain.

WOOLWICH

Beresford Square, SE18; indoor market off Plumstead Road.

Transport: ⇌ *Woolwich Arsenal; buses 51, 53, 54, 96, 99, 122, 161, 177, 178, 180, 244, 272, 291, 380, 386, 422, 469, 472.*

Open: *Tues, Wed, Fri and Sat 8.30am–5.30pm; Thurs 8.30am–2pm.*

Best time to go: *Saturday.*

Parking: *There are some meters along Woolwich New Road.*

Main wares: *Fruit and vegetables, household goods, clothes, CDs and tapes.*

Specifics: *Fish, cut flowers, low-priced fruit and veg, wool, fabrics.*

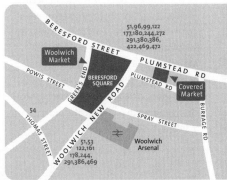

It's a grim walk down Beresford Street to Woolwich's market: featureless grey buildings, no shops, no people, just cars. It doesn't prepare you for the market, a lively, friendly place, and about the nearest you'll get in London to the atmosphere of a market town. This isn't surprising, really, as Woolwich is far enough from central London to have a distinct character and history. There's been a market in the borough since the Middle Ages. Until the 19th century it was held in the High Street and Market Hill (near the river ferry landing stage), but by the 1850s unofficial stalls were trading on Beresford Square, close to the Royal Arsenal and its thousands of munitions workers.

The square, surrounded mostly by 19th-century buildings, has now been pedestrianized and is, in truth, rather genteel: more like Greenwich than Deptford. At its northern end, the **Royal Arsenal Gatehouse** remains. This impressive structure, built in 1829, has recently been restored as part of the Woolwich Revival scheme.

Like a small-town market, Beresford Square concentrates on the needs of its locals. There are about 120 pitches in all, selling household goods, clothing for men, women and children, electrical goods, CDs, books, rugs, an impressive range of fish, and a good choice of low-priced fruit and veg. Some of the costermongers have their produce beautifully arranged on synthetic grass, vying with the cut-flower stalls in their displays. One has a good range of Asian vegetables: tiny aubergines, okra and chillies. The fabric stalls also seem popular with local Asian women.

Food and Drink

Kenroy's pie and mash shop, at 5 Woolwich New Road, is a newly refurbished café popular among traders.

The **Ordnance Arms** and the **Elephant and Castle** pubs are both in Beresford Square. The best pub in the area, however, is probably the **Earl of Chatham** on Thomas Street, with its beautiful curved glass frontage.

There's little reward in exploring the concrete shopping precinct at the western end of the market on Powis Street. It's better to walk along the pedestrianized area to the east, beside the Plumstead Road. There are some stalls outside selling clothes and mobile phone accessories. Inside a dour 1930s structure, you'll find a **covered market** containing 42 lock-ups. The traders sell clothing, drapery (including net curtains), trainers, furniture, and Christian and secondhand books (mainly paperbacks).

One lock-up sells fishing equipment and offers rod and reel repairs; another, **Stat's Trophies**, specializes in pool cues, dartboards and flights, as well as old sporting trophies, tankards and hip flasks – engraving is available at 20p a letter. There is also a specialist in Afro-Caribbean and European hairstyles, with a sign outside saying 'come for a touch of class', and a manicurist. Hot food is served at the **Cabin Café**.

Long impoverished, Woolwich seems to be coming out of the shadow of its wealthy neighbour Greenwich. Its two markets may not be able to compete in terms of size or scope with what Greenwich can offer, but they are nonetheless thriving and attractive.

Other Markets Within the M25 Area

08

The following markets were either too small or too distant from central London to be included in the main body of this book. Be aware that opening times at the smaller markets might vary from week to week.

Barnet

St Albans Road, High Barnet, Hertfordshire, **t** *(020) 8441 7234.* **Open** *Wed and Sat 8.30am–4.30pm.*

An outdoor general market consisting of about 50 stalls, with the emphasis on fruit and veg.

Broadway Market

Broadway, E8, **t** *07709 311 869, www. broadwaymarket.co.uk.* **Open** *Sat 9am–5pm.*

The original market (trading since Victorian times) petered out at the end of the 20th century. There is now a farmers' style market on the newly regenerated site with lots of organic produce on offer. There are a few clothes stalls too, selling new and 'vintage' clothes.

Bromley

Station Road car park, Bromley, Kent, **t** *(020) 8313 4768.* **Open** *Thurs 9am–3pm.*

A good local general market that just celebrated its 800th birthday. There are 65 stalls selling new goods only. Haberdashery is a highlight.

Bromley High Street, Kent, **t** *(020) 8313 4580.* **Open** *Sat 9am–5.30pm.*

An arts and crafts market takes place on the pedestrianized section of the High Street every Saturday. For details of the farmers' market on Friday, *see* p.180.

Catford Broadway

Catford Broadway, SE6, **t** *(020) 8314 2050.* **Open** *Mon and Thurs–Sat 9am–5.30pm.*

About 35 stalls congregate on a pedestrianized street. Traders deal in household goods, clothes, flowers and food (including fish and Afro-Caribbean ingredients).

Chalton Street

Chalton Street, NW1, **t** *(020) 7974 6917.* **Open** *Fri lunchtime.*

The descendant of the riotous Victorian Brill market now takes place only on Fridays, when about 60 stalls sell new goods only: household products, cheap tinned food and also cheap women's clothes.

Chrisp Street

Chrisp Street, E14, **t** *(020) 7377 8963.* **Open** *Tues–Sat 8am–6pm.*

A fair-sized general market, partly of lock-ups, partly of stalls, trading under a new awning in a postwar concrete square. It's good for children's clothes, Asian food, traditional fruit and veg and household goods. In the summer, they hold Super Saturdays, complete with street performers.

Collyer Place

Collyer Place, off Peckham High Street, **t** *(020) 7525 7665.* **Open** *Sun 8am–2pm.*

A new arts and crafts market with around a dozen stalls selling handmade items from silver and crystal jewellery to traditionally crafted ceramics, woodwork and clothes.

Croydon

Surrey Street, Croydon, Surrey, t (020) 8686 4433. Open Mon–Sat 7.30am–5pm.

A busy, traditional street market over 700 years old which inspired the song *The Streets of London*. There are 60 pitches, most dealing in good-quality, low-priced fruit and veg, but you can also buy flowers, plants, bread, meat, eggs, cards, travel bags, shoes and toiletries.

Dartford

Priory Centre car park, Dartford, Kent, t (01322) 343812. Open Thurs 9am–3.30pm.

A large general market with about 250 pitches, many of them under a canopy.

High Street, Dartford, Kent, t (01322) 343812. Open Sat 9am–5.30pm.

An open-air general market with about 100 pitches.

East Ham

Shopping Hall, Myrtle Road, E6, t (01708) 740492. Open Mon–Sat 9am–5.30pm.

An old-established general indoor market containing about 130 traders, selling a wide range of goods, from greengrocery to computer games.

Edmonton

Edmonton Green Shopping Centre, South Mall, Edmonton, Middlesex, t (020) 7499 5666. Open Mon–Sat 9am–5.30pm.

A general market with 45 pitches within the shopping centre.

Elephant and Castle

Outside Elephant and Castle Shopping Centre, SE1. Open Mon–Sat 9am–5pm. Within the congestion charge zone.

About 30 stalls selling new clothes, electrical goods, cosmetics, hair-care products, trainers, rugs, scarves, sports-wear, CDs and Nigerian films. There's also a pretty good Caribbean food stall.

Enfield

Market Place, Enfield, Middlesex, t (020) 8367 8941. Open Mon, Thurs and Fri 8am–4pm, Sat 8am–4pm.

A traditional outdoor general market, with 90-odd stalls, that recently celebrated 400 years. The market is run by a charitable institution and proceeds from pitch rentals help local people in need.

Epsom

Beside the clocktower, Market Place, Epsom, t (01372) 732562. Open Thurs 9am–4pm, Sat 9am–4pm.

A general outdoor market with about 30 stalls in a newly restored charter marketplace. Best on Saturday.

Erith

Pier Road, Erith, Kent. Open Wed, Thurs and Sat 9am–5pm.

A fair-sized outdoor general market in the town centre. On Thursdays around 40–50 bric-a-brac traders turn up.

Feltham

Bedfont Lane, Feltham, Middlesex, t (020) 7739 9900. Open Mon–Sat 9am–6pm.

A market containing 80 pitches.

Finchley

Tally-Ho Corner, Kingsway, N12. Open Tues, Fri and Sat 9am–4pm; car boot sale Sun 9am–2pm.

A general market attracting about 45 traders during the week. Secondhand goods are sold at the car boot sale held on Sunday.

Finsbury Park

Finsbury Park, main entrance, N4. **Open** *Sun 8am–2pm.*

A new general market, with 72 stalls selling fruit and veg, clothes, jewellery and CDs, and there are some hot-food stalls.

Harringay

Harringay Football Club, N17, t (020) 7739 9900. **Open** *Thurs 9am–5pm.*

An open-air general retail market with around 100 stalls.

Harrow

Elmgrove Road, Harrow, Middlesex, t 0800 3583434. **Open** *Thurs 9am–4pm.*

An outdoor general market with around 100 pitches.

Hounslow

Ashford railway station car park, Hounslow, Middlesex, t (01895) 639 912. **Open** *Sat and Sun 9am–4pm.*

A general market with 100 pitches.

Kingston

Charter Market and Apple Market: Market Place, Kingston, Surrey, t (020) 8547 4625. **Open** *Mon–Sat 9am–5pm.*

A traditional town-centre market with 23 stalls; good for fruit and veg.

Fairfield Market: Surface level of multi-storey car park, Fairfield North Kingston, Surrey. **Open** *Mon 9am–1.30pm.*

A large general market held on the site

of the old cattlemarket (now a car park). Over 200 stalls.

Lambeth Walk

Lambeth Walk shopping precinct (between Black Prince Road and Old Paradise Street), SE11, t (020) 7926 2530. **Open** *Tues, Wed and Fri 10am–3pm. Within the congestion charge zone.*

As in the song. A small general market of only two stalls trades here.

London Bridge

Outside London Bridge Underground station, SE1. **Open** *Sat 10am–4.30pm (a few stalls other days). Within the congestion charge zone.*

A small collection of crafts and souvenir stalls joins the flower-seller on a Saturday.

New Addington

Central Parade, New Addington, Surrey, t (01895) 639 912. **Open** *Tues and Fri 9am–4pm.*

A medium-sized general market: clothes, children's clothes, watches, leather goods, bedding, general household goods, fruit and veg, bread and cakes.

Penge

Maple Road, Penge, SE20, t (020) 8313 4768. **Open** *Tues–Sat 8am–5pm.*

A small open-air market just off the High Street.

Potters Bar

Parts Lane, Potters Bar, Hertfordshire, t (020) 7739 9900. **Open** *Sat 7am–5pm.*

An open-air general retail market with around 50 traders.

Rathbone

Off the south side of Barking Road, E16, **t** *(020) 8430 5760.* **Open** *Tues, Thurs, Fri and Sat 8am–6pm.*

Canning Town's market has most everyday commodities among its 83 stalls: fish, meat, fruit and veg, crockery, pots and pans, music cassettes and clothes. There are also a couple of secondhand goods pitches.

Richmond

The Square, Richmond. **Open** *Mon–Sat 9am–5pm.*

A small general market occupying permanent lock-up stalls in an alley.

Romford

Open-air: Market Place, Romford, Essex, **t** *(01708) 432373.* **Open** *Wed and Fri 8am–5pm, Sat 8am–5.30pm.*

A huge open-air market with nearly 300 stalls selling food, clothing and bric-a-brac. It's well worth the trip out from London.

Indoor: 33 Market Place, Romford, Essex, **t** *(01708) 740492.* **Open** *Mon–Sat 9am–5pm.*

An indoor general market with about 50 stalls.

Southall

Car park off South Road (High Street end), Southall, Middlesex. **Open** *Tues, Wed and Sat 9am–3pm, Fri 9am–1pm.*

The Tuesday poultry market and Wednesday's horse market bring country people and travellers into Southall. There's a junk market on Friday and a general market on Saturdays.

South Harrow

Northolt Road, opposite South Harrow tube station, Middlesex, **t** *(020) 7739 9900.* **Open** *Mon–Sat 9am–6pm.*

About 70 kiosks under cover.

Southwark Park Road

Market Place, off Southwark Park Road between Blue Anchor Lane and St James' Road, SE16, **t** *(020) 7525 5000.* **Open** *Mon–Sat 8am–4pm.*

Around 50 food and clothes traders gather at this old market, known as 'The Blue'. Busiest on Saturday. Also sells flowers, plants, cards and stationery.

Staines

Market Square, High Street, Staines, Middlesex, **t** *(0118) 945 1799.* **Open** *Wed and Sat 9am–5pm.*

An open-air general retail market with about 30 traders in the town centre selling garden ornaments, fruit and veg, flowers and greetings cards.

Stoke Newington

117–19 Stoke Newington High Street, N16, **t** *(020) 7739 9900.* **Open** *Mon–Sat 9am–6pm.*

A small outdoor market just off the High Street.

Stratford Mall

Stratford Shopping Centre, E15, **t** *(020) 8430 5760.* **Open** *Mon–Sat 9am–5.30pm.*

About 80 brightly lit stalls transform the drab 1960s concourse of Stratford's shopping centre into something more enticing. Fruit and veg, fish, clothing and handbags are among the wares.

Swanley

London Road, Swanley, Kent, t (01895) 632 221. Open Wed 9am–5pm.

A busy general market with about 140 pitches.

Uxbridge

Pavilion Shopping Centre, Uxbridge High Street, Middlesex, t (01767) 683777. Open Mon–Wed 9am–5.30pm.

A small crafts market.

Watford

Beechen Grove, Watford, Herts, t (01923) 246066. Open Tues, Fri and Sat 7am–6pm.

A large general market with over 120 different stalls in the centre of Watford.

Watney

Watney Market, off the south side of Commercial Road, E1, t (020) 7377 8963. Open Tues–Sat 8am–6pm.

Up to 90 stalls trade on this concrete pedestrian precinct. Two of the best sell Asian fruit and veg and clothing. You can also buy fish, chickens and eggs, crockery, pet foods, household goods and traditional greengrocery.

Wealdstone

31–35 High Street, Wealdstone, Middlesex, t (020) 863 8806. Open Mon–Sat 9am–5.30pm.

An indoor market with 36 pitches.

Wembley

Car park opposite Wembley Stadium, Wembley, Middlesex, t (01895) 632 221. Open Sun 9am–4pm.

Over 500 stalls and parking for up to 4,000 cars. General market with electrical goods, fashion and even food.

West Drayton

High Street, West Drayton, Middlesex, t (01895) 632221. Open Thurs 9am–4pm.

An open-air general market in the town centre with 15 stalls selling meat, fish, fruit and veg and clothing.

Wood Green

Wood Green Shopping City, High Road, N22, t (020) 8888 6667. Open Mon–Sat 9.30am–6pm, Sun 11am–5pm.

A small general market within the shopping centre.

Farmers' Markets

The first of the modern-day farmers' markets in Britain opened in Bath in 1997. By the start of the 2001 foot-and-mouth epidemic (which temporarily closed most markets) there were more than 250. Now there are an estimated 550 around the country. Such success not only shows the need of farmers to sell directly to the public (bypassing the often draconian conditions they must meet when selling to a supermarket), but also the desire of the British public for high-quality, fully traceable fresh food.

Farmers' markets were first set up in the USA in the 1980s, but in essence they emulate the markets of pre-industrial times, when farmers and producers brought their own wares to sell at the local market. The National Association of Farmers' Markets (NAFM) lists four main criteria with which farmers' markets must comply. They are:

• food must be locally produced, within a pre-defined area;

• all produce sold must be grown, reared, caught, brewed, pickled, baked, smoked or processed by the stallholder;

• the stall must be attended by the principal producer or a representative directly involved in the production process;

• information should be made available to customers at each market about the rules of the market and the production methods of the producers.

In the case of London farmers' markets (most of which are run by private operators), all the produce is grown within 100 miles of the M25. This means that you won't find yams or mangoes at these markets and they only have fruit and vegetables that are in season, so no strawberries in December. They do, however, sell many different varieties of fruit and vegetables that you don't usually see in supermarkets, and the food tends to be much fresher because it is transported and sold on the same day.

The farmers' markets don't just sell fruit and veg. Expect to find cut flowers, plants, meat, fish, cheese, eggs, bread, cakes, pies, jams, honey, English wines, cider, beer and perry. The meat and eggs tend to be free-range and much of the produce is organic. A great advantage of farmers' markets is that the consumer can talk to the farmer directly and find out how the food is produced. Many of the stalls will have samples of their wares for you to taste.

It's not all just food and drink, however; other products such as honey-based cosmetics and beeswax furniture polish are also sold.

A list of London farmers' markets is given below. However, new markets are starting up all the time. To check for new markets, visit the website for the National Association of Farmers' Markets on *www.farmersmarkets.net*, or contact the association on **t** 0845 45 88 420, *nafm@farmersmarkets.net*. The London Farmers' Markets organization operates many of the markets in London; visit *www.lfm.org.uk* or contact them on **t** (020) 7833 0338.

Blackheath

Railway station car park, Blackheath Village, SE3, **t** *(020) 7833 0338.* **Open** *Sun 10am–2pm.*

Bromley

Bromley High Street, Kent, **t** *(020) 8466 0719.* **Open** *Fri 9am–5pm.*

Chiswick

Next to Cavendish School, entrance on Edensor Road, W4, **t** *(020) 8747 3063.* **Open** *Sun 10am–2pm.*

Ealing

Leeland Road, West Ealing, W13, **t** *(020) 7833 0338.* **Open** *Sat 9am–1pm.*

Hammersmith

Hammersmith Town Hall forecourt, King Street, W6, **t** *(020) 8878 5132.* **Open** *Thurs 11am–4pm.*

Islington

William Tyndale School, behind Islington Town Hall, N1, **t** *(020) 7833 0338.* **Open** *Sun 10am–2pm.*

Marylebone

Cramer Street car park, off Marylebone High Street, W1, **t** *(020) 7833 0338.* **Open** *Sun 10am–2pm.*

Notting Hill

Car park off Kensington Place, on the corner of Kensington Church Street, W8, **t** *(020) 7833 0338.* **Open** *Sat 9am–1pm.*

Paddington

Next to canal to rear of Paddington Station, in Sheldon Square, W2, **t** *(020) 7833 0338.* **Open** *Thurs 12pm–5pm.*

Palmers Green

Palmers Green railway station car park, N13, **t** *(020) 7833 0338.* **Open** *Sun 10am–2pm.*

Parson's Green

Lady Margaret School, Irene Road, SW6, **t** *(020) 8878 5132.* **Open** *Sat 1–5pm.*

Peckham

Peckham Town Square, Peckham High Street, SE15, **t** *(020) 7833 0338.* **Open** *Sun 9.30am–1.30pm.*

Pimlico

Orange Square, junction of Pimlico Road and Ebury Street, SW1, **t** *(020) 7833 0338.* **Open** *Sat 9am–1pm.*

Pinner

Queen's Head car park, High Street, Pinner, **t** *(020) 7833 0338.* **Open** *Sun 10am–2pm.*

Putney

St Mary's Church, Putney High Street, SW15, **t** *(020) 8392 0631.* **Open** *Fri 11am–3pm.*

Queen's Park

Salusbury Primary School, Salusbury Road, NW6, **t** *(020) 7833 0338.* **Open** *Sun 10am–2pm.*

Richmond

Heron Square, off Hill Street, **t** *(020) 8878 5132.* **Open** *Sat 11am–3pm.*

Stoke Newington

William Patten School, Stoke Newington Church Street, N16, **t** *(020) 7502 7588, www.growingcommunities.org.* **Open** *Sat 10am–2.30pm. All organic produce.*

Swiss Cottage

*Car park of the O2 centre, Finchley Road, NW3, t (020) 7833 0338. **Open** Wed 10am–3pm.*

Twickenham

*Holly Road car park, TW1, t (020) 7833 0338. **Open** Sat 9am–1pm.*

Uxbridge

*High Street, outside Civic Centre, UB8, t (020) 7833 0338. **Open** Sun 10am–2pm.*

Whetstone

*Whetstone High Road (opposite Waitrose), N20, t (020) 7833 0338. **Open** Fri 11am–5pm.*

Wimbledon Park

*Wimbledon Park First School, Havana Road, SW19, t (020) 7833 0338. **Open** Sat 9am–1pm.*

The Best of London's Markets

Antiques
Bermondsey (New Caledonian), Church Street, King's Road Antiques, Portobello

Art
Bermondsey (New Caledonian), King's Road Antiques

Books
Riverside Walk

Bric-a-brac
Brick Lane, Greenwich (flea market)

Clothes

New
Cheap: Roman Road, Wembley; fashionable: Camden, Portobello

Secondhand
Cheap: Brixton, Westmoreland Road; fashionable: Camden, Greenwich, Portobello

Crafts
Camden, Greenwich, Merton Abbey Mills

Fabrics
Brixton, East Street, Ridley Road

Farmers' Markets
Islington, Marylebone, Palmers Green, Stoke Newington

Fish
Brixton, Chapel Market, Ridley Road, Tooting

Flowers
Columbia Road, East Street (Blackwood Street)

Food

Afro-Caribbean
Brixton, Ridley Road, Shepherd's Bush

Asian
Brixton, Queen's Market, Tooting

Delicatessen
Borough

Organic
Portobello, Spitalfields Market

Fruit and Vegetables
Berwick Street, Lewisham, North End Road, Walthamstow

Junk
Brick Lane, Hackney, Portobello (Acklam Road), Westmoreland Road

Kitchenware
New: Shepherd's Bush, Wembley; antique cutlery: Camden Passage

Leatherwear
Brick Lane, Camden, Petticoat Lane , Roman Road, Wembley

Meat
Brixton, Ridley Road

Pet Foods and Provisions
Brick Lane (Sclater Street), Tooting

Records
Berwick Street, Brixton, Camden

Tools and Hardware
Secondhand: Hackney, Kingsland Waste; new: Brick Lane, Wembley

Days to Go

Monday

Central London

Berwick Street and Rupert Street
The Courtyard, St Martin's
Covent Garden: Apple Market and
  Jubilee Market
Earlham Street
Grays Antiques
Leadenhall
Leather Lane
Strutton Ground
Tachbrook Street
Whitecross Street

West London

Portobello: Food Market and
  Golborne Road
Queensway Market

North London

Camden: Camden Lock, Camden Market
  and The Stables
Church Street (Alfie's Antiques)
Inverness Street
Nag's Head

East London

Bethnal Green
Hoxton Street
Petticoat Lane: Wentworth Street
Ridley Road
Roman Road and Globe Town
Spitalfields Market
Walthamstow
Whitechapel

Southwest London

Brixton
Hildreth Street
King's Road Antiques
North End Road

Northcote Road: General Market and
  Antiques Market
Tooting

Southeast London

Lewisham
Lower Marsh
Peckham

Other Markets Within the M25

Bexleyheath
Broadway Market
Camberwell
Catford Broadway
Croydon
East Ham
Edmonton
Elephant and Castle
Feltham
Hammersmith
Kingston
Richmond
South Harrow
Southwark Park Road
Stoke Newington
Stratford Mall
Wealdstone
Well Street
Wood Green

Tuesday

Central London

Berwick Street and Rupert Street
The Courtyard, St Martin's
Covent Garden: Apple Market and
  Jubilee Market
Earlham Street
Grays Antiques
Leadenhall
Leather Lane

St James's (antiques)
Strutton Ground
Tachbrook Street
Whitecross Street

West London
Portobello: Food Market and
    Golborne Road
Queensway Market
Shepherd's Bush

North London
Camden: Camden Market, Camden Lock,
    The Stables
Chapel Market
Church Street (Alfie's Antiques)
Hampstead Community Market
    (permanent stalls)
Inverness Street
Nag's Head
Swiss Cottage

East London
Bethnal Green
Hoxton Street
Petticoat Lane: Wentworth Street
Queen's Market
Ridley Road
Roman Road and Globe Town
Spitalfields Market
Walthamstow
Whitechapel

Southwest London
Brixton
Hildreth Street
King's Road Antiques
North End Road
Northcote Road: General Market and
    Antiques Market
Tooting

Southeast London
East Street
Lewisham
Lower Marsh
Peckham

Westmoreland Road
Woolwich

Other Markets Within the M25
Bexleyheath
Broadway Market
Camberwell
Chrisp Street
Croydon
East Ham
Edmonton
Elephant and Castle
Feltham
Finchley
Hammersmith
Kingston
Lambeth Walk
New Addington
Penge
Rathbone
Richmond
South Harrow
Southwark Park Road
Stoke Newington
Stratford Mall
Watford
Watney
Wealdstone
Well Street
Wembley
Wood Green

Wednesday
Central London
Berwick Street and Rupert Street
The Courtyard, St Martin's
Covent Garden: Apple Market and
    Jubilee Market
Earlham Street
Grays Antiques
Leadenhall
Leather Lane
St James's (arts and crafts)
Strutton Ground

Tachbrook Street
Whitecross Street

West London

Portobello: Food Market and
   Golborne Road
Queensway Market
Shepherd's Bush

North London

Camden: Camden Market, Camden Lock,
   The Stables
Camden Passage (antiques and
   bric-a-brac)
Chapel Market
Church Street (Alfie's Antiques)
Hampstead Community Market
   (permanent stalls)
Inverness Street
Nag's Head (secondhand and antiques)
Willesden

East London

Bethnal Green
Hoxton Street
Petticoat Lane: Wentworth Street
Ridley Road
Roman Road and Globe Town
Spitalfields Market
Walthamstow
Whitechapel

Southwest London

Brixton
Hildreth Street
King's Road Antiques
North End Road
Northcote Road: General Market and
   Antiques Market
Tooting

Southeast London

Deptford
East Street
Lewisham
Lower Marsh
Peckham

Westmoreland Road
Woolwich

Other Markets Within the M25

Barnes
Bexleyheath
Broadway Market
Camberwell
Chrisp Street
Croydon
East Ham
Edmonton
Elephant and Castle
Erith
Feltham
Hammersmith
Kingston
Lambeth Walk
Penge
Richmond
Romford
South Harrow
Southwark Park Road
Staines
Stoke Newington
Stratford Mall
Swanley
Watney
Wealdstone
Well Street
Wood Green

Thursday

Central London

Berwick Street and Rupert Street
The Courtyard, St Martin's
Covent Garden: Apple Market and
   Jubilee Market
Earlham Street
Exmouth Market
Grays Antiques
Leadenhall
Leather Lane
St James's (arts and crafts)

Strutton Ground
Tachbrook Street
Whitecross Street

West London
Portobello: Food Market and
    Golborne Road
Queensway Market
Shepherd's Bush

North London
Camden: Camden Market, Camden Lock,
    The Stables
Camden Passage (books)
Chapel Market
Church Street (Alfie's Antiques)
Hampstead Community Market
    (permanent stalls)
Inverness Street
Kilburn Square
Nag's Head
Queen's Crescent

East London
Bethnal Green
Hoxton Street
Petticoat Lane: Wentworth Street
Queen's Market
Ridley Road
Roman Road and Globe Town
Spitalfields Market
Walthamstow
Whitechapel

Southwest London
Brixton
Hildreth Street
King's Road Antiques
North End Road
Northcote Road: General Market and
    Antiques Market
Tooting

Southeast London
East Street
Lewisham
Lower Marsh

Peckham
Westmoreland Road
Woolwich

Other Markets Within the M25
Bexleyheath
Broadway Market
Bromley
Camberwell
Catford Broadway
Chrisp Street
Croydon
Dartford
East Ham
Edmonton
Elephant and Castle
Enfield
Epsom
Erith
Feltham
Hammersmith
Harringay
Harrow
Kingston
Penge
Rathbone
Richmond
South Harrow
Southwark Park Road
Stoke Newington
Stratford Mall
Uxbridge
Watney
Wealdstone
Well Street
Wembley
West Drayton
Wood Green

Friday
Central London
Berwick Street and Rupert Street
The Courtyard, St Martin's

Covent Garden: Apple Market and
  Jubilee Market
Earlham Street
Exmouth Market
Grays Antiques
Leadenhall
Leather Lane
St James's (arts and crafts)
Strutton Ground
Tachbrook Street
Whitecross Street

West London

Portobello: Food Market; Clothes,
  Crafts and Bric-a-brac Market; and
  Golborne Road
Queensway Market
Shepherd's Bush

North London

Camden: Camden Market, Camden Lock,
  The Stables
Chapel Market
Church Street (Alfie's Antiques)
Hampstead Community Market
  (permanent stalls)
Inverness Street
Kilburn Square
Nag's Head (new goods)
Swiss Cottage

East London

Bethnal Green
Hoxton Street
Petticoat Lane: Wentworth Street
Queen's Market
Ridley Road
Roman Road and Globe Town
Spitalfields Market
Walthamstow
Whitechapel

Southwest London

Brixton
Hildreth Street
King's Road Antiques

North End Road
Northcote Road: General Market and
  Antiques Market
Tooting

Southeast London

Bermondsey (New Caledonian)
Borough
Deptford
East Street
Greenwich: Village Market
Lewisham
Lower Marsh
Peckham
Westmoreland Road
Woolwich

Other Markets Within the M25

Bexleyheath
Broadway Market
Camberwell
Catford Broadway
Chalton Street
Chrisp Street
Croydon
East Ham
Edmonton
Elephant and Castle
Enfield
Feltham
Finchley
Hammersmith
Grove Park
Kingston
Lambeth Walk
New Addington
Penge
Rathbone
Richmond
Romford
South Harrow
Southwark Park Road
Stoke Newington
Stratford Mall
Uxbridge

Watford
Watney
Wealdstone
Well Street
Wembley
Wood Green

Saturday

Central London

Berwick Street and Rupert Street
Charing Cross Collectors' Fair
The Courtyard, St Martin's
Covent Garden: Apple Market and
  Jubilee Market
Earlham Street
Exmouth Market
St James's (arts and crafts)
Tachbrook Street

West London

Portobello: Antiques Market; Food Market;
  Clothes, Crafts and Bric-a-brac Market;
  and Golborne Road
Queensway Market
Shepherd's Bush

North London

Camden: Camden Canal Market, Camden
  Lock, Camden Market, The Stables
Camden Passage (antiques and
  bric-a-brac)
Bell Street
Church Street (Alfie's Antiques)
Hampstead Community Market
Inverness Street
Kilburn Square
Nag's Head (new goods) and Grafton
  School Market
Queen's Crescent
Willesden

East London

Bethnal Green
Hoxton Street
Kingsland Waste

Queen's Market
Ridley Road
Roman Road and Globe Road
Walthamstow
Whitechapel

Southwest London

Brixton
Hildreth Street
King's Road Antiques
Merton Abbey Mills
North End Road
Northcote Road: General Market and
  Antiques Market
Tooting

Southeast London

Borough
Deptford
East Street
Greenwich: Antiques Market; Weekend
  Market; Crafts Market; Organic Food
  Market; Village Market
Lewisham
Peckham
Riverside Walk
Westmoreland Road
Woolwich

Other Markets Within the M25

Barnet
Bexleyheath
Broadway Market
Camberwell
Catford Broadway
Chrisp Street
Croydon
East Ham
Edmonton
Elephant and Castle
Enfield
Epsom
Erith
Feltham
Finchley
Hammersmith

Hounslow
Kingston
London Bridge
Penge
Potters Bar
Rathbone
Richmond
Romford
South Harrow
Southwark Park Road
Staines
Stoke Newington
Stratford Mall
Uxbridge
Watford
Watney
Wealdstone
Well Street
Wembley
Wood Green

Sunday

Central London

The Courtyard, St Martin's
Covent Garden: Apple Market and
   Jubilee Market
Piccadilly

West London

Bayswater Road
Portobello: Clothes, Crafts and
   Bric-a-brac Market

North London

Camden: Camden Canal Market,
   Camden Lock, Camden Market,
   Electric Ballroom, The Stables
Chapel Market
Kilburn Square
Nag's Head (flea market)
Swiss Cottage
Wembley

East London

Brick Lane
Columbia Road
Hackney Stadium
Petticoat Lane: Wentworth Street
Spitalfields Market

Southwest London

Merton Abbey Mills
Nine Elms Sunday Market
Northcote Road Antiques Market
Wimbledon Stadium

Southeast London

East Street
Greenwich: Antiques Market, Central
   Market, Crafts Market, Village Market
Riverside Walk
Westmoreland Road

Other Markets Within the M25

Borough Green (end Mar–Oct)
Camberwell
Finchley Car Boot Sale
Finsbury Park
Wood Green

Where to Buy

Accessories

Camden Market
Camden Passage
Deptford High Street
East Street
Leather Lane
Peckham
Portobello: Antiques Market
Strutton Ground
Walthamstow
Whitechapel
Whitecross Street

Antiques

Bermondsey
Church Street
Covent Garden: Jubilee Market
Grays Antiques
Greenwich: Antiques Market
King's Road Antiques
Northcote Road
Spitalfields Market
Tachbrook Street
Westmoreland Road

Art

Bayswater Road
Bermondsey
King's Road Antiques
Merton Abbey Mills
St James's and Piccadilly
Spitalfields Market

Books

Brick Lane
Deptford High Street
Greenwich: Weekend Market and
   Village Market
Hampstead Community Market
Leather Lane
Merton Abbey Mills
Nine Elms Sunday Market
Riverside Walk
Swiss Cottage
Westmoreland Road

Bric-a-brac

Brick Lane
Brixton
Camden: The Stables
Covent Garden: Jubilee Market
Deptford: Douglas Way
East Street
Greenwich: Village Market
Kingsland Waste
Nag's Head
Nine Elms Sunday Market
Portobello: Clothes, Crafts and Bric-a-brac
Spitalfields Market
Swiss Cottage
Walthamstow

Cards

Deptford High Street
Strutton Ground
Tachbrook Street
Whitecross Street
Wimbledon Stadium

CDs

Brick Lane
Brixton
Greenwich: Village Market
Kilburn Square
Lower Marsh
Queensway Market

Ridley Road
Rupert Street
Westmoreland Road
Wimbledon Stadium
Woolwich

Clothes

New

Bethnal Green
Brick Lane
Brixton
Camden: Camden Canal Market, Camden Lock, Camden Market, Electric Ballroom, The Stables
Chapel Market
Church Street
The Courtyard, St Martin's
Covent Garden: Apple Market and Jubilee Market
Deptford High Street
Earlham Street
East Street
Greenwich: Crafts Market
Hackney Stadium
Hoxton Street
Kilburn Square
Leadenhall
Leather Lane
Lewisham
Lower Marsh
Merton Abbey Mills
Nag's Head
Nine Elms Sunday Market
North End Road
Northcote Road
Peckham
Petticoat Lane
Portobello: Clothes, Crafts and Bric-a-brac; and Golborne Road
Queen's Crescent
Queen's Market
Ridley Road
Roman Road

Rupert Street
Shepherd's Bush
Strutton Ground
Tooting
Walthamstow
Wembley
Whitechapel
Whitecross Street
Willesden
Wimbledon Stadium
Woolwich

Secondhand

Bell Street
Brixton
Camden: Camden Canal Market, Camden Lock, Camden Market, Electric Ballroom, The Stables
Deptford: High Street and Douglas Way
Greenwich: Antiques Market, Village Market
Hackney Stadium
Kingsland Waste
King's Road Antiques
Merton Abbey Mills
Nag's Head and Grafton School
Nine Elms Sunday Market
North End Road
Northcote Road
Portobello: Clothes, Crafts and Bric-a-brac
Queen's Crescent
Rupert Street
Swiss Cottage
Tooting
Westmoreland Road
Whitechapel
Wimbledon Stadium

Computers

Hackney Stadium
Queensway Market

Crafts

Camden: Camden Lock, The Stables
The Courtyard, St Martin's
Covent Garden: Apple Market and
  Jubilee Market
Greenwich: Antiques Market,
  Crafts Market
Hampstead Community Market
Merton Abbey Mills
Portobello: Clothes, Crafts and Bric-a-brac
Spitalfields Market
St James's and Piccadilly

DVDs

See Videos

Electrical Goods

Brixton
Camden Canal Market
Hackney Stadium
Kingsland Waste
Leather Lane
Lower Marsh
Nag's Head and Grafton School
Petticoat Lane
Ridley Road
Shepherd's Bush
Strutton Ground
Walthamstow
Wembley
Whitechapel
Wimbledon Stadium

Fabrics

Berwick Street
Brixton
Deptford High Street
East Street
Lewisham
Lower Marsh
Ridley Road

Roman Road
Shepherd's Bush
Tooting
Walthamstow
Whitechapel
Willesden
Woolwich

Fish

Berwick Street
Brixton
Chapel Market
Church Street
East Street
Hampstead Community Market
Leadenhall
Lewisham
Nag's Head
North End Road
Northcote Road
Peckham
Queen's Crescent
Ridley Road
Tachbrook Street
Tooting
Woolwich

Flowers and Plants

Church Street
Columbia Road
Deptford High Street
Earlham Street
East Street
Hildreth Street
Leadenhall
Leather Lane
Lewisham
Merton Abbey Mills
Northcote Road
Queen's Crescent
Strutton Ground
Swiss Cottage
Tachbrook Street

Walthamstow
Woolwich

Food

Afro-Caribbean
Brixton
Hildreth Street
Northcote Road
Peckham
Portobello: Golborne Road
Queen's Market
Ridley Road
Shepherd's Bush
Tooting
Willesden

Asian
Brixton
Queen's Market
Tooting
Whitechapel

Delicatessen
Borough
Exmouth Market
Greenwich: Crafts Market
Portobello: Food Market
Tachbrook Street
Walthamstow

Organic
Borough
Camden: The Stables
Greenwich: Central Market and
  Crafts Market
Portobello: Food Market
Spitalfields Market

Fruit and Vegetables

Berwick Street
Bethnal Green
Brixton
Chapel Market
Church Street

Deptford High Street
East Street
Hampstead Community Market
Hildreth Street
Hoxton Street
Inverness Street
Leather Lane
Lewisham
Lower Marsh
Nag's Head
Nine Elms Sunday Market
North End Road
Northcote Road
Peckham
Portobello: Food Market and
  Golborne Road
Queen's Crescent
Queen's Market
Ridley Road
Roman Road
Rupert Street
Shepherd's Bush
Strutton Ground
Tachbrook Street
Tooting
Walthamstow
Westmoreland Road
Whitechapel
Whitecross Street
Willesden
Wimbledon Stadium
Woolwich

Furniture

Brick Lane
Camden: The Stables
Greenwich: Village Market
Tooting

Household Goods

Bethnal Green
Chapel Market
Church Street

Deptford High Street
East Street
Greenwich: Village Market
Hackney Stadium
Hoxton Street
Inverness Street
Kilburn Square
Lower Marsh
Nag's Head and Grafton School
North End Road
Peckham
Petticoat Lane
Portobello: Golborne Road
Queen's Market
Queen's Crescent
Ridley Road
Roman Road
Shepherd's Bush
Tooting
Walthamstow
Wembley
Willesden
Woolwich

Jewellery and Watches

Bermondsey
Camden Passage
Deptford High Street
East Street
Grays Antiques
Greenwich: Central Market
King's Road Antiques
Leather Lane
Merton Abbey Mills
Northcote Road
Rupert Street
Whitechapel
Whitecross Street

Junk

Bell Street
Camden: Camden Canal Market, Camden Lock, The Stables
Charing Cross Collectors' Fair

Covent Garden: Jubilee Market
Greenwich: Antiques Market, Greenwich Village Market
Hackney Stadium
Nag's Head: Grafton School
Nine Elms Sunday Market
Portobello: Clothes, Crafts and Bric-a-brac
Westmoreland Road

Kitchenware

Camden Passage
Greenwich: Weekend Market
Roman Road
Shepherd's Bush
Walthamstow
Wembley

Leatherware

Brick Lane
Camden
Petticoat Lane
Wembley

Meat

Brixton
Church Street
Leadenhall
Nine Elms Sunday Market
Peckham
Queen's Crescent
Ridley Road
Tooting

Novelty Goods

The Courtyard, St Martin's
Covent Garden: Apple Market

Pet Foods and Provisions

Brick Lane
East Street
Kilburn Square

Tooting
Walthamstow
Wimbledon Stadium

Records

Berwick Street
Brixton
Camden: Camden Canal Market,
  Camden Market, The Stables
Covent Garden: Jubilee Market
Deptford: Douglas Way
Greenwich: Village Market
Merton Abbey Mills
Ridley Road
Tooting
Whitechapel

Souvenirs

Camden: The Stables
The Courtyard, St Martin's
Covent Garden: Jubilee Market
Petticoat Lane
Queensway Market

Tools and Hardware

Brick Lane
Hackney
Kingsland Waste
Nine Elms Sunday Market
Walthamstow
Wembley
Wimbledon Stadium

Toys

Merton Abbey Mills
Wimbledon Stadium

Videos/DVDs

East Street
Rupert Street
Queensway Market
Wimbledon Stadium

Learning the Lingo

The language used on the markets continually changes. Rhyming slang, though still much used in TV sitcoms, is not heard as often as you may think on East End markets. Along with backslang (such as 'reeb' for beer and 'esclop' for police), it was used by traders to confuse outsiders. Most Londoners know what it is to take a butcher's (butcher's hook: look) or when to close their north and south (mouth), so the point is lost. However, several words used among London's traders survive. The following list is a collection of market jargon, some of which you may hear, some of which has almost died out, some of which can only be heard in certain districts, notably the East End. As can be seen, there's a strong Yiddish influence, a result of immigration by Jewish cloth traders from Eastern Europe.

Some of the best spiels on London markets can be heard at Brick Lane (on the wasteland off Bacon Street) and Wembley, both on a Sunday; and at Church Street (the toy seller), Deptford and Hoxton Street, all on a Saturday.

bat price
billig cheap price
bin pocket
bunce profit
burster good day's trade
carpet £3
casual newcomer/occasional trader
clocking looking
cockle £10
cow's 50p
demic damaged, broken
demmer trader who demonstrates wares (usually vegetable peelers or window cleaning devices)
deuce £2
edge crowd gathered round a stall, i.e. 'getting an 'edge' (hedge)
exis £6
fence buyer/seller of stolen goods
fents remnants of material
fiddle a fair day's profit
flash a display of goods
flim £5
flyer fast-selling line
funt £1
gaff open market

ganiff thief
gelt money
grafter speciality seller
grand £1,000
jacks £5
joint stall
kipper season January and February (the low season for markets)
kite cheque
knocking out selling goods off cheap
line type of goods
monkey £500
nause complaint, problem
neves £7
nicker £1
oncer £1
packing setting goods out in a display
    down/out (the opposite: packing up or in)
patter sales talk
pitch allotted space on market
pitching method of selling using sales talk to attract crowd
plunder goods sold at or below cost to attract custom
poke money

pony £25
punter customer
readies paper money
ream gear quality goods
rouf £4
score £20
shmatty poor quality
snides unserviceable goods

spiel sales talk
strike £1
swag cheaper lines
tilt stall cover
toby or tobé formerly a worker who set up a trader's stall; now a market superintendent
ton £100

Further Reading

Adburgham, A., *Shops and Shopping 1800–1914* (George Allen & Unwin, 1964).

Benedetta, M., *Street Markets of London* (John Miles, 1936).

Britnell, R. H., *The Commercialisation of English Society 1000–1500* (Cambridge University Press, 1993).

Burke, T., *The Streets of London* (Batsford, 1940).

Cousins, E. F. and Anthony, R., *Pease and Chitty's Laws of Markets and Fairs* (Charles Knight, 1993).

Davis, D., *A History of Shopping* (Routledge & Kegan Paul, 1966).

Drummond, J. C. and Wilbraham, A., *The Englishman's Food* (Pimlico, 1994; first published 1939).

Fisher, F. J., 'The Development of the London Food Market, 1540–1640' in *Economic History Review V*, 1935.

Forshaw, A. and Bergström, T., *The Markets of London* (Penguin, 1983).

Hammond, D., *London, England: A Day-Tripper's Travelogue from the Coolest City in the World* (Mainstream, 1998).

Howse, C., 'A Dying Market', *Sunday Telegraph Magazine* (5 November 1995).

Jasper, A. S., *A Hoxton Childhood* (Centerprise, 1969).

Kershman, A., *The London Market Guide* (Metro, 2003).

Lang, T., *Putting the Market back into the Market Economy: A Report to the Association of Metropolitan Authorities* (Centre for Food Policy, Thames Valley University, 1996). Unpublished commissioned research.

Mayhew, H., *London Labour and the London Poor* (1851).

Perlmutter, K., *London Street Markets* (Wildwood House, 1983).

Phillips, C. (ed.), *Time Out Eating & Drinking Guide 2006* (Time Out).

Raven, H. et al, *Off Our Trolleys?: Food Retailing and the Hypermarket Economy* (Institute for Public Policy Research, 1995).

Shore, W.T., *Touring London* (Batsford, 1930).

Stow, J., *The Survey of London* (J. M. Dent, 1912; first published 1598).

Urban and Economic Development Group (URBED), *Vital and Viable Town Centres* (HMSO, 1995).

Weinreb, B. and Hibbert, C., *The London Encyclopedia* (Macmillan, 1983).

Index of Markets

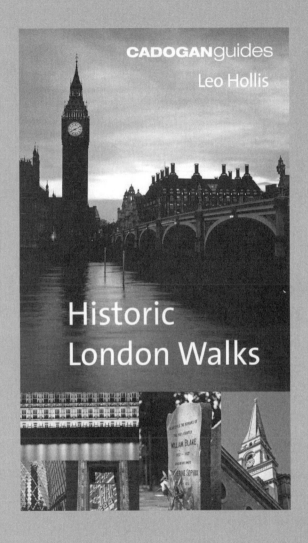